# THE
# OXYRHYNCHUS PAPYRI
## VOLUME XL

# THE
# OXYRHYNCHUS PAPYRI

## VOLUME XL

EDITED WITH TRANSLATIONS AND NOTES BY

## J. R. REA

Graeco-Roman Memoirs, No. 56

———

PUBLISHED FOR
## THE BRITISH ACADEMY
BY THE
EGYPT EXPLORATION SOCIETY
3 DOUGHTY MEWS, LONDON WC1N 2PG
1972

PRINTED IN GREAT BRITAIN
AT THE UNIVERSITY PRESS, OXFORD, BY VIVIAN RIDLER
PRINTER TO THE UNIVERSITY
AND PUBLISHED FOR
THE BRITISH ACADEMY
BY THE EGYPT EXPLORATION SOCIETY
3 DOUGHTY MEWS, LONDON WC1N 2PG
ALSO SOLD BY
BERNARD QUARITCH, 5–8 LOWER JOHN STREET, GOLDEN SQUARE, W1V 6AB

# PREFACE

THIS part is exclusively documentary and devoted to a homogeneous group of texts from a short period in the late third century after Christ. They have been assembled, transcribed, translated, and interpreted by Dr. John Rea, who first realized their purport and isolated them as an archive. Identification of the documentation in Oxyrhynchus of the institution in that town of a corn dole apparently modelled on that of Rome itself is a considerable gain for historical studies. It is particularly felicitous that this discovery should be published in the 75th anniversary year of the opening of work at Behnesa.

The index has been made by Dr. John Rea himself. He would like to thank Mr. W. E. H. Cockle for cleaning the originals. And Dr. Rea and the general editors are grateful to the University Press, Oxford for their care over the printing.

P. J. PARSONS
J. R. REA
E. G. TURNER
*General Editors of the*
*Graeco-Roman Memoirs*

*May 1972*

# CONTENTS

# TABLE OF PAPYRI

[1] All dates are A.D.

# LIST OF PLATES

# NUMBERS AND PLATES

# NOTE ON THE METHOD OF PUBLICATION
## AND ABBREVIATIONS

THE method of publication follows that adopted in Part XXXVIII. As there, the dots indicating letters unread are printed slightly below the line; but the dots inside square brackets to estimate the number of lost letters are printed on the line. The texts are printed in modern form, with accents and punctuation, the lectional signs occurring in the papyri being noted in the *apparatus criticus*, where also faults of orthography, &c., are corrected. Iota adscript is printed where written, otherwise iota subscript is used. Square brackets [ ] indicate a lacuna, round brackets ( ) the resolution of a symbol or abbreviation, angular brackets ⟨ ⟩ a mistaken omission in the original, braces { } a superfluous letter or letters, double square brackets ⟦ ⟧ a deletion, the signs ‘ ’ an insertion above the line. Dots within brackets represent the estimated number of letters lost or deleted, dots outside brackets mutilated or otherwise illegible letters. Dots under letters indicate that the reading is doubtful. Heavy Arabic numerals refer to Oxyrhynchus papyri printed in this and preceding volumes, ordinary numerals to lines, small Roman numerals to columns.

The abbreviations used are in the main identical with those in E. G. Turner, *Greek Papyri: an Introduction* (1968). It is hoped that any new ones will be self-explanatory.

# PUBLIC DOCUMENTS: THE CORN DOLE IN OXYRHYNCHUS, AND KINDRED DOCUMENTS

## 2892–2940. CORN DOLE ARCHIVE

This group of documents reveals that a corn dole was distributed in Oxyrhynchus in the reigns of Claudius II and Aurelian and adds significantly to the otherwise not very extensive evidence for the existence of corn doles in the cities of Egypt in the third century. In the authoritative work on the Roman corn dole the Egyptian evidence was not considered and, though a definite statement about the third century was not made, it was implied that nowhere in the empire were there corn doles comparable with the Roman one until the time of Diocletian (D. van Berchem, *Les distributions de blé et d'argent à la plèbe romaine sous l'empire*, p. 102). The new evidence, however, shows that the Oxyrhynchite dole followed the Roman model closely. The same may well have been true of those in Alexandria and Hermopolis.

### *Alexandria and Hermopolis*

For Alexandria our evidence is a passage of a paschal letter of Dionysius, bishop of Alexandria, quoted by Eusebius (*HE* vii 21, 9). It refers to a time just after Gallienus had recovered control of Alexandria from the supporters of Macrianus and Quietus and when plague as well as war had reduced the population of the city, that is, to A.D. 261 or not much later.

εἶτα θαυμάζουσι καὶ διαποροῦσι . . . διὰ τί μηκέτι τοσοῦτο πλῆθος οἰκητόρων ἡ μεγίστη πόλις ἐν αὐτῇ φέρει, ἀπὸ νηπίων ἀρξαμένη παίδων μέχρι τῶν εἰς ἄκρον γεγηρακότων, ὅσους ὠμογέροντας οὓς ἐκάλει πρότερον ὄντας ἔτρεφεν, ἀλλ' οἱ τεσσαρακοντοῦται καὶ μέχρι τῶν ἑβδομήκοντα ἐτῶν τοσοῦτον πλέονες τότε ὥστε μὴ συμπληροῦσθαι νῦν τὸν ἀριθμὸν αὐτῶν προσεγγραφέντων καὶ συγκαταλεγέντων εἰς τὸ δημόσιον σιτηρέσιον τῶν ἀπὸ τεσσαρεσκαίδεκα ἐτῶν μέχρι τῶν ὀγδοήκοντα, καὶ γεγόνασιν οἷον ἡλικιῶται τῶν πάλαι γεραιτάτων οἱ ὄψει νεώτατοι.

'Men wonder and debate . . . why (our) greatest city no longer bears in it as great a total of inhabitants—beginning from infant children and including the very oldest—as it once maintained of those whom it called "elderly" (ὠμογέροντες), but (on the contrary) the people of forty to seventy years of age were then so much more numerous that nowadays an equal number cannot be made up when everyone from fourteen to eighty years of age is enrolled and mustered for the public corn dole, and the youngest looking have turned into the contemporaries, as it seems, of those who have long been old.'

Wilcken took this to mean that a corn dole distributed originally to persons of forty to seventy years of age was widened to include everyone from fourteen to eighty (*Archiv* iv 546). The new papyri show that the arrangements for distribution depended

in some way on age, e.g. **2902** 5 seqq. ταγείς ... πρὸς τὴν τῶν ἐκκαιδ[ε]κ[α-]⁷ετῶν ϲιτο-
δοϲίαν. I take it to mean, therefore, that though it was necessary before the troubles
to divide the population according to age for the distribution of the corn, afterwards
persons of every age could be seen collecting the dole at the same time in the same
place and their total number was less than had formerly been found in a single category,
that of the ὠμογέροντες.

The evidence for a dole in Hermopolis comes from a single document of the
same period. In A.D. 261 a citizen registered himself [εἰς] τὴν ἐπ᾽ ἀγαθοῖ[ς] ⁸ [ἐϲομέν]ην
διάδοϲιν τοῦ ἐπὶ ⁹ [πλείϲτοις ἀ]γαθοῖς ϲυνχωρη¹⁰[θέντο]ς ἡμῖν ϲιτηρεϲίου ἐκ ¹¹ [τῆ]ς μεγαλο-
δωρίας τῶν ¹² [κυρί]ων ἡμῶν Μακριανοῦ ¹³ [καὶ] Κυ[ή]του Καιϲάρων Ϲεβαϲτῶν (WChr. 425
= P. Lond. 955, vol. iii pp. 127 seq.). Wilcken took this as a temporary measure as
he did the very fragmentary reference to *tesserae* and corn of the first year of Claudius II
which he cited from a Leipzig papyrus in the introduction to his republication of the
London document as WChr. 425 (P. Lips. inv. 483 = SB i 4514).[1] The Alexandrian
dole he visualized as standing and long established (*Archiv* iv 546). In Oxyrhynchus the
dole was a standing arrangement; the dates of the new papyri range from 1 Claudius II[2]
to 3 Aurelian[3] and the distribution was on a monthly basis.

Perhaps the most likely hypothesis is that all these doles were arranged in much the
same way. The earliest date that we have is in the reign of Macrianus and Quietus,
but this may easily be accidental and the Alexandrian evidence may imply the existence
of a dole there before them. We have relatively very little information about what
begins to bear the appearance of an institution widespread in the cities of Egypt.[4]

*Oxyrhynchus*

It appears that these new documents all come from a single archive, probably
from the records of the magistrates in charge of the dole. The slight doubt of their
unity arises from the fact that though the inventory numbers indicate that the bulk of
them were dug up during the third season of excavations at Behnesa, a few come from
the first season and one from the fourth. The range of dates, however, is the same and
some of the same documentary types occur in the pieces from the first and third seasons.
The singleton from the fourth season (**2923**) is of the same period but of a type not
occurring elsewhere in the group.

*Qualifications*

(a) ἐπικριθέντες

For receipt of the dole the usual basic qualification was the possession of a certain
class of citizenship in Oxyrhynchus, expressed by the claim to have undergone scrutiny

---

[1] The provenance of the Leipzig scrap is unknown. The date of it suggests the obvious possibility
that it is a stray from the present archive, and it is certainly to be compared with **2924**, see ibid. 6 n.

[2] For the possible implication of a slightly earlier date see **2903** 10 n.

[3] Expressions of the form '1 Claudius, II', '3 Aurelian', etc., are used throughout to represent briefly
'the first Graeco-Egyptian regnal year of Claudius II', 'the third Graeco-Egyptian regnal year of
Aurelian', etc.

[4] See now below, **2941–2942,** for new evidence of a dole—though perhaps a different sort of dole—
in Antinoopolis.

(ἐπίκρισις). There were two types of scrutiny that might be in question here, that for admission to the μητροπολῖται, and that for admission to the more restricted class of οἱ ἐκ τοῦ γυμνασίου or ἀπὸ γ., see Mertens, *Les services de l'état civil*, pp. 98–128, esp. pp. 127–8. The Hermopolite applicant was of the ἀπὸ γυμνασίου class, but one Oxyrhynchite describes himself in his application as a μητροπολίτης (**2895** ii 5), which implies that the eligible class was the wider one. Nor are there any here who claim to be of the gymnasium class.

The number of recipients was limited. Places fell vacant by death and were filled by lot. If **2929** is rightly included here, the ideal number was 3,000 and the actual number in Payni of 2 Claudius II (May/June, A.D. 270) was slightly over 2,900.

The lottery was held annually at Rome in the time of Caesar (Suet. *Jul.* 41, 'quotannis'). At Oxyrhynchus applications from persons who had been successful in the lot were submitted in the months Thoth, Phaophi, Tybi, and Mecheir, which might suggest that the lottery was held more often. On the other hand, since eligibility did not depend at all on means, it is likely that a proportion of recipients had no urgent need of an extra food supply. It is probably better to suppose, therefore, that those who entered their petitions in Tybi and Mecheir were simply slow to apply, see also **2894** ii 13 n., **2929** introd.

Citizens of Rome and Alexandria were also admitted to the dole and listed with the ἐπικριθέντες (**2927** 3 n.). Applications from Alexandrians refer to resolutions of the Oxyrhynchite city council which declared them eligible to share. No application from a Roman citizen *domo Roma* survives, but their case may have been the same. However, the grain was the gift of the emperor (**2898** 10 n.) and it is reasonable to wonder, therefore, whether the city decree was not merely the endorsement of measures which owed their real authority to him.

Part of the qualification of Alexandrians was residence (ἑστία, ἐφέστιον) in Oxyrhynchus. It is uncertain whether this means permanent residence or not, see the divergent views in Braunert, *Binnenwanderung*, p. 25 n. 39, and Hombert–Préaux, *Recensement*, p. 67.

There is also a fragmentary application from a citizen of Antinoopolis (**2917**), but he claims to have done public service in Oxyrhynchus and this appears to be the ground of his appeal, see next paragraph. According to the Antinoite privileges he should have been exempt from public service in other cities, but voluntary liturgy by exempt persons is known (*BASP* vi (1969), pp. 20–1). An Alexandrian also applies on grounds of public service (**2915**).

(b) ῥεμβοί

The other large category of persons entitled to the dole consisted of those who had performed a public service, the λελειτουργηκότες. It appears that these were not merely persons with the appropriate citizen rights (ἐπικριθέντες), whose service entitled them to receive the dole without taking part in the lottery for a place, but were admitted solely on grounds of public service without regard to hereditary rights. The normal applications for admission on grounds of public service do not mention citizen rights, though two, perhaps three, petitioners refer both to their *epicrisis* and to their public service (**2899**, cf. **2900**; **2918**). However another person described as ἀνεπίκριτος was admitted to this category (**2908** iii). One application (**2907** ii) from a liturgist whose name had been mistakenly omitted from the list uses the formula for enrolment in the place of a dead man, which is seen elsewhere only in the cases of ἐπικριθέντες. The name of the dead man was omitted and a space left for it was never filled, so that there is a strong probability that the formula was completely inappropriate here.

Freedmen were also admitted, but only, it seems, those who had performed a liturgy. The phrase ἀπελευθέρων λελειτουργηκότων unfortunately occurs only in the genitive; it is a less likely possibility that it means 'freedmen of those who have performed a liturgy'. Together the liturgists and the freedmen formed a group called the ῥεμβοί, which I have translated by 'sundries'.

The ideal number of the ῥεμβοί appears to have been nine hundred. This comes from a much damaged application (**2908** iii), but it does seem clear that the petitioner asks for his foster-brother to be enrolled 'among the nine hundred'—ἐν τοῖς (ἐννακοσίοις) —and the official subscription at the foot of the sheet runs: παρεδεξάμην ἐν [τῇ τά]ξει τῶν ῥεμβῶν—'I admitted (him) in the category of the sundries.' One actual list of numbers of ῥεμβοί from the various quarters of the city counts only six hundred and thirty five (**2928** i). But another figure implies that in May/June, A.D. 270, there were about 750 of them, see **2929** 18 n.

It seems to follow from the absence of the ἀντὶ τοῦ δεῖνα τετελευτηκότος formula, except in the case mentioned above where the name was never added, that the lot did not apply to the ῥεμβοί. Probably a share in the dole was offered as an inducement to attract prospective liturgists or to console those appointed against their will. In respect of exemption from the lot the whole class of the ῥεμβοί is parallel to the freedmen at Rome (sch. Persius v 73). There the numbers were probably kept within manageable bounds by the residence requirement and by the legal restrictions on the granting of full citizenship by manumission (A. M. Duff, *Freedmen*, pp. 72 seqq.). Freedmen of the inferior Latin status, called *Latini Juniani*, could acquire full citizenship by various types of public service, specified in Gaius, *Inst.* i §§ 32b–34. It may be that the classification of the ἀπελεύθεροι λελειτουργηκότες was derived from this Roman model.

### (c) ὁμόλογοι

Not included among the ἐπικριθέντες or the ῥεμβοί were the ὁμόλογοι, who formed the third and last category according to the terminology of the documents. Their ideal number was only one hundred and on one occasion the actual number was ninety-three (**2928** ii). They are more fully described in a formulary as ὁμόλογοι ἀπογραφέντες καὶ ἀπὸ γραφῆς ἀφηλίκων προσβάντες (**2927** 4). This means that they were admittedly liable for poll-tax and that they were of age to be promoted from the list of minors. I supposed at first that these were young boys who were qualified by birth and age but who had not yet undergone their *epicrisis*. However when one applicant who probably fell in this class made his application in 1 Claudius II (A.D. 268/9), he set his promotion from the list of minors in 1 Decius and Herennius (A.D. 249/50), almost twenty years earlier. He does not describe himself specifically as ὁμόλογοc but begins his petition with the words ἀπογραφεὶc καὶ προcβ(ὰc) ἀπὸ γραφῆc ἀφηλίκων τῷ α (ἔτει) Δεκίων (**2913** ii 7–9), which repeats the major part of the formulary's description of the ὁμόλογοι. The most noteworthy fact about him is that he was illegitimate and therefore debarred from *epicrisis*. This is expressed by the phrase χρηματίζων μητρὸc ᾽Ιcειτοc, 'officially known by the name of his mother Isis', which precludes his fulfilling the requirement of being officially ἐξ ἀμφοτέρων γονέων μητροπολιτῶν, 'born of parents both of the metropolite class', cf. **1306**, PSI x 1109, 10. The ὁμόλογοι therefore seem to be persons who were not qualified to share the corn dole by their citizen status, but who were admitted as a concession. The manner of their selection is not known. One may reasonably suspect that the mother at least was of the metropolite class.

The only applicant who is specifically said to belong to the category of the ὁμόλογοι uses the same words ἀπογραφεὶc καὶ προcβὰc ἀπὸ γραφῆc ἀφηλίκων and likewise seems to be illegitimate, though this conclusion is based on the shortness of the lacuna between his name and his mother's. He claims to have been registered in the phylarch's records ἐν τῇ τάξε[ι τῶν ὁ]μολόγ[ων (**2912** 11), but says nothing of his age. He has been away from Oxyrhynchus and reports his return in order to collect his dole.

*Procedures*

The procedures for the distribution of the dole cannot be recovered in much detail but the allusions in the documents are sufficient to build up a general picture. The phylarchs were responsible for drawing up lists of eligible persons in their districts under the three heads of ἐπικριθέντεc (including Romans and Alexandrians), ὁμόλογοι and ῥεμβοί (comprising λελειτουργηκότεc and ἀπελεύθεροι λελειτουργηκότεc). For this purpose they consulted the public records contained in the δημοcία βιβλιοθήκη. Before they were listed the applicants for the dole had to undergo a special screening process called διάκριcιc, which entailed the presentation of documentary evidence, in one case specifically a certificate of *epicrisis* and proofs of lineage (**2898** 15–17). There are three other cases of the production of documents to support applications and these same documents may well have been produced again for the διάκριcιc. An Alexandrian produced something called τοῦ ἐφεcτί[ου] τὸ ἀντίγραφον, perhaps an official authority to reside in Oxyrhynchus, perhaps simply a certificate of actual residence there (**2916**). Another Alexandrian produced an extract from his nomination to an Oxyrhynchite liturgy (**2915**). And in the third case an Oxyrhynchite is ordered to produce τὰ cύμβολα τῆc πολιτείαc (**2908** ii 32–3). The process of the διάκριcιc was controlled by διακριταί, officials appointed by the city council (**2913**).

The successful candidates also had to answer to their names at a roll call, the ἀναγορία. The conditions and the purpose of it are uncertain. Probably its main object was to prevent impersonation. It may also have been an opportunity for public objections to be heard. Every qualified person who had not yet been successful in the lottery would have an interest in preventing the admission of unqualified candidates. The use of the present tense of ὑπακούω in certain formulas indicates that the roll call took place regularly and involved not only the newly qualified applicants but all of them (**2927** 19 n.). There may have been a regular meeting for the distribution of tokens at which a roll call was taken. Or alternatively it may have been taken at a general business meeting of the citizen body and not have been concerned, or not primarily concerned, with the corn dole, though we should observe the wording of, e.g., **2913** ii 14–16, ἀξιῶ ἐνταγῆναι ἐν τοῖc ἀναγορευομένοιc πρὸc διάδοcιν τοῦ cιτηρεcίου ὀνόμαcι.

That distribution was based on a monthly ration is clear from the fragments of registers where each man's name is followed by a series of month names for keeping account of the distributions (**2934–2937**). The monthly ration may have been one artaba, because in **2908** iii it appears that nine hundred men receive nine hundred artabas. Professor Youtie has pointed out to me that this is an amount sometimes met with as a monthly allowance, drawing my attention to P. Mich. v 355 (duplicated in PSI viii 902) and **994**; see also CPLat. 136, PSI ix 1050 and, strikingly, SB X 10567 19–21, δίδου δὲ αὐτῷ τὴν εἰωθυεῖαν πᾶcι δίδοcθαι [[πᾶcι]] ἀρτάβην μηνιαίαν; for more references see the note on this passage in *CÉ* xliv (1969), 321–2.

At Rome the monthly allowance was five *modii* (van Berchem, *Les distributions*, p. 15). Because various types of artaba and *modius* were in use, it is hard to be sure of the relation between these two rations, but if one accepts the apparently reasonable assumptions that the artaba in question was the most usual one, the ἀρτάβη μέτρῳ δημοcίῳ, and that the *modius* was the one described in Egypt as the μόδιοc Ἰταλικόc, they were exact equivalents. The artaba μέτρῳ δημοcίῳ was the equivalent of 72 Alexandrian *sextarii* (Segrè, *Metrologia*, p. 35), while the μόδιοc Ἰταλικόc contained exactly one fifth of that amount, $14\frac{2}{5}$ Alexandrian *sextarii* (ibid. p. 37).

The distribution was managed by officials appointed by the city council (**2918**, **2924**). In **2924** the distributors warned those who had received *tesserae* (τάβλαι) from them but had not yet collected their corn to present the *tesserae* immediately, because they had served their term of office and new distributors had been appointed. There is a clear implication in this that a *tessera* was a token to be produced in exchange for a certain quantity of corn, as in the Roman dole of the time of Augustus, cf. van Berchem, *Les distributions*, p. 85, citing Suet. *Aug.* 40. The terminology indicates that the distributors were liturgists of the curial class, appointed by the council probably for the usual annual term, and they address their warning only to τοὺc παρ' ἡμῶν τάβλαc . . . ἐcχηκόταc. It is clearly implied that the *tesserae* were valid only for the term of the officials who issued them.

*Quarters and tribes*

From the two calculations of area totals we may draw some tentative conclusions about the organization of the tribes and the quarters.

Both **2928** and **2929** list twelve areas. From the sum totals—2,928 for an ideal 3,000 in **2929** and 93 for an ideal 100 in **2928** ii—we may conclude that the calculations were complete for the whole city and that the city was divided for this purpose into twelve areas. Since the number of quarters named in the papyri is more than twice that, see Rink, *Strassen- und Viertelnamen*, p. 52, some at least of the twelve areas will have included more than one quarter, and it will have been only for convenience that they were designated by the name of a single quarter.

It has already been established that an Oxyrhynchite φυλή consisted of ἄμφοδα (e.g. Mertens, *Les services*, pp. 15, 24, 129), so that the question naturally arises whether these twelve areas correspond to the tribes, as might be suggested by the title of the phylarch in **1119** 13 τῷ τῶν μελλόντων λειτουργεῖν ἀμφόδων φυλάρχῳ, and of the *systates*, the phylarch's successor, in PSI 1108, 5–6 and **2715** 5–6, cυcτάτηc φυλῆc Δρόμου Γυμναcίου καὶ ἄλλων ἀμφόδων, cf. **1116** 5–6; P. Flor. 39 4. That they do correspond to the tribes seems to be confirmed by **2930**, which is a piece from the beginning of a list of recipients, compiled by a person described as γενομέ[νου φυλάρχου] 3 φυλῆc Δρόμου Θοήριδοc καὶ Λυ[κίων (Παρεμβολῆc?). This evidence, together with the separate responsibility of the phylarchs for compiling the registers of corn dole recipients in this archive, strongly inclines me to think that these areas are equivalent to tribes and that there were twelve tribes at this period.

The Oxyrhynchite tribal system is imperfectly understood, but we know from the document published in *TAPA* xcix (1968), pp. 259–63, and from three others to be published along with a reprint of it in a forthcoming volume, that it began in A.D. 206/7 with six tribes, each of which provided public servants for a year in rotation till A.D. 229/30. In the next three years A.D. 230/1–232/3 the tribes acted in pairs. A little later we find a nine-year rotation period in effect, at least between A.D. 244/5 and A.D. 253/4 (**1119**). Nothing more is known except that there were at least three tribes in the reign of Aurelian (**1413** 12, 13) and that a tribal system continued as late as A.D. 396 (P. Flor. 39). If PSI 86 is from Oxyrhynchus there were at least sixteen tribes *c.* A.D. 367–75.

It is rather uncertain how much support the evidence in this archive provides for the view that the Roman corn dole was organized on the basis of the Roman tribes, see **2928** introd. and below, pp. 14 seq.

*The phylarch in Oxyrhynchus*

This official has been well investigated by Professor Mertens, *Les services*, pp. 16–30. At the time of his work, however, there were no dated mentions of the phylarch between A.D. 254 and the appearance of his successor the *systates* (A.D. 287, Mertens, p. 19). These papyri, together with P. Wis. 2 (Aurelian; see *BASP* iv 34, *CÉ* xliv (1969), pp. 134–8) and **2764** (Probus), fill that gap to some extent.

One additional point of importance emerges. The phylarch was thought to function only in years in which his tribe had the duty of providing public servants (Mertens, pp. 22–4). From this archive it is clear that even in years in which his tribe was not serving the phylarch was responsible for keeping records, at least of the corn dole. In this situation, however, he called himself an ex-phylarch, see e.g. **2930** 2, where the corn dole list of ῥεμβοί is submitted by a γενόμενος φύλαρχος. A subscription to **2908** ii may even indicate that they acted together as a college. It runs (31–4) παρόντων τῶν φυλάρχ(ων) καὶ τῶν γνωστήρων παρεχέτω τὰ σύμβολα τῆς πολειτείας. Outside Oxyrhynchus collegiate activity is attested for phylarchs (P. Eitrem 6 = SB 7375; Hermopolis?) and for their successors the *systatae* (P. Beatty Panopolis i 180, 195, 338). In **2908** ii, however, it is possible that there is a mistake for τοῦ φυλάρχ(ου). The γνωστῆρες can remain in the plural: compare the two subscribing to **2892** i 28–30.

## The Roman dole

Perhaps the most important aspect of the new archive is the possibility which it affords of confirming or correcting our views of the Roman corn dole. There can hardly be any doubt that the Oxyrhynchite dole is modelled closely on the Roman system. As in Rome the basic qualifications are citizenship and residence, freedmen are admitted, the distributions are calculated by the month, probably at the same rate, and controlled in some way by tokens. It is regarded as a gift from the emperor, as in Rome at least from the time of Severus.

There are local differences, as we might expect. We know of nothing in Rome to correspond to the λελειτουργηκότες and the ὁμόλογοι and there is so far nothing to suggest that children could draw the Oxyrhynchite dole, a puzzling aspect of the Roman system. But the resemblances are more important. It is very clearly confirmed, for instance, that the doles were not a provision for the very poor, but a perquisite of the already privileged middle classes of the cities, as in Rome. On the other hand there is no sign that the dole was available to the city councillors or magistrates, and we may probably conclude from the Roman situation that it was not.

The received view of the lottery is the first one which seems to need modification. Van Berchem concluded (p. 27) that the fixed number of recipients and the lottery for places did not last beyond Caesar's reform of the dole as described in Suet. *Jul.* 41. The passage runs: *recensum populi nec more nec loco solito sed vicatim per dominos insularum egit; atque ex viginti trecentisque milibus accipientium frumentum e publico ad centum quinquaginta retraxit; ac ne qui novi coetus recensionis causa moveri quandoque possent, instituit, quotannis in demortuorum locum ex iis qui recensi non essent subsortitio a praetore fieret.* 'He held a registration of the people not in the usual way or in the usual place, but street by street through the landlords, and reduced the number of persons receiving corn from the state from 320,000 to 150,000. To prevent the calling of future meetings for registration at any time he also laid it down that a lottery for the places of the deceased should be held by the praetor every year among those who had not been enrolled.'

The Oxyrhynchite regulations for the compilation of lists by the phylarchs according to districts and for the control of the numbers by lottery are clear reflections of Caesar's. It is hard to believe that the Oxyrhynchites would imitate regulations that had gone out of use at Rome by the date their dole was established. Of course that date is not known, but since our evidence is confined to the second half of the third century it would be implausible to set it as early as the reign of Augustus, who is supposed to have abolished the *subsortitio*. In fact it is hard to resist the conclusion that an institution so intimately connected with the Roman citizenship as the corn dole could not have spread beyond the city before the *constitutio Antoniniana*.[1] The obvious implication is that the lot continued in Rome well into the imperial period.

Because there is no actual mention of the *subsortitio* except in connection with Caesar's reform van Berchem explained away the two passages which imply its continuance in Rome. The first is Dio–Xiph. lv 10, 1 ὁ δὲ Αὔγουστος τὸ τοῦ δήμου τοῦ ϲιτοδοτουμένου πλῆθος ἀόριϲτον ὂν ἐϲ εἴκοϲι μυριάδαϲ κατέκλειϲε, 'Augustus closed the number of the *plebs frumentaria*, which was unlimited, at 200,000.' Xiphilinus seems to contradict Suetonius when he says that the number had been unlimited before, but we can probably rely on the statement that in Augustus' time the number was fixed, which implies a lottery.

The second passage occurs in Pliny's panegyric on Trajan (ch. 25) and refers to a *congiarium* issued in A.D. 99. It is known that *congiaria* were distributed to the *plebs frumentaria* only, see van Berchem, pp. 127–130, citing especially Fronto, *Princ. hist.* 18: *congiariis frumentariam modo plebem singillatim placari ac nominatim* etc. The passage of Pliny runs: *datum est his, qui post edictum tuum in locum erasorum subditi fuerant, aequatique sunt ceteris illi etiam, quibus non erat promissum*, 'It was given to persons who had been substituted in place of those whose names had been erased and even those to whom it had not been promised were made equal with the rest.' Van Berchem claimed that the number of the additional names need not have equalled the number of those erased. His argument (p. 29) is that if the number was fixed, Trajan's generosity in giving to those enrolled between the announcement of the *congiarium* and its distribution would not have been great enough to merit Pliny's praise. But we should note that on a similar occasion Augustus did not admit the newly enrolled. Suetonius' words are quite parallel with Pliny's: *negavit accepturos quibus promissum non esset* (*Aug.* 42, 2). Augustus' reason was that many new freedmen, to whom the lot did not apply, see below, pp. 11 seq., had been admitted to citizenship expressly to collect the money for their patrons. Clearly Trajan's generosity was worthy of some remark, and he may have broken a custom established by Augustus. For his panegyric Pliny naturally chose to praise Trajan's benefaction as it applied to citizens rather than freedmen.

It seems to me that the words '*in locum erasorum*' imply very strongly that the number of new recipients, excluding freedmen, had to be the same as the number of the dead, and that the new evidence from Oxyrhynchus justifies us in believing that the lottery for places was a standing feature of the Roman dole.

The archive also gives us reason to reconsider the function and form of the *tesserae* in the Roman dole. The context of the single mention of them, under the name of τάβλαι,

---

[1] There is now evidence of a corn dole distributed in Antinoopolis in the period A.D. 166–9, see **2941–2942** introd. and p. 117 n. 1, but it is still not known whether it was organized on the Roman model or on a Greek one.

is enough to make it clear that they were tokens or coupons to be exchanged for a quantity of corn and that their validity lasted only as long as the term of the officials who distributed them (**2924**, see above, p. 6). In Augustus' time they were coupons too, as we learn clearly from Suetonius' account of the emperor's unsuccessful attempt to simplify the administration of the dole by distributing *tesserae* for a four months' supply three times a year (*Aug.* 40).

According to van Berchem's account, pp. 87–8, it was before the end of the first century after Christ that the *tessera* changed into an identity document which was retained permanently by the person named in it and presented at the *porticus Minucia* on a fixed day in the month and at a fixed counter (*ostium*).

Once again, therefore, the conditions in Oxyrhynchus seem to reflect an early state of the corn dole in Rome and not a late one. We are faced with the three-fold choice of believing that the Oxyrhynchite corn dole was instituted before the end of the first century and that it preserved, until the second half of the third century, conditions that soon changed at Rome; or that it was founded nearer to the period for which we have evidence and reflected contemporary conditions at Rome; or that it was founded late but used an early Roman set of regulations. I continue to find the hypothesis that it was founded relatively late and in imitation of the contemporary Roman dole the most probable one, certainly probable enough to justify doubting the change in the function of the *tessera*.

The theory that the *tessera* was a document like an identity card goes back to Rostowzew, though he had the best of both worlds by supposing that the earlier tokens continued in use under the same name, e.g. *Röm. Bleitesserae*, pp. 16 seq., 38, *RE* vii 179. It rests on the following four passages of the *Digest* that speak of the buying and bequeathing of the *tessera*:

xxxi 49, 1. *Si Titio frumentaria tessera legata sit et is decesserit, quidam putant exstingui legatum, sed hoc non est verum, nam cui tessera vel militia legatur, aestimatio videtur legata* (Paul). 'If the *tessera frumentaria* is bequeathed to Titius and he dies, some people think that the legacy is extinguished, but this is not true, for if anyone is left the *tessera* or a post in the public service it is as if he were left the monetary value of it.'

xxxi 87 pr. *Titia Seio tesseram frumentariam comparari voluit post diem trigesimum a morte ipsius: quaero, cum Seius viva testatrice tesseram frumentariam ex causa lucrativa habere coepit, nec possit id quod habet petere, an ei actio competat. Paulus respondit ei, de quo quaeritur, pretium tesserae praestandum, quoniam tale fidei commissum magis in quantitate quam in corpore consistit.* 'Titia wished that the *tessera frumentaria* should be bought for Seius after thirty days from her own death. I put the question whether, in the event that he begins to hold the *tessera* during the lifetime of the testatrix by paying for it, an action is available to him, since he cannot claim the privilege which he already holds. The response of Paul was that the cost of the *tessera* should be given to the person concerned in the question, because the substance of such a trust lies more in the value than in the nature of it.'

xxxii 35 pr. *Patronus liberto statim tribum emi petierat: libertus diu moram ab herede patroni passus est, et decedens heredem reliquit clarissimum virum: quaesitum est an tribus aesti-*

*matio heredi eius debeatur. respondit deberi. idem quaesivit an et commoda et principales liberali-*
*tates, quas libertus ex eadem tribu usque in diem mortis suae consecuturus fuisset, si ei ea tribus*
*secundum voluntatem patroni sui tunc comparata esset, an vero usurae aestimationis heredi eius*
*debeantur. respondit quidquid ipse consecuturus esset, id ad heredem suum transmittere* (Scaevola).
'A patron had required that a (place in a) tribe should be bought for his freedman
immediately. The freedman was subjected to a long delay by his patron's heir and died
leaving a senator as his heir. The question was put whether the value of the (place
in a) tribe is owing to his heir. (Scaevola's) response was that it was. The same person
inquired whether there were also owing to his heir the advantages and the principal
largesses which the freedman would have obtained from the same tribe up to the day
of his death, if (a place in) that tribe had been bought for him at the time in accordance
with his patron's will, and indeed whether the interest on their value was owing. The
response was that the man passed to his heir whatever he would have obtained himself.'

v 1, 52, 1 *Si libertis suis tesseras frumentarias emi voluerit, quamvis maior pars hereditatis*
*in provincia sit, tamen Romae debere fidei commissum solvi dicendum est, cum apparet id testatorem*
*sensisse ex genere comparationis* (Ulpian). 'If a man wills that *tesserae frumentariae* be
bought for his freedmen, even if the greater part of the estate lies in the provinces, still
it must be stated that the trust is to be executed at Rome, since it is apparent from the
nature of the provision that that was the testator's intention.'

It seems to me that in these cases the word *tessera* is used as a simple and intelligible
metaphor for the right to draw the corn dole. One of the above passages uses instead
of '*tesseram emere*' the expression '*tribum emere*', which may mean exactly the same thing,
see Cardinali in *Diz. Epigr.* iii 269–71. Whether it does or not, the usage is metaphorical
and seems to me to supply a good parallel to '*tesseram emere*'. 'To buy the tribe' means
to buy a place in a tribe, more particularly to buy the advantages of belonging to a
tribe, as the text goes on to specify: *commoda et principales liberalitates quas libertus ex eadem*
*tribu . . . consecuturus fuisset.* There seems no need at all to suppose that the *tessera*
changed its nature.

But even on this interpretation of *tessera* the allusions to buying and bequeathing
the right to the corn dole are hard to understand, because they seem to contradict
what we already know of the qualifications for it. Van Berchem believed that the state
sold the right to citizens newly settled at Rome (pp. 49–53). It seems to me that this
is inconsistent with the operation of the lot and would represent a diminution of the
privileges of the citizens born in Rome too serious to be passed over in silence. The
lot, however, did not apply to freedmen, as we see from the scholia to Persius, *Sat.* v 73:
*Romae autem erat consuetudo ut omnes qui ex manumissione cives Romani fiebant in numero civium*
*Romanorum frumentum publicum acciperent.* The tense of the verbs and the prominent
position of '*Romae*' tend to show that this comment is late and provincial, but the fact
is confirmed by passages where it is alleged that Romans freed their slaves in order to
take advantage of the doles that freedmen received (Suet. *Aug.* 42, 2; Dion. Hal. *Ant.*
*Rom.* iv. 24, 5).

Two of the *Digest* passages specifically relate to freedmen (v 1, 52, 1 ; xxxii 35 pr.), and in the other two (xxxi 49, 1 ; xxxi 87 pr.) there is no obvious obstacle to supposing that the legatees were freedmen, on whom the patron could confer a status that automatically entitled them to the dole. This could be done by will and in that sense the *tessera*, the right to the dole, could be bequeathed. The question of buying the right to the dole arose only, I suggest, when the freedman had Latin status to begin with. He could acquire full citizen rights by certain public services (Gaius, *Inst.* i §§ 32b–34), which resolve themselves into a question of money. If the patron could provide capital enough to do one of these services, he could in effect buy his freedman citizen status with the unconditional right to the dole. Similarly in the second *Digest* passage (xxxi 87 pr.) I suggest that the freedman himself 'bought' the right by way of public service before the death of his patroness, who had left money for this purpose in her will.

In xxxii 35 pr. the object of the purchase is not the *tessera* but the *tribus*. From which Mommsen concluded that in the principate a place in one of the thirty-five Roman tribes could be bought by or for a freedman[1] and this place, together with his status as a freedman and official domicile at Rome, entitled him to a share in the dole (*Staatsrecht* iii 447, cf. *RE* xiii col. 107 fin. s.v. *Libertini*). It is not, however, certain that this is right: the *liberalitates* need not include the state corn dole. If it is right, it may be only another way of referring to the process suggested above, with the emphasis laid on the tribal affiliation of a full citizen, and perhaps with the implication that the Roman dole was somehow organized by tribes, see below, pp. 14 seq.

The purchase of a place in a tribe perhaps has its counterpart in Oxyrhynchus, where it seems that only freedmen who had performed a liturgy were entitled to the dole. The main function of the Oxyrhynchite tribes was to provide liturgists during the year that the tribe had its turn in office. It seems quite possible that for a freedman there the performance of an expensive liturgy was the equivalent of buying a place in a Roman tribe for a freedman at Rome.

Juvenal advised a teacher of declamation to change his job '*summula ne pereat qua vilis tessera venit frumenti*' (*Sat.* vii 174 seq.). I would agree with van Berchem (pp. 52–3) that this refers to a nest-egg from which the man hoped to buy the right to the corn dole rather than to the purchase of the use of *tesserae*. I conclude that the man was a freedman, but I can see no corroboration from the rest of the satire.

These are admittedly speculative interpretations of the puzzling *Digest* passages, but they do at least provide a reasonable explanation for the references to the inheritance and purchase of the right to the corn dole without contradicting what we know about how the right could be acquired by the ordinary citizen. The important point is that these passages do not actually describe the *tessera* as a sort of identity document and do not necessarily imply a *tessera* of that sort.

There is still great uncertainty about the form of the *tesserae*. Rostowzew thought

---

[1] Mommsen may mean to include also other 'persons of low degree'—'Personen niederen Standes'. If so, I would disagree. The passage in question specifies freedmen.

that they could be identified with some of the many types of bronze and lead pieces shaped like coins, particularly with those carrying devices suggesting a connection with the corn supply, such as the *modius* or ears of corn (*Röm. Bleitesserae*, pp. 1–4). Van Berchem rejected this interpretation of the metal pieces, explaining them as counters for use with an abacus (*Rev. Num.* 1936, pp. 297 seqq.). He suggested that the *tesserae* were wooden rectangles, later diptychs, and claimed to find them represented on certain coins and works of art (*Les distributions*, pp. 92–5).

If van Berchem is right, there is some hope of finding a wooden *tessera* surviving in Egypt, but so far there is nothing that I can discover that could be a *tessera* of the sort he envisages.

If Rostowzew is right, some of the lead tokens from the Egyptian nome capitals, which often do indeed bear suitable devices such as Nilus, Euthenia, a reaper, ears of corn, may be the tokens used in the Graeco-Egyptian corn doles (*Num. Chron.* 1908, pp. 287–310; 1930, pp. 300–15; *Ancient Egypt*, 1915, pp. 107–20). However these have been taken by J. G. Milne to be coins made locally to supply the general lack of small change, and this explanation certainly holds good for such few of them as bear an indication of monetary value, e.g. *JEA* xxi (1935), pp. 213–14 and pl. xxvi 1–6.

The Palmyrene inscriptions on two lead tokens of Zenobia from Antioch are doubtfully interpreted as meaning 'grain', which may possibly be relevant (Comte du Mesnil du Buisson, *Les tessères . . . de Palmyre*, pp. 757–8).

One puzzling piece of our information about the Roman dole becomes even more suspect when compared with the Oxyrhynchite documents, namely the statement in Suet. *Aug.* 41 that the age of entitlement was at one time ten. Suetonius says that Augustus admitted children to the *congiaria*, and consequently to the dole, see above, p. 9, which previously could not be drawn '*nisi ab undecimo aetatis anno*'. In Rome as in Oxyrhynchus the fundamental qualification was citizenship. In Oxyrhynchus a boy became a citizen after undergoing *epicrisis* in his fourteenth year; in Rome he became one after assuming the *toga virilis* at an age which varied in practice, but which was sometimes set conventionally by the jurists at fourteen (van Berchem, p. 33; see Ulpian, fr. 11, 28 = FIRA ii p. 276).

I hope it will not seem unreasonable to suggest, therefore, that the figure in Suetonius has been corrupted from one that represented the age of majority, most probably '*quarto decimo*'. There are two ways in which the corruption might easily have occurred. The one that first suggested itself to me was a misreading of the four minims of the form '*iiii decimo*' as '*un*'. It is notoriously easy to misread these minims, to confuse, for example, *nimis* and *minus*. A simpler alternative and perhaps on that account a better one was suggested to me by Dr. M. Winterbottom, that is, that the form '*xiv*' might have lost its last element.

So emended the passage of Suetonius can be matched with Dio Cassius li 21, 3: τῷ τε δήμῳ καθ᾽ ἑκατὸν δραχμάς, προτέροις μὲν τοῖς ἐς ἄνδρας τελοῦσι, ἔπειτα δὲ καὶ τοῖς παισὶ διὰ τὸν Μάρκελλον τὸν ἀδελφιδοῦν, διένειμε.

There are two alternatives to emending Suetonius' text; namely, to continue to suppose that the two passages refer to the same occasion and that by the phrase οἱ ἐς ἄνδρας τελοῦντες Dio means boys above the age of ten, or to suppose that there were two stages by which Augustus admitted first boys from ten to the age of maturity and afterwards those below ten. Neither of these is wholly impossible, but much complication is avoided if we replace '*undecimo*' with a figure for an age that can credibly be attributed to τοῖς ἐς ἄνδρας τελοῦσιν.

The archive also raises, somewhat remotely, the debated question whether the Roman dole was organized on the basis of the thirty-five tribes (For: Mommsen, *Staatsrecht* iii 444, cf. 195; Cardinali, *Diz. Epigr.* iii 269–71. Against: Hirschfeld, *Philologus* 1870, p. 13. Undecided: Rostowzew, *RE* vii 182). For the Oxyrhynchite dole the evidence discussed above seems to indicate that the lists drawn up by the phylarchs were done on the basis of twelve tribes, see pp. 6–7. *CIL* vi 10211, quoted in **2928** introd., resembles **2928** and **2929**, a fact which may support Mommsen's restoration of it as a list of numbers of tribesmen entitled to the corn dole.

Gifts to the people could be distributed by way of the tribe. Augustus is said to have distributed the proceeds of the sale of Caesar's estate to the φύλαρχοι (Appian, *BC* iii 23). The empress Eusebia distributed largesse in Rome in A.D. 357 to τῶν φυλῶν τοῖς ἐπιστάταις (Julian, *Or.* iii 129 C–D). Compare Suet. *Aug.* 101 and Tac. *Ann.* i 8 on Augustus' bequests to the people.

In *Digest* xxxii 35 pr., quoted above, pp. 10–11, the *liberalitates* which a freedman might receive after being enrolled in a tribe have been held to include the state corn dole because of wording similar to the other passages concerning *tesserae frumentariae*, but it is not absolutely necessary to accept this; the word can quite well refer only to private acts of generosity.

In Persius v 73 seqq. the tribe name which appears prominently may be taken to indicate that the tribe played a special part in the dole.

> *libertate opus est. non hac ut quisque Velina*[1]
> *Publius emeruit scabiosum tesserula far*
> *possidet.*

'There is need of freedom. Not the sort we have nowadays when any nonentity in the Velina tribe who has served his time (as a slave?) can get the mouldy corn with a free ticket.'

But the inference does not need to be drawn. The *praenomen* and tribe may stand there merely to indicate that only the freedman with full citizen rights could draw the dole.

---

[1] In view of the connection that I have suggested between the tribe and the possibility of gaining full citizenship by public service (above, p. 12), it is very tempting to emend the text to '*Velinam...emeruit*' and translate 'who has earned (a place in) the Velina tribe', i.e. by public service. But the whole subject is too uncertain to justify any confidence about altering the text.

Similarly the inscription proudly claiming '*tri[bu]m ingenuam, frumentum [publ]icum*' falls short of proof (*CIL* vi 10220). The Oxyrhynchite evidence too falls far short of proof, but its tendency is to reinforce the implications that at Rome the tribe was a factor in the organization of the lists of recipients, see above, pp. 6–7.

It has been suggested by G. Raffo in an article on the distribution of provisions in third-century Rome (*Giornale Italiano di Filologia* iv (1951), pp. 250–5) that the corn dole ceased to be distributed at Rome some time after Alexander Severus and was eventually replaced by Aurelian's dole of bread (Zos. i 61; SHA *Aur.* 35, 1; 47, 1–2). The new documents from Oxyrhynchus have nothing positive to say on this, but one might reasonably argue that the abolition of the original Roman dole would have been likely to lead to a speedy end to its poor relations in Egypt.

*The chronology*

This archive has produced about thirty date clauses in the reigns of Claudius II and Aurelian. One contains the earliest known date for Aurelian, which turns out a surprise in itself, but the greatest importance lies in the five dates early in the first year of Claudius II, which are, like some already known particularly from the Strasbourg papyri, very hard to fit into a coherent scheme for the two reigns.

For convenient consultation a table of the dates of the new documents is put first. Each item is given a number in chronological order for easy reference within this section (Table I overleaf).

The problem of the period is that there appear to be too many Egyptian regnal years for the available Julian years. If one puts the evidence apparently available from all the papyri into a scheme, working forward from the regnal years of Gallienus for which the Julian equivalents are firmly established, one reaches this result:

$$15 \text{ Gallienus} = 267/8$$
$$16 \text{ Gallienus} = 268/9 \ = 1 \text{ Claudius}$$
$$269/70 = 2 \text{ Claudius}$$
$$1 \text{ Aur. \& Vab.}; 1 \text{ A. } 4 \text{ V.} = 270/1 \ = 3 \text{ Claudius}$$
$$2 \text{ Aur. } 5 \text{ Vab.} = 271/2$$
$$3 \text{ Aur.} = 272/3$$
$$4 \text{ Aur.} = 273/4$$
$$5 \text{ Aur.} = 274/5$$
$$6 \text{ Aur.} = 275/6$$
$$7 \text{ Aur.} = 276/7$$

But Aurelian's successor Tacitus, whose short reign was contained within a single Graeco-Egyptian year, was *consul ordinarius* as emperor in Jan., A.D. 276, and consequently 1 Tacitus (= 7 Aurelian = 1 Probus) must be A.D. 275/6, not A.D. 276/7.

The explanation which passes current was set out by A. Stein in *Archiv* vii (1924), pp. 30–51, depending heavily on the work of Grenfell and Hunt in *P. Oxy.* xii (1916),

## TABLE I

| Item number | Year | Month | Day | Publication number |
|---|---|---|---|---|
| | | Claudius II | | |
| 1 | 1 | Tybi (Dec./Jan.) | 4 | **2901** |
| 2 | 1 | Mecheir (Jan./Feb.) | 25 | **2913** ii |
| 3 | 1 | Mecheir | lost | **2913** iii |
| 4 | (1) | Mecheir | lost | **2914** i |
| 5 | 1 | Mecheir | lost | **2914** ii |
| 6 | 2 | Thoth (Aug./Sept.) | 27 | **2892** i |
| 7 | 2 | Thoth | damaged | **2892** ii |
| 8 | 2 | Thoth | 28 | **2893** i |
| 9 | 2 | Phaophi (Sept./Oct.) | not given | **2892** i |
| 10 | 2 | Phaophi | not given | **2892** ii |
| 11 | 2 | Tybi (Dec./Jan.) | 19 | **2894** ii |
| 12 | 2 | Tybi | 19 | **2895** ii |
| 13 | 2 | Mecheir (Jan./Feb.) | not given | **2894** iii |
| 14 | 2 | Payni (May/June) | not given | **2929** |
| 15 | 2 | not given | not given | **2895** i |
| 16 | lost | Phaophi (Sept./Oct.) | lost | **2896** |
| | | 'Interregnum' | | |
| 17 | ἐπὶ ὑπάτων etc. | Hathyr (Oct./Nov.) | damaged | **2907** i |
| 18 | ,, | Hathyr | damaged | **2907** ii |
| 19 | ,, | Hathyr | 6 | **2906** ii |
| | | Aurelian and Vaballathus | | |
| 20 | 1[1] | Choeac (Nov./Dec.) | 11–19 | **2921** |
| 21 | 1[1] | Tybi (Dec./Jan.) | not given | **2908** ii |
| 22 | 1[1] | lost | lost | **2898** |
| 23 | 1[1] | not given? | not given? | **2908** iii |
| 24 | 2 & 5 | Tybi (Dec./Jan.) | not given? | **2936** |
| 25 | 2 & 5 | Pharmouthi (Mar./Apr.) | 22 | **2904** |
| 26 | lost | lost | lost | **2916** |
| 27 | lost | lost | 26 | **2906** |
| 28 | lost | Tybi (Dec./Jan.) | 15 | **2922** |
| | | Aurelian | | |
| 29 | 3 | Payni (May/June) | 30 | **2902** |

[1] A separate figure for the reign of Vaballathus is not included in these papyri. His titles are given in the form usual in later documents where the regnal year number precedes them. Similarly there are among the Alexandrian coins some of 1 Aur. and Vab. and some of 1 Aur. 4 Vab. (Vogt, *Die alex. Münzen* ii 160).

pp. 229–35. It is that the date of Claudius' accession was actually shortly before 29 August, A.D. 268, on which date by the usual and official system his second Egyptian regnal year began. Because the news was not known in the remoter parts of Egypt until after 29 August, the theory runs, the scribes of the Strasbourg papyri reckoned A.D. 268/9 as 1 Claudius instead of 2 Claudius and in order to avoid confusion in their rent receipts carried this system through into the reign of Aurelian, giving him only six years. Further, since in **1208**, a document of A.D. 291, it is plainly stated that the second year of Claudius became the first of Aurelian, he suggested that a third reckoning, also unofficial, might have been in use. I reproduce his table from *Archiv* vii 37.

TABLE II

|  | *c* | *a* | *b* |
|---|---|---|---|
| 266/7 | 14 Gallienus | 14 Gallienus | 14 Gallienus |
| 267/8 | 15 Gallienus | 15 Gallienus<br>1 Claudius | 15 Gallienus |
| 268/9 | 16 Gallienus<br>1 Claudius | 2 Claudius | 16 Gallienus<br>1 Claudius |
| 269/70 | 2 Claudius<br>1 Aurelian | 3 Claudius<br>1 Aurelian | 2 Claudius |
| 270/1 | 2 Aurelian | 2 Aurelian | 3 Claudius<br>1 Aurelian |
| 275/6 | 7 Aurelian<br>1 Tacitus | 7 Aurelian<br>1 Tacitus | 6 Aurelian<br>1 Tacitus |

*a*. Official: coins and most papyri. *b*. P. Strasb. 7 (2 payments for 15 Gall., 2 for 1 Claudius, 2 for 2 Claudius, 1 for 3 Claudius); P. Strasb. 10 (1 Claudius, Phaophi); P. Strasb. 11 (1 Claudius, Phamenoth; reference to 'past 15th year'); P. Tebt. 581 (16 Gallienus); P. Flor. 265 (16 Gallienus); P. Lips. inv. 483 (WChr. p. 503: 1 Claudius, 6 March). *c*. **1208** 11 (2 Claudius = 1 Aurelian).

This complicated scheme can be accepted only if there is very good evidence for it. The most disturbing part of it is the premiss that at the beginning of a new reign the numbering of the years might depend on the time the news reached any particular place. By this method the Delta might be dating by year 2 while the Thebaid dated by year 1 simply because of the time the news would take to travel up the Nile. My premiss is that everyone in Egypt dated from the emperor's *dies imperii* and that no one invented a date for himself. Officials dated in accordance with instructions and the rest of the population followed their practice. Dates by dead emperors are possible because of the time taken by news to travel and indeed they are well attested, see, e.g., *Klio* xxi (1927), p. 80, but once the news had officially arrived one must presume that the proper method was followed, barring error. It was always improbable that an aberrant system should have been adopted and allowed to continue into the reign of

Aurelian. Now that Oxyrhynchus has produced dates early in Claudius' first year, impossible in Stein's 'official' system and just like the 'unofficial' dates in the Strasbourg papyri, it is time to examine the evidence again.

Before we can move forward we must be certain that the chronology of the previous reign is firmly based. Stein's theory was attacked at this point by Mattingly, who maintained that the reign of Valerian and Gallienus began shortly before 29 August, A.D. 253 and that consequently their Graeco-Egyptian year numbers should all be put back by one.[1] Quite properly Stein's view has prevailed. The most important and unambiguous pieces of evidence are three, **1476**, **1563**, and **1201**. The first two are horoscopes which give astronomical proof that 1 Macrianus and Quietus (= 8 Gallienus) was A.D. 260/1 and that 6 Valerian and Gallienus was A.D. 258/9. By giving a consulship as well as a regnal year **1201** confirms that 6 Valerian and Gallienus was A.D. 258/9. A papyrus from Oxyrhynchus, soon to be published as **2951**, adds its statement that 31 May in the consulship of Paternus and Arcesilaus, A.D. 267, fell in 14 Gallienus, which was consequently A.D. 266/7.

On that basis, then, we may take the first step forward and examine the relationship between the reigns of Gallienus and Claudius II, beginning with the evidence for the extent of Claudius' first year.

The first five items in the above table of the new Oxyrhynchus papyri show that it ran at least from 30 December to 19 February, and from the other papyri of the first year (table III below) we can extend that period in both directions. It ran at least from 16 October to 21 May. This year therefore cannot be the same as 15 Gallienus, which began on 30 August,[2] A.D. 267 and is attested on 20 March, A.D. 268 (P. Strasb. 7, 16). A short year 16 Gallienus is mentioned in two[3] papyri, P. Flor. 265 (Thoth 21 = 18 September, A.D. 268) and P. Tebt. 581 (Phaophi 1[4] = 28 September, A.D. 268). This will fit just before and in the same Graeco-Egyptian year as 1 Claudius, A.D. 268/9, and this relationship is strongly supported by P. Strasb. 11, which gives two dates in Phamenoth (Feb./March), 1 Claudius, and refers to 'the produce of the past 15th year'.

Here is a table of the papyri of 1 Claudius, omitting the five new items from Oxyrhynchus, for which see Table I.

---

[1] The controversy continued over several years: Mattingly, *Num. Chron.* 1924, p. 119, *JEA* xiii (1927), pp. 14–18, xiv (1928), p. 19; Stein, *Archiv* viii (1927), pp. 11–13, *JEA* xiv (1928), pp. 16–18. Cf. on the same topic Milne, *JEA* xiv (1928), pp. 20–1, and Tait, *Archiv* vii (1924), p. 224.

[2] In the year preceding the Julian leap year the Graeco-Egyptian year began one day later than usual after an extra intercalary day.

[3] The reading Ἔτου[ϲ ι]ϛ ϛ τοῦ κυρίου ἡμῶν [2] [Γαλ]λιηνοῦ Ϲεβαϲτοῦ, Ἀθὺρ ιη in P. Strasb. inv. P. gr. 1234 (*Recherches de Papyrologie* iii 62, no. 7) is suspect because comparison of the documents (P. Tebt. 581 of 16 Gallienus, Phaophi 1, and P. Strasb. 10 of 1 Claudius, Phaophi 19) indicates that in the Fayum the change from Gallienus to Claudius took place in Phaophi, the month before Hathyr. See plate iii ibid. for the poor state of the papyrus at this point. Professor Schwartz very kindly supplied me with a new photograph and examined the papyrus again for me. He suggests the revised reading Ἔτου[ϲ] αϛ ϛ τοῦ κυρίου ἡμῶν [2] [Κ]λαυδίο[υ] Ϲεβαϲτοῦ, Ἀθὺρ ιη, pointing out at the same time that the day number may be ιβ, since there is no trace of the crossbar of the supposed *eta*.

[4] See *P. Oxy.* xii p. 233.

TABLE III

| Reference | Month | Day | Conversion |
|-----------|-------|-----|------------|
| P. Strasb. 10, 23 | Phaophi[1] | 19 | 16 Oct., A.D. 268 |
| P. Strasb. 7, 17 | Hathyr | 9 | 5 Nov., A.D. 268 |
| P. Strasb. inv. P. gr. 1207,[2] 27 | Choeac | not given | 27 Nov.–26 Dec., A.D. 268 |
| P. Strasb. inv. P. gr. 1197,[3] 4 | Choeac[4] | not given | 27 Nov.–26 Dec., A.D. 268 |
| P. Strasb. 11, 7 | Phamenoth | 7 | 3 Mar., A.D. 269 |
| P. Lips. inv. 483[5] | (Phamenoth) | (10) | 6 Mar., A.D. 269 |
| P. Strasb. 11, 15 | Phamenoth | 14 | 10 Mar., A.D. 269 |
| P. Strasb. 7, 18 | Phamenoth | 30 | 26 Mar., A.D. 269 |
| P. Ryl. 117, 29 | Pachon | 17 | 12 May, A.D. 269 |
| P. Ryl. 117, 4 | Pachon | 26 | 21 May, A.D. 269 |
| PSI 457,[6] 20 | Epeiph | 18 | 12 July, A.D. 269 |

According to these dates interpreted in the traditional way Claudius II acceded between 28 August and 16 October, A.D. 268 and his first Graeco-Egyptian regnal year ran from the *dies imperii* to 28 August, A.D. 269.[7]

[1] 1 Claudius, Thoth is referred to in retrospect in SB 8086, 9. Reason appears above (p. 18 n. 3) for thinking that a document actually of that date would have been assigned to 16 Gallienus. Similarly **1698** 27 of Thoth 13 of the first year of an unnamed emperor is probably not to be assigned to Claudius II, though the right explanation remains to be found. Personally I incline to regard it as a mistake for year two, because it would require a journey of almost miraculous speed to bring news of a new accession from Rome to Oxyrhynchus in thirteen days or less.

[2] *Recherches de Papyrologie* iii 63–4 = SB 8086.

[3] *Recherches de Papyrologie* iii 67.      [4] This date is retrospective in its context.

[5] WChr. p. 503 = SB 4514. Only the Julian conversion is given.

[6] PSI 457 is attributed to the reign of Tacitus. It is obvious from line 17—ὀμνύω τὴν Κλαυδίου καίσαρος τοῦ κυρίου Cεβαστοῦ τύχην—that the correct reading in line 6 must be πρὸς τὸ ἐνεστὸς α (ἔτος) Κ[λαυδίου and in lines 20–1 αὐτοκράτορος καίσαρος Μάρκου [Αὐρηλίου] [21] Κλ[αυδίου etc., not Μάρκου [Κλαυδίου Ta-][21]κί[του. The circumstance that a man who had his *epicrisis* in 1 Decius and Herennius (A.D. 249/50) had a son of age for *epicrisis* in 1 Claudius (A.D. 268/9) means that the son was born probably in A.D. 255/6 and the father married about that year or the year before, in his 19th or 20th year. There is no difficulty in that; see Hombert–Préaux, *Recensement*, p. 160.

[7] According to *AÉ* 1944, no. 85 a new reading in *CIL* iii 3525 (= 10492) = D. 2457 gives the day as [*pr*]*idie kal. Iuli.* The consuls are those of A.D. 268 and the *legio II Adiutrix* has the cognomen *Claudiana*. Professor Alföldi concluded that Claudius acceded before this date, 30 June, A.D. 268. This is incompatible with the evidence of the papyri. If the text of line 8 is correctly read and supplemented as *militib*[*us iuss*]*it* [*pr*]*idie kal*(*endas*) *Iuli*(*as*), the day might tolerably be taken as the date of the order rather than the date of the inscription, which must be put after the accession of Claudius. However the text as it stands in *AÉ* 1944, no. 85 is unintelligible—for instance, there is no subject and no room for a subject

His second year will be A.D. 269/70. Besides the new Oxyrhynchus papyri of that year (items 6 to 16 in Table I), we have five other papyrus dates—Thoth 1 (**1561** 21), Thoth 24 (P. Strasb. 7, 19), Choeac 14 (P. Flor. 50, 117), Mecheir 23 (P. Strasb. 7, 20, 'E[π]είφ ed. pr.; Mε[χ]είρ *Recherches* iii 55) and, rather doubtfully read, Payni 30 (P. Erlangen 101 i 2). In fact there is every reason to believe that, as far as the Egyptians knew, it was a complete year, since it is attested from Thoth (August/September) to Payni (May/June, Table I, item 14) and there are two mentions of a third year on Thoth 23 (P. Strasb. 7, 21) and Phaophi 23 (?; second digit uncertain, **1646** 33), i.e. 20 September and on or near 20 October, A.D. 270.

Before using the names of Aurelian and Vaballathus Egyptian scribes dated for a short time by the formula ἐπὶ ὑπάτων τοῦ ἐνεστῶτος ἔτους, which probably means that agreement had not yet been reached between the Palmyrenes and the Romans. In the new archive there are three examples (Table I, items 17–19). It was previously known only in P. Strasb. inv. P. gr. 1238 (*Recherches* iii 62–3, no. 8) and in the unpublished P. gr. 2550 (ibid. pp. 93–4).[1] The context of the first makes it clear that this formula precedes dating by the titles of Aurelian and Vaballathus. The document is a note of a series of half-yearly payments for rent of livestock. The last instalment was paid in 1 Aur. 4 Vab. on Phamenoth 18 (14 March, A.D. 271). The preceding payment is dated ἐπὶ ὑπάτων τοῦ ἐνεστῶ(τος) ἔτους, Ἀθὺρ ιϛ, i.e. 11 November, A.D. 270.

The name of Claudius' brother and successor, Quintillus, has not so far appeared in the papyri. The coins show that his short reign was acknowledged in Alexandria (J. Vogt, *Die alex. Münzen* i 212, ii 160).

The new archive gives us the earliest papyrological date in the reign of Aurelian, between 11 and 19 Choeac[2]—7 and 15 December—year 1; the second digit of the day number is damaged (Table I, item 20). Other papyri attest for this year the months Tybi (item 21), Phamenoth (*Recherches* iii 62–3), Pharmouthi (P. Strasb. 8 i 1), Pachon (*Recherches* iii 67; **1200**, corrected in *P. Oxy.* xii p. 223), and Payni (O. Mich. 1006),[3] i.e. December to June. From which it is clear that 1 Aur. (4) Vab. cannot overlap in any way with 2 Claudius, A.D. 269/70. It follows the short year 3 Claudius and falls in the same Graeco-Egyptian year, A.D. 270/1.

This new date for Aurelian's earliest appearance in the papyri is significant in itself, because it suggests two arguments that help to confirm that 1 Aur. (4) Vab. is A.D. 270/1. Firstly, since Claudius reached a third tribunician power (*CIL* ii 1672, iii 3521, viii 4876) and acceded sometime in A.D. 268, whether before or after 29 August,

---

for *refeci*[*t*] (6) and [*iuss*]*it* (8)—and the texts given in *CIL* and *ILS* suggest that the reading of the date is far from certain.

[1] A possible third example is **1544** 11 ἐπὶ ὑπ[ά]των Φαῶφι κγ. The first editors placed this under Diocletian but the persons concerned seem to have been active rather earlier than that, see **2775** 5 n.

[2] CPR i 9, 8 refers retrospectively to Hathyr of 1 Aur. 4 Vab., but this is not necessarily a real date. The document itself is dated 2 Aur. 5 Vab., month and day lost.

[3] Professor Youtie has informed me by letter and in another connection that instead of καὶ β(αϲιλέωϲ) in O. Mich. 1006, 3 we should read καὶ Οὐ(αβαλλάθου). This has no effect on the date.

he must on the usual theory of the renewal of the tribunician power have lived beyond 10 December, A.D. 269. News of the succession could not have reached Oxyrhynchus in less than five days, so if Claudius' third *trib. pot.* is correctly dated, the December of this papyrus cannot be that of A.D. 269 and must be that of A.D. 270.

Secondly, every other third-century emperor from Gordian III with the sole exception of Diocletian was *consul ordinarius* in the January after he came to power. There is a strong implication that Aurelian acceded in A.D. 270 since he was consul in January, A.D. 271. If he had succeeded in or before December, A.D. 269, he would in all probability have been consul in January, A.D. 270, which he was not. For this argument I am indebted to the good advice of Dr. T. D. Barnes.

Neither of these arguments constitutes absolute proof, but each of them lends valuable weight to the system proposed here.

In SHA *Claud.* 11, 3 (cf. 12, 2) we are given the consular year A.D. 270 for Claudius' last campaign and death. However pleased we would be to accept the statement, the SHA notoriously requires rather than affords support. It has it, I believe, from the papyri.

Corroboration of this account of the overlapping of the three reigns is available from two items of the archive. In these the petitioners give the year of their *epicrisis* and their age at the time of submitting their applications to be admitted to the corn dole. The normal age for *epicrisis* was in the 13th or 14th year; the 12th year appears to be attested once (P. Haw. 401 = *Archiv* v 395) and for accidental reasons a later age was possible,[1] but both examples work well for our scheme if they were in their 14th year at *epicrisis*. One (**2894** ii) had his *epicrisis* in 11 Gallienus and was in his 20th year (ἐτῶν κ) in 2 Claudius; the other (**2908** ii) had his in 13 Gallienus and was in his 19th year in 1 Aur. (4) Vab.[2] It may be put schematically as follows:—

| A's age | B's age | Regnal year | | Julian year |
|---------|---------|-------------|---|-------------|
| <u>14</u> | | 11 Gallienus | | 263/4 |
| 15 | | 12 | | 264/5 |
| 16 | <u>14</u> | 13 | | 265/6 |
| 17 | 15 | 14 | | 266/7 |
| 18 | 16 | 15 | | 267/8 |
| 19 | 17 | 16 G. = 1 Claudius | | 268/9 |
| 20 | 18 | | 2 Claudius | 269/70 |
| <u></u> | <u>19</u> | 1 Aur. (4) Vab. = 3 Cl. | | 270/1 |

In a third case the applicant underwent *epicrisis* in 1 Aurelian and was in his 16th year in 3 Aurelian (**2902**). This has no bearing on the relation between the reigns,

---

[1] See *CÉ* xxxi (1956), pp. 109–17, both for late *epicrisis* in unusual circumstances and the latest list of *epicrisis* documents; add newly P. Wis. 17.

[2] The official method of reckoning age was much like that of regnal years; the child was 'in his first year' as soon as he was born and began to be 'in his second year' at the next new year's day, Thoth 1. See *BICS* xiv (1967), pp. 53–5, and a very good new example in BGU xi 2020, a declaration of birth for a pair of twins and two other children.

but it does appear to support the regularity of the scheme. He was in his 14th year in 1 Aur., in his 15th in 2 Aur., and in his 16th in 3 Aur. I believe that this is in fact true, but the interpretation of the dates is not so straightforward as it appears at this stage and it will be necessary to return to the case later.

This scheme is the only one that will make sense of all the numerous items of evidence without distorting them, but it brings us up very forcibly against the original problem. Seven years of Aurelian are attested and if we follow 1 Aur. (4) Vab. = A.D. 270/1 by a normal succession of years we find that 7 Aurelian should begin on 29 August, A.D. 276. And yet Tacitus was consul as emperor in January, A.D. 276.

The problem is a real one. The seventh[1] year of Aurelian is attested by the coins (Vogt, *Die alex. Münzen* ii 163), by **2338** ii 39 and by **1455**, which adds a month and day, Phaophi 21 = 19 October. **1633** of Mesore 30 in Aurelian's sixth year, i.e. only six days before the end of the sixth year, is also worth citing, since if we count forward from what we have already worked out it appears to be of 23 August, A.D. 276. Similarly P. Cair. Isid. 85, of Epeiph 29, 6 Aurelian, appears to be of 23 July, A.D. 276.

And in case any doubt should arise about the accuracy of the consular *fasti* we have astronomical evidence for the reign of Probus to supplement the *fasti*, the coins, and the ordinary papyri. **2557** is a horoscope for 4 Probus, Thoth 24. Agreement of the text and modern computation is very good for 21 September, A.D. 278. It would be very bad for A.D. 279, with only two of the six legible placings of the heavenly bodies in the signs of the zodiac correct. This confirms that 4 Probus was A.D. 278/9 and that 1 Probus = 1 Tacitus = 7 Aurelian was A.D. 275/6. A similar proof is available from another horoscope PSI 764 = Neugebauer and van Hoesen, *Greek Horoscopes*, p. 61, no. 277. In short, at the end of the reign we find that 6 and 7 Aurelian were A.D. 274/5 and 275/6, which appears to contradict the evidence that 1 Aur. (4) Vab. was A.D. 270/1.

Another way out of the impasse was suggested by P. Schnabel in *Klio* xx (1926), pp. 363-8. Stein made a characteristically vigorous rejoinder in *Klio* xxi (1927), pp. 78-82, and perhaps on this account Schnabel's view has received less attention than I believe it deserves.[2] Before setting out his explanation it may be helpful to recapitulate one of his arguments against Stein's theory which has gained yet more force from the new Oxyrhynchus papyri. He pointed out that in P. Strasb. 7, 21 the date 3 Claudius, Thoth 23 equals 20 September, A.D. 270, as the series of half-yearly payments complete from the ninth year of Gallienus plainly shows.[3] But in **1200** (corrected in *P. Oxy.* xii p. 223) 1 Aur. 4 Vab., Pachon 30 would on Stein's system of official dates be equal to 25 May, A.D. 270. Stein admitted (*Klio* xxi 81) that it was odd to have dates by Claudius II in the Fayum four months after Aurelian's accession was

---

[1] The alleged mention of an eighth year in O. Mich. 157, 3 cannot be accepted for a moment; see *BL* iii 262, based somewhat loosely on *TAPA* lxxvi (1945), p. 146.

[2] It was adopted, however, by D. Schlumberger in *Bull. Ét. Orient.* ix (1942-3), pp. 46-8.

[3] Professor Schwartz has suggested in *Recherches* iii 93 that the last three entries on this sheet of papyrus refer to years of Aurelian and were added in error to the wrong sheet. This is both unlikely in itself and unhelpful in resolving the contradiction of the regnal years.

known in Oxyrhynchus, which is more remote than the Fayum, but he appealed to other examples of the irregular spread of news. Now, however, we have from Oxyrhynchus documents of Claudius' first year (Table I, items 1–5) that evidently follow the same system as P. Strasb. 7, and with them we have the earliest document in 1 Aur. (4) Vab. (Table I, item 20), which would on Stein's official system date from December, A.D. 269, nine to ten months earlier than the date by Claudius II in P. Strasb. 7, 21.

Schnabel's suggestion was that Aurelian's accession actually fell shortly before 29 August, A.D. 270 but that during the Palmyrene domination in Egypt his years were incorrectly counted 1 Aur. (4) Vab. = A.D. 270/1, 2 Aur. 5 Vab. = A.D. 271/2 until the recovery of Egypt, when A.D. 271/2 was correctly called 3 Aurelian even though it came at the end of the same Graeco-Egyptian year as 2 Aur. 5 Vab. He considered that there was documentary proof of this in **1208** of A.D. 291, where it is specifically stated that 2 Claudius II became 1 Aurelian—line 11 τῷ β (ἔτει) Κλαυδίου, ὃ ἐγέ[νετο] α (ἔτος) Αὐρηλιανοῦ, [μ]ηνὶ Τῦβι.

This theory continues to satisfy all the documentary evidence. The latest date in 2 Aur. 5 Vab. is now Pharmouthi 22 (17 April; Table I, item 25). The earliest date by 3 Aurelian is now Payni 30 (24 June; Table I, item 29). The other dates by 3 Aurelian are from Mesore (July/August). The documents are P. Strasb. 280, 21 of Mesore 3rd intercalary day, P. Oslo 96, 10 (day lost), and P. Wis. 2, 35 (day not given; for the reading see ed pr., plate i, and *CÉ* xliv (1969), p. 136). In P. Flor. 26, 11 Aurelian's third year is mentioned retrospectively without month or day.

This is not a theory that one can feel completely comfortable with, unless a satisfying explanation for the change of reckoning can be found. Schnabel offered no detailed explanation, and one is left in doubt whether he ascribed the initial 'error' to the Palmyrene domination or to faulty communication with Egypt. Stein was particularly scathing about the absence of a reason—'Warum Aurelian dem Jahr, das er als sein zweites bezeichnete, solang er Vaballath anerkennte, dann lieber die Ziffer 3 verlieh, das bleibt Schnabels Geheimnis' (*Klio* xxi (1927), p. 78).

D. Schlumberger, who accepted Schnabel's chronology, suggested that Aurelian never recognized Vaballathus and therefore never recognized the Egyptian computation of his years, *Bull. Ét. Orient.* ix (1942–3), p. 46. However that may be—and it is not the usual view—I see no reason why the Palmyrenes should have attributed an unofficial *dies imperii* to Aurelian, though it is conceivable that they were reluctant on practical grounds to alter the formula 1 Aurelian, 4 Vaballathus once it was proclaimed. If a change of computation was made, therefore, I would attribute it to Aurelian's own policy, and a possible reason for it can be discerned. Aurelian presented himself as the legitimate successor of Claudius, not of Quintillus. Nevertheless it is clear from the coins that Quintillus was widely recognized without demur for a while and that it was only after some lapse of time that Aurelian was proclaimed by the soldiers (Damerau, *Kaiser Claudius II Goticus*, p. 90). Whereupon Quintillus either committed suicide or was killed. If we postulate that the death of Claudius took place shortly before 29 August,

A.D. 270 and the proclamation of **Aurelian** after that date, we begin to see how a problem might arise for Egyptian officials. If Aurelian first set his *dies imperii* on the day the troops proclaimed him and subsequently put it back to the day of Claudius' death, claiming what Zonaras relates, that the dying Claudius declared him worthy to be emperor (xii 26), the effect would be to change the enumeration of his Egyptian regnal years. The Egyptians, however, might well be reluctant to make the confusing change from 1 Aur. 4 Vab. to 2 Aur. 4 Vab., and since the Palmyrenes controlled the country his preference would not necessarily have been respected.

We must examine how the reign of Quintillus might fit into this hypothesis. It is clear from the existence of Alexandrian coins both of 3 Claudius and of 1 Quintillus that the latter's *dies imperii* did not fall before 29 August, A.D. 270. Claudius died in Pannonia at Sirmium on the Save (Zonaras xii 26). Quintillus was apparently in Italy (SHA *Aur.* 37, 5 '*in praesidio Italico*'). It is acceptable then that his *dies imperii* can have fallen later than the day of Claudius' death. We may compare Hadrian's *dies imperii*, which he fixed on the day that news of Trajan's death reached him (SHA *Hadr.* 4, 7). In my hypothesis 29 August will have fallen in the interval required for the news to reach Quintillus.

The scheme that I propose, following Schnabel, for the dating of papyrus documents is this:

```
       15 Gallienus = 267/8
       16 Gallienus = 268/9   = 1 Claudius
                       269/70 = 2 Claudius
1 Aurelian (4) Vaballathus = 270/1 = 3 Claudius (= 1 Quintillus)
2 Aurelian 5 Vaballathus  = 271/2 = 3 Aurelian
                            272/3 = 4 Aurelian
                            273/4 = 5 Aurelian
                            274/5 = 6 Aurelian
                            275/6 = 7 Aurelian ( = 1 Tacitus = 1 Probus)
```

This will be adequate to deal with dates which refer to the time of writing. For those writing in or after 3 Aurelian, however, the proper designations of the Egyptian years A.D. 269/70 and A.D. 270/1 were 1 Aurelian and 2 Aurelian. So in **1208** 11 the year A.D. 269/70 is described as τῷ β (ἔτει) Κλαυδίου, ὃ ἐγέ[νετο] α (ἔτος) Αὐρηλιανοῦ. A document actually of that date would have been dated in 2 Claudius. The double version may have been fossilized into this document of A.D. 291 and no longer of much practical importance, but on the other hand it may have been essential for anyone who wanted to consult the public records of twenty years before.

Similarly, in the single item of the new Oxyrhynchite archive that is dated in 3 Aurelian, the applicant says that he had his *epicrisis* in 1 Aurelian and was 16 years old in 3 Aurelian (Table I, item 29). By 1 Aurelian he will mean, if Schnabel and I are right, A.D. 269/70. An indication that may favour this view is his explanation that he has not answered to his name when it was called 'because of having been away from home on unavoidable duty following the army'—τῷ ἐπὶ τῆς ἀλλοδαπῆς ἀναγκαίας χρείας χάριν παρεϲτρατεῦϲθαι. I take this to refer to the military activity connected with Aurelian's recovery of Egypt, which fits very nicely with the view that it has only just been completed at the end of A.D. 271/2. But of course this falls far short of proof that that actually was the case.

It may be useful to list the main conclusions reached in what precedes:

1. Gallienus lived beyond 28 August, A.D. 268 into the 16th year of his reign.

2. Claudius II acceded between 28 August and 16 October, A.D. 268.

3. Claudius II probably died shortly before 28 August, A.D. 270, that is, before the end of his second year. His third year is attested because news of his death did not reach Egypt till after 28 August, A.D. 270.

4. Quintillus succeeded as emperor after 28 August, A.D. 270, as shown by Alexandrian coins both of 3 Claudius and of 1 Quintillus. He has not yet appeared in the papyri.

5. After a short period during which Quintillus was widely acknowledged on the coinage Aurelian acceded.

6. Before dates by Aurelian and Vaballathus appear in the papyri scribes used the formula ἐπὶ ὑπάτων τοῦ ἐνεϲτῶτος ἔτουϲ in Hathyr (Oct./Nov.) and perhaps also in Phaophi (Sept./Oct.; **1544** 11), A.D. 270. The exact significance of it in the minds of its users is uncertain, but it presumably reflects the Palmyrene challenge to Rome in the East.

7. By December Egyptian scribes were dating by the first year of Aurelian and Vaballathus, implying that Aurelian succeeded after 28 August, A.D. 270. Later in the Egyptian year this was emended to 1 Aurelian, 4 Vaballathus. The earliest papyrus using the emended formula is P. Strasb. inv. P. gr. 1238 of 14 March, A.D. 271 (*Recherches* iii 62–3, no. 8). CPR i 9, 8 mentions Hathyr of 1 Aur. 4 Vab., but retrospectively.

8. Aurelian appears to have put back the date of his *dies imperii* to before 29 August, A.D. 270, probably to the date of Claudius' death and probably in order to avoid recognizing the reign of Quintillus. As a result he reached a seventh Graeco-Egyptian year though he ruled only from late A.D. 270 to after, presumably not long after, 29 August, A.D. 275.

At this point it may be worth quoting two passages from J. G. Milne's *Catalogue of Alexandrian Coins in the Ashmolean Museum* relating to the amount of coinage in the reigns of Claudius II and Aurelian, but with the warning that unexplained fluctuations in the output of the Alexandrian mint are not uncommon.

The passages are:

p. xxiv, paragraph 51,

'The activity of the Alexandrian mint continued under Claudius Gothicus: during the months which counted as his first year, it was about equal to what it had been in the preceding months which formed the fifteenth year of Gallienus, and in year 2 it rose still farther.'

p. xxiv, paragraph 53,

'In year 3 of Aurelian another drop brought the coinage to a lower figure than had been recorded for several years, about a quarter of that of year 2: then a rise began, the output being doubled in year 4, doubled again in year 5 and increased further by about a quarter in year 6.'

It may fairly be claimed without pressing these passages too hard that the first one is consistent with the conclusion that year 15 of Gallienus and year 1 of Claudius II were separate years, and the second one consistent with the conclusion that year 3 of Aurelian represents only the end of the same Graeco-Egyptian year as 2 Aur. 5 Vab.

What I hope to have shown by the cumulation of the new evidence on the old is that there is no reason to accept that there were two reckonings in use at the same time. These Oxyrhynchus papyri are quite plainly using the same system as the Strasbourg papyri and their context is an official one, so that the relation between the reigns of Gallienus, Claudius, and Aurelian is as unambiguous as the proof that 6 and 7 Aurelian were A.D. 274/5 and 275/6. Consequently we are obliged to recognize that there was a change of reckoning between 2 Aur. 5 Vab. and 6 Aurelian. In amplifying Schnabel's hypothesis with my own conjectures I hope to have shown a plausible way in which the change might have taken place.

The chronology of Aurelian's early years will be especially affected by this interpretation of the papyri. A proper study will be needed, but it may be useful to point out that the recovery of Egypt in A.D. 272 instead of A.D. 271 leaves a little more room to accommodate the numerous early campaigns against the northern invaders, see Walser and Pekáry, *Die Krise*, p. 52 = A. Alföldi, *Studien z. Geschichte d. Weltkrise des 3. Jahrh.*, pp. 427–30, esp. 429–30.

## APPENDIX

*Consul and* trib. pot. *numbers in the inscriptions and coins of Aurelian*

For real precision this question requires a thorough investigation by an epigraphist able and willing to check the originals or photographs of as many as possible of the items of evidence, some of which are now lost or otherwise dubious. However I have a suggestion to make which has not previously been considered.

From the list compiled by L. Bivona in *Epigraphica* 28 (1966), p. 107, of 33 items containing indications of *tribuniciae potestates* and consulships one can extract 25 which contain both, falling into 11 combinations as shown in Table A opposite.

Everyone who has treated the question so far has considered that there is no doubt about what is meant by the consulship numbers 1, 2, and 3. According to the *fasti* they mean A.D. 271, 274, and 275 respectively. But unless the inscriptions and coins teem with errors this is impossible. The tribunician power is assumed by an emperor at the beginning of his reign and in the ordinary way is renewed either annually on the *dies imperii*, as Mattingly and his followers would have it, or on the 10 December next following the accession and subsequently on each succeeding 10 December, according to Mommsen and his school of thought. In some cases an extra *trib. pot.* can be assumed to mark a special event, as was done by Decius (Walser–Pekáry, *Die Krise*, p. 23) and by Maximinus (Bersanetti, *Massimino*, p. 66 n. 4). If Aurelian acceded about September, A.D. 270 and died sometime between 29 August and 10 December, A.D. 275, as the papyri seem to indicate, he would by either system have had six grants of tribunician power. Seven are attested. Presumably he had one extra, perhaps to celebrate his defeat of Zenobia or Tetricus, or to celebrate his *quinquennalia*—so Laffranchi, *Riv. Ital. Num.* xliii (1941), p. 131. But by no possible scheme can he have passed through grants 3, 5, 6, and 7 in his second consulship in A.D. 274 and through grants 3?, 4, 5, 6, and 7 in his third consulship in A.D. 275. The only hope of constructing a coherent scheme is to allow that there was some doubt about the numbering of his consulships.[1]

TABLE A

|  | cos. | trib. pot. |  |
|---|---|---|---|
| 1 | 1 | 2 | Sotgiu 42[2] |
| 2 | 1 | 3 | *CIL* iii Suppl. 1, 7586, viii 2, 9040[3] |
| 3 | 2 | 3 | *CIL* viii 2, 10017, xii 5511 |
| 4 | 2 | 5 | Sotgiu 38, *CIL* viii 2, 10177, 10217, Suppl. 3, 22449, vi 1112 (*cos. des. III*) |
| 5 | 2 | 6 | Cohen 178, *RIC* 185 |
| 6 | 2 | 7 | Rohde 32?[4], *RIC* 16, *RIC* 186 |
| 7 | 3 | 3? | *CIL* ii 4506 |
| 8 | 3 | 4 | Cohen 177, *CIL* xii 5456 |
| 9 | 3 | 5 | *CIL* v 1, 4319, xiii 2, 2, 8904, xii 5548 (both figures uncertain)? |
| 10 | 3 | 6 | Sotgiu 2, *CIL* viii 1, 5143, xiii 2, 2, 8997? |
| 11 | 3 | 7 | *CIL* xiii 2, 2, 8973 |

Interesting parallels are provided by the neighbouring reigns of Claudius II and Tacitus. Tacitus was *consul ordinarius* in A.D. 273 and again as emperor in A.D. 276, at which point the *fasti* give him the iteration figure *II*. He died in the course of the same year, yet some of his coins describe him as *consul III* (Webb, *RIC* v i Tac. nos. 120, 121). He can hardly have demeaned himself to be a suffect consul in the same year in which he was *ordinarius*. The explanation has been advanced that he was suffect consul at the end of A.D. 275, when his reign began (Degrassi, *Fasti*, p. 73). If this is right it seems that there was some doubt about how it should affect the iteration figure. Perhaps it

[1] The mention of a suffect consulship of A.D. 258 in SHA *Aur.* 11, 8 is generally regarded as an invention and it certainly cannot be used unless corroborated by some reliable evidence.
[2] G. Sotgiu, *Studi sull'epigrafia di Aureliano*, Cagliari, 1961.
[3] For the uncertainty of this item see now *Hermes* xcviii (1970), pp. 121–4.
[4] This is placed by Dr. Bivona under *trib.pot. V cos. II*, but it appears to have a legend wrongly struck or wrongly read indicating *trib.pot. VII* (TB [sic] p. v· ii cos· ii).

arose because of the relatively low prestige of the suffect consulship, so that people were not sure if they would be flattering the emperor if they counted a suffect consulship in the iteration figure. However when I showed a draft of this appendix to Dr. T. D. Barnes he put forward the suggestion that the uncertainty about iteration figures might arise rather from *ornamenta consularia* than from suffect consulships held at the beginning of a reign. The custom of including *ornamenta consularia* in the iteration figure began with the indulgence shown by Septimius Severus to Plautianus, who was proclaimed *consul II* by reason of the *ornamenta* when he held his first real consulship in A.D. 203 (Dio xlvi 46, 4). Macrinus refused to count his *ornamenta* because they were acquired under the distasteful regime of Caracalla (Dio lxxviii 13). However in inscriptions from the first Julian year of his reign he is called both consul designate and consul designate II, the latter because of the *ornamenta*, according to Dessau (*ILS* 465 n. 2).

In favour of this explanation rather than Degrassi's is the fact, if it is not too early to be relevant, that when Elagabalus began his reign by replacing Macrinus as consul in the middle of A.D. 218 there was no hesitation in counting that consulship towards the subsequent iteration figures.

Whatever the reason for the uncertainty, it extends also to the reign of Claudius II, who appears in the *fasti* only for A.D. 269 and without an iteration figure. He was not *consul ordinarius* in A.D. 270. Yet he is given the title *cos. II* in four inscriptions (*CIL* ii 3619, 3834, 4505, viii 4876).[1] Other inscriptions with *trib. pot. II* and *III* give him no iteration figure, e.g. *ILS* 569, 570.

**2710** has recently revealed another instance which may be of the same sort. It is dated 17 May, A.D. 261 by Egyptian regnal year and day of the month, and also in the consulships of Macrianus for the second time and of Quietus. The iteration figure in the case of Quietus is lost. It seems unlikely that these persons had been consuls before they became unsuccessful rivals to Gallienus at the end of A.D. 260. They do not appear in the *fasti*. They presumably pretended to regard themselves as the ordinary consuls for A.D. 261 and Macrinus at least had some claim to be *consul iterum* based on the events of the end of A.D. 260.

If we allow the hypothesis that two reckonings of Aurelian's consulships were in use at the same time, as it seems there were two reckonings for Claudius and Tacitus, it becomes possible to accommodate most of the 11 combinations of consulship and tribunician power. The critical factor now becomes the dating of the extra grant of tribunician power. No date assigned to it can produce absolute consistency among the documents, but a very promising solution can be found in the following scheme, based on the hypotheses that Aurelian acceded in A.D. 270, renewed his *trib. pot.* on 10 December, A.D. 270, and on the same day annually thereafter, and allowed himself an extra grant in the course of A.D. 274, perhaps to celebrate his defeats of Zenobia and Tetricus or to mark his *quinquennalia*.

---

[1] We can probably neglect the single coin of poor workmanship that calls him *cos. III* (Webb, *RIC* v i Cl. no. 177).

TABLE B

| | trib. pot. | consul (a) | consul (b) |
|---|---|---|---|
| August,    A.D. 270 | I | O | I |
| December       270 | 2 | O | I |
| January        271 | 2 | I | 2 |
| December       271 | 3 | I | 2 |
| December       272 | 4 | I | 2 |
| December       273 | 5 | I | 2 |
| January        274 | 5 | 2 | 3 |
| ?              274 | 6 | 2 | 3 |
| December       274 | 7 | 2 | 3 |
| January        275 | 7 | 3 | 4 |

Using one or other of the consular figures this scheme will accommodate all the combinations in Table A but 7 and 8, i.e. *trib. pot. III, cos. III* and *trib. pot. IIII, cos. III*. Both of these are represented by suspect documents, 7 by *CIL* ii 4506 and 8 by Cohen 177 and *CIL* xii 5456. The first is now lost, the second was suspected by Cohen of error or falsity and has not been verified and incorporated into *RIC*, and the third is also lost.

If the argument so far is correct the iteration figure for the tribunician power is more reliable for assessing the date of an inscription or a coin than that of the consulship, though it cannot be precise until the date of the extra grant is ascertained rather than assumed. For the moment I assign it to A.D. 274, because that requires the rejection of the fewest and the least reliable documents. It would not be worth while to reproduce all the possible schemes but their effects can be summed up.

We may take first the group of schemes that assumes renewal on 10 December. If the extra grant is assigned to any year before A.D. 274 it is not possible to accommodate group 9, i.e. *trib. pot. V, cos. III*, represented by *CIL* v 1, 4319 and xiii 2, 2, 8904. Both of these are still extant and reliably read.[1] If we put it later than A.D. 274, that is, in A.D. 275, we exclude group 6, *trib. pot. VII, cos. II*, represented by *RIC* 16 and *RIC* 186.

If we make an analogous scheme supposing that the tribunician power was renewed on the *dies imperii* and the extra grant made in A.D. 274, we find again that group 6, *trib. pot. VII, cos. II*, is excluded. The same would be true for any similar scheme that fixed the extra grant of *trib. pot.* earlier than A.D. 274, and one that placed the extra grant in A.D. 275 would exclude groups 5 and 6, as well as the doubtful group 7.[2]

[1] Sotgiu, p. 16, regards them as mistaken, however.
[2] The pretended proof of Kramer and Jones (*AJP* lxiv (1943), pp. 83–6) that Aurelian renewed his tribunician power on the *dies imperii* consists only in manipulating the inconvenient evidence, disregarding especially the evidence for the seventh tribunician power. Dr. Bivona's idea that in A.D. 272 Aurelian began to count a new series of *trib. pot.* is unsatisfactory, because the prestige of the title increased as the number grew higher. For an emperor to go back to number 1 without some very special mark of a new era would be to diminish his own reputation.

It may be useful to set out the propositions of this appendix in general terms. The main contention is that there are strong indications, both in the apparent inconsistencies of the documents and in the analogous confusions over consulships in the preceding and succeeding reigns, that there were two sets of iteration figures for Aurelian's consulships, one that of the *fasti* and another giving a figure one higher at each stage.

If this is accepted, the outstanding problem is to date the extra grant of tribunician power which brings Aurelian's total to the attested 7 instead of the 6 that strictly annual renewal would have produced. Absolute consistency among the documents cannot be attained, but if we assign the extra grant to A.D. 274 we need reject only three documents and they are documents which are now unverifiable. If we assign the extra grant to other years, more documents must be rejected, including some that are still extant and reliably reported.

## 2892–2922. Applications

These applications form the bulk of the corn dole archive. Most of them bear clear indications that they come from τόμοι cυγκολλήcιμοι, files made up in roll form by glueing together side by side the individual sheets on which the applications are written. Clearly some effort was made to arrange them by area. In five cases (**2892–2894**, **2906**, and **2908**) there are two adjacent items from persons listed in the same quarter. In one case (**2913**) adjacent items concern different quarters, but this may be because both these quarters fell in one of the twelve areas into which the city was divided for the purposes of the corn dole and which are perhaps identical with the tribes (**2928–2929**; Introd. pp. 6 seq).

It is not clear whether there were files devoted to each area or whether the local arrangement was made within each file. In either case the length of the period of time which they cover makes it very probable that several files are represented.

There may also have been an effort to arrange them according to the official to whom they were addressed. In four cases (**2892–2894, 2908**) adjacent items are addressed to the same official. In one case the officials in adjacent items are different (**2906**).

The standing and relation to one another of the several officials and boards to whom the applications are addressed are far from clear. It may be that the distinction between the individuals is solely one of time and that they succeeded one another in the same office. This may be supported by **2906** ii and iii, two petitions addressed to different officials, stuck together and evidently coming from the same roll file. Plution's is dated in the period of indecision between the reigns of Claudius and Aurelian, while Horion's is dated in the first year of Aurelian and Vaballathus. However there are differences of terminology which might be taken to indicate that the situation is more complex.

Ten applications are addressed to Aurelius Plution, who is always described simply as γραμματεὺϲ ϲιτηρεϲίου, 'secretary of the corn dole'. Most of the dated ones fall in the second year of Claudius II, one is dated in the period of indecision between Claudius and Aurelian (**2906** ii), and a damaged one is dated at some now irrecoverable time in the reign of Aurelian and Vaballathus (**2916**).

Eight are addressed to Calpurnius Horion, a synthesis of whose titles would be ὁ κράτιϲτοϲ ὑπομνηματογράφοϲ βουλευτὴϲ τῆϲ λαμπροτάτηϲ πόλεωϲ τῶν Ἀλεξανδρέων, νεωκόροϲ τοῦ μεγάλου Ϲαράπιδοϲ. All those dated by reign and year fall in the first year of Aurelian and Vaballathus, so that he could have succeeded Plution directly some time after the beginning of that year.

Three dateless applications (**2915, 2918, 2930**) are addressed to Marcus Aurelius Achilles, ὁ κράτιϲτοϲ ὑπομνηματογράφοϲ, who is once given an alias beginning with *alpha* (**2918**). In one of the documents he is associated with a board of commissioners, οἱ αἱρεθέντεϲ ὑπὸ τῆϲ κρατίϲτηϲ βουλῆϲ διάδοϲιν ποιήϲαϲθαι τοῦ ϲιτηρεϲίου.

A fourth damaged document may be attributable to Achilles (**2899**). It is addressed to an official described as νεωκόροϲ τοῦ μεγάλου Ϲαράπιδοϲ ὁ κράτιϲτοϲ ὑπομνηματογράφοϲ and bearing the *nomen* Aurelius. He is associated with a board of διακριταί. He can hardly be Aurelius Plution, who is always called only γραμματεὺϲ ϲιτηρεϲίου. The final formula of another **document**, unfortunately headless, is very much like this one except that it preserves the date, 1 Claudius, Tybi (**2901**). It may be, therefore, that Achilles' term of office fell even before Plution's, but this guess depends on a very tenuous connection of a headless document with a damaged name in another.

One application dated in 2 Aurelian 5 Vaballathus (17 April, A.D. 272; **2904**) is addressed to Aurelius Eudaemon *alias* Helladius, ἄρξαϲ βουλευτὴϲ Ἀλεξανδρείαϲ καὶ ὡϲ χρηματίζει. He is already known from **1412** as a *prytanis*, about A.D. 283/4, and as a property registrar from MChr. 196 of A.D. 309 (see Lallemand, *L'Administration*, p. 261, for the date). According to **1412** he was an ex-*hypomnematographus* about A.D. 283/4, as well as having held other Alexandrian and Oxyrhynchite magistracies. He could therefore have been, like Horion and Achilles, a *hypomnematographus* when he received this application.

There is still a good deal of uncertainty surrounding the *hypomnematographus*. Three types have been distinguished, two in Alexandria and one in the nome capitals. A much simpler account by Oertel, *Die Liturgie*, pp. 351–4, suggests very convincingly that there is evidence for only one sort in the Roman period, an Alexandrian citizen appointed for various administrative and judicial duties often, perhaps even always, outside Alexandria. The more complicated view may be represented by Stein, *Ägypten unter röm. Herrschaft*, pp. 191–201. It is still sometimes accepted that they were municipal officers, e.g. P. Herm. Rees 18, 5 n., and most lately in Braunert, *Binnenwanderung*, pp. 349–52.

A significant collocation of the names of Horion and Achilles is found in **2568** of A.D. 264. The owner of a requisitioned boat gave an acknowledgement of its return

to Καλπουρνίῳ Ὡρίωνι τῷ ἀξιολογωτάτῳ εἰρηνάρχῃ καὶ Αὐρηλίῳ Ἀχιλλεῖ τῷ καὶ Ἀμμω-
νίῳ τῷ κρατίστῳ (1–6). If these are the same as our Horion and Achilles, as seems
likely, the natural conclusion is that they were Alexandrian citizens resident in Oxyrhynchus who took a continuing active part in the administration of the area in which they
lived. Two more occurrences of the name Aurelius Achilles may also concern this
man, namely **1444** 15, **1534** 21.

Perhaps the most likely view of these officials, then, is that they were all local
residents of good standing who served as secretary of the corn dole at different times in
the succession Achilles(?), Plution, Horion, Eudaemon.

Inevitably, however, the differences of the terminology of their titles leave some
doubt. A broad difference can be detected between the petitions addressed to the
officials actually called *hypomnematographus*, Achilles and Horion, and those addressed
to the others, Plution and Eudaemon. The second pair receive for the most part straightforward applications from persons whose qualifications are not in doubt, while the
*hypomnematographi* receive petitions from people who have been out of Oxyrhynchus or
whose names have been omitted from the lists or who have failed in the first instance
to provide the documentary evidence of their qualifications. An exception to this may be
**2906** ii, which is rather doubtfully read, but the single clear exception is addressed to
Plution from an applicant who claims to have been left out of the list by mistake (**2905**).
This document has an unusual docket in the upper margin, unfortunately damaged
and incomprehensible. There is a possibility that it was addressed to the wrong
official. At any rate if we could explain this document away, we might put forward
the alternative hypothesis that Plution and Eudaemon were administrators of the routine
affairs of the dole, while Horion and Achilles had a commission to hear and settle
doubtful claims. This might well be consistent with what we hear of the judicial
activities of *hypomnematographi*, cf. Oertel, p. 353, citing P. Tebt. 286, **1102**, P. Strasb. 22,
and (doubtfully) P. Théad. 18.

The boards to which some applications are addressed are more straightforward.
A single application (**2918**) is addressed to τοῖς αἱρεθεῖσι ὑπὸ τῆς κρατίστης βουλῆς
διάδοσιν ποιήσασθαι τοῦ σιτηρεσίου together with an official who is νεωκόρος τοῦ μεγάλου
Σαράπιδος and whose *nomen*, Aurelius, alone survives. This is probably the same board
which issues the warning about the use of *tesserae* (**2924**), though this document seems
to allude to a διάδοσις of *tesserae* which is different from the διάδοσις of the grain itself.

At first sight there appears to be a different board called the διακριταί, whose
business was to check the credentials of the recipients. They are called in **2899** ii οἱ
αἱρεθέντες ὑπὸ τῆς κρατίστης βουλῆς διακριταί and in **2913** οἱ διακριταὶ ἄρχοντες σιτηρεσίου.
From their resemblance to **2899**, it seems likely that **2900** and **2901** were also addressed
to them. But all the applications mentioned are from persons whose names had been
omitted from the lists of recipients, which implies rather that there was only a single
board of magistrates addressed in different terms. If **2924** is rightly assigned to them,
they dealt with the issue of *tesserae* as well as controlling the lists of recipients.

## 2892

22 3B.14/F(9)a                    18 × 28·5 cm.                    24 Sept., A.D. 269;
                                                                   (?) Sept., A.D. 269

i

(m. 9?)                          κζ

(m. 1?)                     α⁻

(m. 1)   Αὐρηλίῳ Πλουτίωνι γρ[α]μματεῖ ϲιτηρεϲίου
          παρὰ Αὐρηλίου Ἀγαθοῦ Δ[α]ίμονοϲ Ἀρείου
5         τοῦ Ϲαραπίωνοϲ μητρ[ὸϲ] Ϲενψόιτοϲ
          ἀπ[ὸ] τῆϲ λαμπρᾶϲ Ὀξυρ[υ]γχειτῶν πόλε[ωϲ.
          Ὀξυρυ[γ]χείτηϲ τυγχάνω[ν] καὶ ἐπικρι[θεὶϲ
          ἐπ' ἀμφόδου Δρόμου Θ[ο]ήριδοϲ καὶ [γενό-
          μενοϲ εἰϲ τὸ ἐνεϲτὸϲ β (ἔτοϲ) (ἐτῶν) κ ἐκ κλή-
10        ρου εἰϲάγω ἐμαυτὸν ἀντὶ Ἀντιό[χου
          Ἀντιόχου τοῦ καὶ Διογέν[ο]υϲ ⟨τοῦ⟩ Ἀντ[ιόχου
          μητρὸϲ Θεοδώραϲ ὄντοϲ ἐπὶ τοῦ [αὐτοῦ
          ἀμφόδου, τετελευτ[ηκό]τοϲ, καὶ ἀξι[ῶ
          δεικνὺϲ ἐμαυτὸν [πο]λίτην ὄν[τα
15        μεταλαβῖν [τῆϲ τοῦ ϲ]ιτηρεϲίου
          διαδόϲεωϲ. (ἔτουϲ) [β Αὐτ]οκράτο[ροϲ
          Καίϲαροϲ Μάρκου Α[ὐρηλίου] Κλαυ[δίου
          Εὐϲεβοῦϲ Εὐτυχοῦϲ Ϲ[εβαϲ]τοῦ,
          Θὼθ κζ̄. (m. 2) Αὐρήλι[οϲ Ἀγα]θὸϲ Δαί-
20        μων Ἀρείου ἐπιδέδωκα. Αὐρ(ήλιοϲ)
          Ἀπολλώνιοϲ ἔγραψα ὑπὲρ αὐτοῦ
          μὴ εἰδότοϲ γράμματα.

     (m. 3)   Αὐρ(ήλιοϲ) Ϲερῆνοϲ ἐπικ(ριτήϲ)· οὗτόϲ ἐϲτιν ὁ ἐπικ(ριθείϲ),
               ὃϲ καὶ ἀναγορευθ(εὶϲ) ὑπήκουϲεν.
                              (vac.)

25 (m. 4)   Αὐρήλ(ιοϲ) Δίδυμοϲ γενό(μενοϲ) φύλ(αρχοϲ)· οὕτωϲ ἔχει
             καί ἐϲτιν αὐτὸϲ ὁ προκ(είμενοϲ), ὃϲ καὶ ἀνα-
             γορευθ(εὶϲ) ὑπήκουϲ(εν).

6 οξυρ[υ]γ'χειτων   7 οξυρυ[γ]'χειτηϲτυγ'χανω[ν]   9 βϲ L κ   16 L [β   20 αυρ'   23 αυρ', επι^κ,
επι^κ   24 αναγορευθ⁻   25 αυρηλ, γενο) φυλ   26 προκ   27 γορευθ υπηκουϲ'

C 8173                                     D

(m. 5)  Αὐρήλ(ιος) Θέων γνωστ(ήρ)· οὗτός ἐστ(ιν) ὁ διακρ(ιθείς),
          ὃν κ(αὶ) γνωρίζω.

30 (m. 6)  Αὐρήλ(ιος) Ϲαρᾶϲ ὁ κ(αὶ) Ἰϲίδω(ρος) γνω(ϲτήρ)· οὗτός ἐστιν ὁ
          διακριθ(είς), ὃν καὶ γνωρίζω.

             (vac.)

(m. 7)  ἐνετάγη β (ἔτους) Φαῶφι.

(m. 8)  Δρό(μου) Θοήριδος.

28 αυρηλ, γνωϲτ', εϲ<sup>τ</sup>, διακρ'    29 ον<sup>κ</sup>    30 αυρηλ, ο<sup>κ</sup> ιϲιδ<sup>ω</sup> γν<sup>ω</sup>    31 διακρι<sup>θ</sup>    32 βϚ    33 δρο⁻

ii

(m. 9?)                κη

(m. 1)  Αὐρηλ(ίῳ) Πλουτίωνι γρ[αμματεῖ ϲιτηρεϲίου
          παρὰ Αὐρηλ(ίου) Κοπρέως Θ[
          Διδύμης ἀπὸ τῆς λ[αμπρᾶς Ὀξυρυγ-
          χειτῶν πόλεως. Ὀξ[υρυγχείτης τυγ-
5       χάνων καὶ ἐπικριθ[εὶς ἐπ' ἀμφόδου
          Δρόμου Θοήριδος κα[ὶ γενόμενος εἰς
          τὸ ἐνεϲτὸϲ β (ἔτος) (ἐτῶν) [.. ἐκ κλήρου
          εἰϲάγω ἐμαυτὸν ἀντ[ὶ c. 7
10      κλᾶ τοῦ Θέωνος μητρ[ὸϲ c. 7
          ὄντος ἐπὶ τοῦ αὐτο[ῦ ἀμφόδου,
          τετελευτηκότος, [καὶ ἀξιῶ δεικνὺϲ
          ἐμαυτὸν πολίτην [ὄντα μετα-
          λαβῖν τῆϲ τοῦ ϲιτ[ηρεϲίου διαδό-
15      ϲεωϲ. (ἔτους) β [Αὐτοκράτοροϲ
          Καίϲαροϲ Μάρκου Αὐρη[λίου
          Κλαυδίου Εὐϲεβοῦϲ [Εὐτυχοῦϲ
          Ϲεβαϲτοῦ, Θὼθ .[

(m. 2)  Αὐρήλ(ιος) Κοπρεὺϲ Θ[.].[ ... ἐπιδέδωκα.
20      Αὐρήλ(ιος) Ἡρακλείδηϲ ἔγραψ[α ὑπὲρ αὐτοῦ
          μὴ εἰδότοϲ γράμματα.
              (vac.)

(m. 3)  Αὐρήλ(ιος) Δίδυμοϲ γεν[ό(μενος) φύλ(αρχος)· οὕτως
          ἔχει καί ἐϲτιν αὐτ[ὸϲ ὁ προκ(είμενος),
          ὃ[ϲ] καὶ ἀναγορευθ(εὶς) ὑ[πήκουϲεν.

25 (m. 4)  Αὐρήλιος Cερῆνος ἐ(πικριτής)· οὗ[τός ἐστιν

ὁ ἐπικ(ριθείς), ὃς καὶ ἀναγορευθ[(εἰς) ὑπήκου-

cεν.

(m. 5)  Αὐ[ρή]λ(ιος) Θέων γνω(cτήρ)· οὗτ(ός) ἐcτ(ιν) ὁ διακρ[(ιθείς),

ὃ[ν κ(αὶ)] γνωρίζω. (m. 6) Αὐρήλ(ιος) Cαρᾶc ὁ [κ(αὶ) Ἰcίδω(ρος) γνω(cτήρ)·

30  οὗτός ἐcτιν ὁ διακριθ(είς), ὃν [κ(αὶ) γνωρίζω.

(m. 7)  ἐνετάγη β (ἔτους) Φαῶφι.

(m. 8)  Δρό(μου) Θοήριδ(ος).

2, 3 αυρη^λ    8 βς L [    15 L β[    19, 20, 22 αυρη^λ    24 αναγορευθ⁻    25 ε)    26 επι^κ
28 αυ[ρη]^λ, γν^ω, ου^τ εc^τ    29 αυρη^λ    30 διακριθ⁻    31 βς    32 δρο⁻ θοηρι^δ

Col. i '(9th hand?) No. 27. (1st hand?) Copy(?). (1st hand) To Aurelius Plution, secretary of the corn dole, from Aurelius Agathus Daemon, son of Areus, grandson of Sarapion, mother Senpsois, from the glorious city of the Oxyrhynchites. Being an Oxyrhynchite, scrutinized in the Thoëris Street quarter and 20 years old in the present second year, I enter myself as a result of the draw in place of Antiochus, son of Antiochus alias Diogenes, grandson of Antiochus, mother Theodora, of the same quarter, deceased, and I ask, having shown myself a citizen, to receive my share of the distribution of the corn dole. Year 2 of Imperator Caesar Marcus Aurelius Claudius Pius Felix Augustus, Thoth 27. (2nd hand) I, Aurelius Agathus Daemon, son of Areus, submitted (the petition). I, Aurelius Apollonius, wrote for him because he does not know letters. (3rd hand) Aurelius Serenus, scrutineer: This is the person scrutinized, who also answered when his name was proclaimed. (4th hand) Aurelius Didymus, formerly phylarch: He is as described (?) and is the aforementioned in person, who also answered when his name was proclaimed. (5th hand) Aurelius Theon, witness of identity: This is the person examined, whom I also identify. (6th hand) Aurelius Saras, alias Isidorus, witness of identity: This is the person examined, whom I also identify. (7th hand) He has been enrolled. Second year, Phaophi. (8th hand) Thoëris Street.'

Col. ii '(9th hand?) No. 28. (1st hand) To Aurelius Plution, secretary of the corn dole, from Aurelius Copres, son of Th . . . (grandson of . . .?), mother Didyme, from the glorious city of the Oxyrhynchites. Being an Oxyrhynchite and scrutinized in the Thoëris Street quarter and aged in the present second year . . . years, I enter myself as a result of the draw in place of . . ., son of . . . clas, grandson of Theon, mother . . ., being of the same quarter, deceased, and I ask, having shown myself a citizen, to receive my share of the distribution of the corn dole. Year 2 of Imperator Caesar Marcus Aurelius Claudius Pius Felix Augustus, Thoth . . . (2nd hand) I, Aurelius Copres, son of Th . . . (submitted this petition). I, Aurelius Heracleides, wrote for him because he does not know letters. (3rd hand) Aurelius Didymus, formerly phylarch: He is as described (?) and is the aforementioned in person, who also answered when his name was proclaimed. (4th hand) Aurelius Serenus, scrutineer: This is the person scrutinized, who also answered when his name was proclaimed. (5th hand) Aurelius Theon, witness of identity: This is the person examined, whom I also identify. (6th hand) Aurelius Saras alias Isidorus, witness of identity: This is the person examined, whom I also identify. (7th hand) He has been enrolled. Second year, Phaophi. (8th hand) Thoëris Street.'

Col. i 1 κζ, cf. ii 1 κη. These are item numbers in a file made of separate documents glued together to form a roll (τόμος cυγκολλήcιμος).

2 α⁻. This presumably means ἀ(ντίγραφον), as it commonly does. The document has a subscription in a second hand and is a copy probably only in the sense that one or more duplicates existed. Less likely possibilities are (πρῶτος) or α(ὐτός) and cases.

12 The clause οὗτος ἐπὶ τοῦ αὐτοῦ ἀμφόδου is sometimes omitted (**2893** i 14, ii 10, **2895** i 10, ii 19). Where it appears the quarter is always the same as the new incumbent's (**2892** i 12, ii 11, **2894** ii 19, iii 17, **2896** 5, **2897** 9). It is doubtful whether one should conclude that the dead had to be replaced

from their own quarter—or perhaps tribe—or not. The numbers of recipients in the twelve divisions were far from equal (**2928**, **2929**), and there is no evidence that there was a fixed maximum for each of them as there was for each whole class. Nevertheless one would not be surprised to find a tendency for each tribe to hold on to its privileges if it could.

25 οὕτως ἔχει. The translation assumes a personal subject here and in ii 23 because of such expressions as γνωρίζω τὸν προκείμενον οὕτως ἔχοντα (**2902** 23–4).

32 Φαῶφι. 28 Sept.–27 Oct., A.D. 269.

## 2893

4 1B.75/G(d)                11 × 14·5 cm.                25 Sept., A.D. 269

### i

Αὐρηλίῳ Πλου]τίωνι γρ(αμματεῖ)
   cιτηρεcίου]       (vac.)
παρὰ Αὐρηλίο]υ Ἰcιδώρου Ἀπολ-
. . . . . . . . . .] . ιτος μητρὸς

5      . . . . . . τῆς κα]ὶ Διδύμης ἀπὸ
τῆς λαμ](πρᾶς) Ὀξυρυγχειτῶν πόλεως. ἀνα]γραφόμενος ἐπ' ἀμφόδου Δ]ρόμου Γυμναcίου ἐπικρι-
θ[ε]ὶ̣[ς] καὶ γενόμενος εἰκοcαετὴς

10      πρὸς τὸ ἐνεcτὸς β (ἔτος) ἰcάγω ἐμαυτὸν ἐκ κλήρου λαχὼν ἀντὶ Κτί-
c]του τοῦ καὶ Ἀμμωνίου Ἡρακλεί-
δ]ου τοῦ Πινδάρου μητρὸς Θα-
ή]cιος τετελευτηκότος καὶ ἀ-

15      ξιῶ ἀναλημφθῆναι πρὸς τὸ
μ]εταcχεῖν τῆς τοῦ cιτηρεcίου
δω]ρεᾶς.       (vac.)
(ἔτους) [β]″ Αὐτοκράτο̣ρ̣[ο]ς
Καί]c̣α̣ρ̣[ος Μάρ]κ̣ου Αὐρηλίου

20      Κλαυδίου Εὐc]ε̣βοῦς Εὐτυχ[οῦς
Cεβαcτοῦ Θ]ὼ̣θ κη⁻[
              ] . . [
              ] . [

          •     •     •     •     •

1 γρϲ̄      3 ϊcιδωρου      6 λαμ]ϲ̄      10 βϲ̄, l. εἰcάγω      18 ↳[β]″

ii

Αὐρηλίῳ Πλ[ουτίωνι γρ(αμματεῖ) cιτηρεcίου

παρὰ Αὐρηλίο[υ

θου τοῦ καὶ .[

τοῦ κ(αὶ) Ποταμ[

5 ἀναγραφόμεν[οc ἐπ' ἀμφόδου Δρόμου

Γυμ]ναcίου ἐπ[ικριθεὶc καὶ γενόμενοc

εἰκ[οc]αετὴc π[ρὸc τὸ ἐνεcτὸc β (ἔτοc)

ἰcάγω ἐμα⟨υ⟩τ[ὸν ἐκ κλήρου λαχὼν

ἀντὶ Ἱερα[

10 ου (vac.) [

τετελευτη[κότοc καὶ ἀξιῶ

ἀναλημφθ[ῆναι πρὸc τὸ μεταc-

χεῖν τῆc [τοῦ cιτηρεcίου

δωρ[εᾶc

.  .  .  .  .  .

4 τουᴷ    8 l. εἰcάγω

Col. i 'To Aurelius Plution, secretary of the corn dole, from Aurelius Isidorus, son of Apol(lonius?), grandson of (Amo?)is, mother ... alias Didyme, from the glorious city of the Oxyrhynchites. Being registered in the Gymnasium Street quarter, scrutinized and aged twenty years in the present second year, I enter myself as a result of success in the draw in place of Ctistes alias Ammonius, son of Heracleides, grandson of Pindar, mother Thaësis, deceased, and I ask to be included so as to share in the gift of the corn dole. Year two of Imperator Caesar Marcus Aurelius Claudius Pius Felix Augustus, Thoth 28.'

Col. ii 'To Aurelius Plution, secretary of the corn dole, from Aurelius ..., son of ... -thus (or -thes?), grandson of ... alias Potamon, mother ... Being registered in the Gymnasium Street quarter, scrutinized and aged twenty years in (the present second year?), I enter myself as a result of success in the draw in place of Hiera ..., ..., deceased, and I ask to be included so as to share the gift of the corn dole.'

Col. i 3–4 Ἀπολ[λωνίου τοῦ Ἀμ]όιτοc would suit very well.

Col. ii 8 ἐμα⟨υ⟩τ[όν. Cf. Mayser, I i 114–15.

9–10 Space has been left for the mother's and perhaps also the grandfather's name. Perhaps they were illegible in the exemplar.

**2894**

22 3B.15/D(21)a                    17×31 cm.                    14 Jan., A.D. 270;
                                                                  26 Jan.–24 Feb., A.D. 270

ii

Αὐρηλίῳ Π[λ]ουτίωνι γραμματεῖ
  ϲιτηρε[ϲίου
παρὰ Αὐρη[λίου Ϲαρα]πίων[οϲ Ἔρω-
  τοϲ τοῦ .[. . . . . . . . .]. . . . . . . .
5   μητρὸϲ [. . . . . . . . .] ἀπὸ τῆϲ
  λαμπρ[ᾶϲ Ὀξυρυγχι]τῶν πόλεωϲ.
  ἀναγραφ[ό]μ[ενοϲ ἐ]π' ἀμφόδου
  Δρόμου Γυμναϲίου ἐπικριθεὶϲ
  τῷ ια (ἔτει) καὶ γενόμενοϲ πρὸϲ
10   τὸ ἐν[εϲτὸϲ] β (ἔτοϲ) (ἐτῶν) κ
  καὶ ἐκ τ[οῦ] γενομένου κλήρου κα[τὰ τ]ὰ δόξαντα τῇ
  κρατίϲ[τῃ] βουλῇ ἐπίλογ-
  χοϲ λα[χὼ]ν χώραϲ παρα-
15   πεϲούϲ[η]ϲ εἰϲάγω ἐμαυτὸν ἀν[τὶ] Θέωνοϲ Διοϲ-
  κουρίδ[ου] τοῦ Θεοξένου
  μητρ[ὸϲ] Θεωνίδοϲ τῆϲ κ(αὶ)
  Ἀρϲινόη[ϲ] ὄντοϲ ἐπὶ τοῦ
20   αὐτοῦ ἀ[μ]φόδου τετελευτηκότο[ϲ, κ]αὶ ἀξιῶ ἐντα[γ]ῆ-
  ναι πρ[ὸϲ τ]ὸ κἀμὲ μετ[αϲ-
  χεῖν τ[ῆ]ϲ τοῦ ϲιτηρεϲί[ο]υ
  δωρε[ᾶϲ .] (ἔτουϲ) β'
25   Αὐτοκράτοροϲ Καίϲαροϲ
  Μάρκου Αὐρηλίου Κλαυδίου
  Εὐϲεβοῦϲ Εὐτυχοῦϲ
  Ϲεβαϲτοῦ, Τῦβι ιθ⁻.

  (m. 2)   Αὐρήλιοϲ Ϲαραπίων Ἔρωτοϲ
30     ἐπιδέδωκα. Αὐρήλιοϲ Ἡρακλῆϲ

ὁ καὶ Δημήτριος Cαραπίωνος
ἔγραψα ὑπὲρ αὐτοῦ μὴ εἰδότος
γράμματα.

(m. 3) Αὐρ(ήλιος) Cε[ρῆ]νος ἐπικ(ριτής)· οὗτός ἐστιν
35       ὁ ἐ(πικριθεὶς) ὃς καὶ ἀναγορευθ(εὶς) ὑπήκουςεν.
                 (vac.)

(m. 4) Αὐρήλ(ιος) Βησάμμων καὶ οἱ
ςὺν ἐμοὶ χειροτονηταί·
οὗτός ἐςτι ὁ προκείμενος
ὁ διακριθεὶς καὶ ἀναγορευ-
40       θεὶς ὑπήκουςε. (m. 5) Αὐρήλ(ιος)
Θέων γνωςτήρ· οὗτός ἐςτιν
ὁ διακριθ(εὶς) ὃν καὶ γν[ωρίζω.

(m. 6) Αὐρήλ(ιος) Ἀντώνιος γνωςτήρ· [οὗτός
ἐ]ςτιν ὁ διακριθ(εὶς) ὃν κ(αὶ) γνω[ρίζω.)

9 ιας″     10 βς L κ     13–14 επιλογ᾿χος     18 τηςκ     24 L β′     32 υπερ     34 αυρ′,
επικ     35 εκ, αναγορευθ⁻     36 αυρηλ     40 αυρηλ     42 διακριθ     43 αυρηλ     44 διακριθον)

### iii

Αὐρηλίῳ Πλου]τίωνι
γραμματεῖ] ςιτηρεςίου
παρὰ Αὐρηλίου Ἀβινούνιος
Ἀμμωνίου τοῦ Διδύμου
5      μητρὸς Ταύριος ἀπὸ τῆς
λαμπρᾶς Ὀξυρυγχιτῶν π[όλε-
ως. ἀναγραφόμενος ἐπ[᾿ ἀμφόδου Δρόμου Γυμναςί[ου
ἐπικριθεὶς τῷ ια (ἔτει) καὶ [γενό-
10     μενος πρὸς τὸ ἐνεςτὸς β (ἔτος) [(ἐτῶν) κ ?
καὶ ἐκ τοῦ γενομένου κλ[ήρου
κατὰ τὰ δόξαντα τῇ κρατί[ςτῃ
βουλῇ ἐπίλογχος λαχ[ὼν
χώρας παραπεςούςης ἰςάγω
15     ἐμαυτὸν ἀντὶ Τρύφωνος

5 ταύριος     9 ιας″     10 βς [     13 επιλογ᾿χος     14 l. εἰςάγω

Ἀπολλωνίου τοῦ Ἀπολλωνίου
μητρὸς Ξεναρχίδος ὄντος
ἐπὶ τοῦ αὐτοῦ ἀμφόδου, τετελευτηκότος, καὶ ἀξιῶ ἐν-
20     ταγῆναι πρὸς τὸ κἀμὲ μετασχεῖν τῆς τοῦ cιτηρεcίου
δωρεᾶ[c. (ἔτους) β Αὐτο]κράτοροc
Καίcα[ροc Μ]άρκου Α[ὐ]ρηλίου
Κλαυδί[ου Ε]ὐcεβοῦc Εὐτυχοῦc
25     Cεβαcτ[ο]ῦ, Μεχείρ    (vac.)

(m. 2)   Αὐρήλιος Ἀβινοῦνιc ἐπιδέδωκα. Αὐρήλιοc Θῶνιc ὁ καὶ
Ἀχιλλᾶc Cαραπίωνοc ἔγρα-
ψα ὑπὲρ αὐτοῦ μὴ ἰδότοc
30     γράμματα.

(m. 3)   Αὐρ(ήλιος) Cερῆνοc ἐ(πικριτής)· οὗτόc ἐcτιν ὁ ἐπι-
κριθ(εὶc) ὃc καὶ ἀναγορευθ(εὶc) ὑπήκουcε[ν.

(m. 4)   Αὐρήλιοc Βηcά[μμων καὶ οἱ
cὺν ἐμο[ὶ

.   .   .   .   .

29 ὕπερ, l. εἰδότοc      31 αυρ΄, ε)      31–2 επικριθ⁻      32 αναγορευθ⁻

Col. ii 'To Aurelius Plution, secretary of the corn dole, from Aurelius Sarapion, son of Eros, grandson of . . ., mother . . ., from the glorious city of the Oxyrhynchites. Being listed in the Gymnasium Street quarter, scrutinized in the 11th year and twenty years old in the present second year, and in the last draw in accordance with the decrees of the most excellent council having obtained the succession to a place which had fallen vacant, I enter myself in place of Theon, son of Dioscurides, grandson of Theoxenus, mother Theonis alias Arsinoe(?), listed in the same quarter, deceased, and I ask to be enrolled so that I too may share the gift of the corn dole. Year 2 of Imperator Caesar Marcus Aurelius Claudius Pius Felix Augustus, Tybi 19. (2nd hand) I, Aurelius Sarapion, son of Eros, submitted (the petition). I, Aurelius Heracles alias Demetrius, son of Sarapion, wrote on his behalf since he does not know letters. (3rd hand) Aurelius Serenus, scrutineer: This is the person scrutinized, who also answered when his name was proclaimed. (4th hand) Aurelius Besammon, and associate electors: This is the aforesaid person, who has been examined and answered when his name was proclaimed. (5th hand) Aurelius Theon, witness of identity: This is the person examined, whom I also identify. (6th hand) Aurelius Antonius, witness of identity: This is the person examined, whom I also identify.'

Col. iii 'To Aurelius Plution, secretary of the corn dole, from Aurelius Abinounis, son of Ammonius, grandson of Didymus, mother Taüris, from the glorious city of the Oxyrhynchites. Being listed in the Gymnasium Street quarter, scrutinized in the 11th year and (twenty?) years old in the present second year, and in the last draw in accordance with the decrees of the most excellent council having obtained the succession to a place which had fallen vacant, I enter myself in place of Tryphon, son of Apollonius, grandson of Apollonius, mother Xenarchis, listed in the same quarter, deceased, and I ask to be enrolled so that I too may share the gift of the corn dole. Year 2 of Imperator Caesar Marcus Aurelius Claudius Pius Felix Augustus, Mecheir (day omitted). (2nd hand) I, Aurelius Abinounis, submitted (the petition). I, Aurelius Thonis, alias Achillas(?), wrote on his behalf since he does not know letters. (3rd hand) Aurelius Serenus, scrutineer: This is the person scrutinized, who also answered when his name was proclaimed. (4th hand) Aurelius Besammon, and associate . . .'

Col. ii 1 There may have been item numbers in the top margins, which are mostly broken away. The traces of col. i are enough to show that it was another application of the same general type but are otherwise negligible.

13 ἐπίλογ'χος. Apart from this and other occurrences in this archive (iii 13, [**2896** 2 ?], [**2897** 6 ?]) the word is known only from P. Ryl. 77, 43, 44, 49. The meaning there is obscure but it is explained by the editors as derived from ἐπιλαγχάνειν in the sense of 'to succeed (someone) in office', which suits very well here. In P. Ryl. 77, ἐκέλευcεν μὴ cυγχωρῖcθαι ἄνευ τριῶν ἐπιλόγχων εἰc ἐξηγ(ητείαν), looks as if it means 'ordered that it was not to be permitted (i.e. no one was to be admitted to the office of *exegetes*) without the backing of three persons (already) designated to that office'. Here it may possibly be an attempt to represent the Latin technical term '*subsortior*', compare the translations in *CGL* of *subcelo*/ἐπικρύπτω (ii 309, 7), *subigo*/ἐπιπέμπομαι (ii 190, 27, perhaps better = *subicio*), *suffundo*/ἐπιχέω (ii 312, 62), *suppedito, subministro*/ἐπιχορηγέω (ii 313, 2), *subministratio*/ἐπιχορηγία (ii 313, 1).

There is also another possibility. The lottery was an annual event at Rome in the time of Caesar (Suet. *Jul.* 41 '*quotannis*'), but at Oxyrhynchus applications as a result of success in the lot cover the months of Thoth, Phaophi, Tybi, and Mecheir. Possibly the main event was in Thoth (**2892** i, ii, **2893** i, ii?), at the beginning of the year, and the others were regarded as supplementary. In that case ἐπίλογχος λαχὼν χώρας might mean 'gaining a place from the supplementary lottery'. This, however, does not appear to suit the passage from the Rylands papyrus very well and here too it is probably better to suppose that those who entered their petitions in Tybi and Mecheir were simply slow to apply, see Introd., p. 3.

37 χειροτονηταί. This word is new in the papyri and exists otherwise only in the glossaries as the equivalent of the Latin '*creator*' in its meaning of 'one who elects or nominates to office', *CGL* ii 476, 43, iii 444, 32; 476, 2. The text of the present subscription makes it clear that they were acting for the phylarch, cf., e.g., **2892** i 25–7. Luckily **2936** illuminates this a little by showing a χιρ(οτονητής) acting for a person who is ill, no doubt the phylarch again (**2936** ii 9, 12, 15, 18, 21). Perhaps **2936** also refers to another person who is 'managing the affairs of the (phylarchy?)'—διοικ(ῶν) τὰ κατὰ τὴν [φυλαρχίαν, ii 28, see n. He may have been, as it were, chairman of a committee deputizing for the phylarch. It is not clear whether Besammon held this post or whether he was just one of the ordinary committee members.

Col. iii 10 [(ἐτῶν) κ? This restoration is probable because scrutiny usually took place at the official age of 14, cf. ii 10 and Introd. p. 21.

## 2895

23 3B.13/E(1–2)a          15 × 25 cm.          A.D. 269/70;
14 Jan., A.D. 270

i

.    .    .    .    .

. . . . . . . .] ἐπικριθεὶς
ἐπὶ τοῦ πρ]οκειμένου
ἀμφό]δου καὶ ὧν πρὸς

τὸ ἐνεϲτὸϲ β (ἔτοϲ) (ἐτῶν) κ

5     καὶ ταχθεὶϲ ἐν τοῖϲ

χλαμυροφορεῖν μ[έλ-

λουϲι χώραν τε ἔχων

ἐκ κλήρου εἰϲάγω ἐμαυ-

τὸν ἀντὶ Χαιρήμονοϲ

10    τοῦ καὶ Βηϲάμμωνοϲ

τετελευτηκότο[ϲ] κ̣α̣ὶ̣

ἀ̣ξιῶ μεταϲχεῖ[ν τῆϲ

τ]οῦ ϲιτηρεϲίου διαδό-

ϲ]εωϲ. (ἔτουϲ) β″ Αὐτοκράτοροϲ

15    Κ]αίϲαροϲ Μάρκου Αὐρηλίου

Κ̣λαυδίου Εὐϲεβοῦϲ Εὐτυ[χο]ῦϲ

Ϲ]εβαϲτοῦ.      (vac.)

(m. 2)   Αὐρήλ(ιοϲ) Ἡρᾶϲ [ἐπι]δ̣έ̣-

δωκα. Τ̣.κλ̣...ι̣

20    ων ἔγραψα ὑπὲ[ρ] α̣(ὐτοῦ)

μὴ ἰδότοϲ γράμ[ματα.

(m. 3)   Αὐ]ρή(λιοϲ) Ϲερῆνοϲ ἐπικ(ριτήϲ)· [οὗτόϲ

ἐϲ]τ̣ιν ὁ ἐπικριθείϲ, [ὃϲ κ(αὶ) ἀνα-

γορ]ευθεὶϲ ὑπήκ[ουϲεν.

25 (m. 4)   Αὐρή]λιοϲ Θέων ὁ̣ [καὶ

....]. ιανὸϲ γνωϲ[τήρ·

οὗτό]ϲ ἐ(ϲτιν) ὁ προκεί[μενοϲ ὁ

διακρι]θείϲ, ὃν κ̣αὶ [γνωρίζω.

(m. 5)   Αὐρ(ήλιοϲ) .]ρίων γνωϲ[τήρ·

30    οὗτόϲ ἐ(ϲτιν)] ὁ προκείμεν[οϲ ὁ

διακριθείϲ,] ὃν καὶ γν[ωρίζω.

(m. 6)   .........].. απο[

............].. [

•    •    •    •

4 βϲ Ⳑ κ    6 l. χλαμυδοφορεῖν    14 Ⳑ β″    18 αυρηλ    20 α̣⁻    21 ἰδοτοϲ    22 αυ]ρη′,
επικ      27 εᵒ

ii

. . . . .

π[αρὰ Αὐρ]ηλίου Π[εκυσίου

ς[αρα]πίωνος τοῦ [ . . . . . .

μη(τρὸς) Θεωνίδος .[ . . . . .

ἀπ[ὸ] τῆς λαμπρᾶς Ὀ[ξ(υρυγχιτῶν) πόλ(εως).

5  μητροπολείτης ὢ[ν καὶ

ἐπικριθεὶς καὶ ἀνα[γρα-

φόμενος ἐπ' ἀμφόδ[ου

Τεμιούθεως ἀκολού[θως

ᾗ ἐπήνεγκα ἐπικρί[σει

10  τῷ ια (ἔτει) καὶ ταχθεὶς ὑπ[ὸ τοῦ

τοῦ] ἡμετέρου ἀμφόδο[υ φυλ(άρχου)

διὰ τῶ]ν ὑπ' αὐτοῦ ἐπιδ[οθέν-

των β]ιβλίων ἐν τάξ[ει . .

. . . . .]ων κατὰ πλάνη[ν . . .

15  . . . . . .] . . . .εως υπ .[ . . . .

. . . . . .] . . καὶ χώραν ἔ[χων

ἀντὶ ] .ιου Κλαυδίο[υ . .

. . . . .] .κ . . . . . .[. τε-

τελευ]τηκότος ε[ἰσά-

20  γω] ἐμαυτὸν πρὸς τ[ὸ κἀμὲ

μετασχεῖ]ν τῆς τοῦ σιτηρ[ε-

σίου] δωρεᾶς.

(ἔτους) β Αὐτο]κράτορος Καίσαρος

Μάρκου] Αὐρηλίου Κλαυδίου

25  Ε]ὐσεβοῦς Εὐτυχοῦ[ς] Σεβαστοῦ

Τ]ῦβι ιθ⁻.

(m. 2)  Α]ὐρήλιος Πεκύσιος [Σαραπί-

ωνος ἐπιδέδωκα.

(m. 3)  Αὐ]ρήλιος Ἀμυντι[α]νὸς

30  γε]νό(μενος) φύλ(αρχος)· ἔστιν ὁ πρ[ . . . ] . .[

. . . .] .γνω .εις ἐπι[

. . . . .

3 μη.    10 ιας    30 γε]ν°?, φυλ

Col. i '. . . scrutinized in the aforesaid quarter and being twenty years old in the present second year and enrolled among those who are to wear the *chlamys* and having a place as a result of the draw, I enter myself in place of Chaeremon alias Besammon, deceased, and ask to share the distribution of the corn dole. Year 2 of Imperator Caesar Marcus Aurelius Claudius Pius Felix Augustus, (month and day omitted). (2nd hand) I, Aurelius Heras, submitted (the petition). I, . . . , wrote on his behalf because he does not know letters. (3rd hand) Aurelius Serenus, scrutineer: This is the person scrutinized, who also answered when his name was proclaimed. (4th hand) Aurelius Theon alias . . . ianus, witness of identity: This is the aforesaid, the person examined, whom I also identify. (5th hand) Aurelius . . . rion, witness of identity: This is the aforesaid, the person examined, whom I also identify. (6th hand) . . .'

Col. ii '. . . from Aurelius Pekysius, son of Sarapion, grandson of . . . , mother Theonis (daughter of . . .?), from the glorious city of the Oxyrhynchites. Being a citizen of the nome capital and one who has been scrutinized and being listed in the Temiouthis quarter in accordance with the (certificate of) scrutiny that I presented in the 11th year and having been enrolled by the phylarch of our quarter in the records submitted by him in the category of . . . by mistake . . . and having a place in the stead of . . . (son of?) Claudius . . . , deceased, I enter myself so that I too may share the gift of the corn dole. Year 2 of Imperator Caesar Marcus Aurelius Claudius Pius Felix Augustus, Tybi 19. (2nd hand) I, Aurelius Pekysius, son of Sarapion, submitted (the petition). (3rd hand) Aurelius Amyntianus, formerly phylarch: He is the aforesaid . . .'

Col. i 6 χλαμυροφορεῖν. Read presumably χλαμυδοφορεῖν. In view of the existence of the words χλαμυρός 'luxurious' and χλαμυρίς 'oats', some sort of pun may have been intended, but more likely it is just an anticipation of the *rho* following soon after. There are other indications that the wearing of the *chlamys* signifies some special rank or privilege in the Egyptian cities but the exact meaning of it is still unknown, see the discussion in *TAPA* lxxi (1940), pp. 383–90.

19 Perhaps read Τι΄. Κλ[΄], i.e. Τι(βέριος) Κλ(αύδιος).

Col. ii 8 Τεμιούθεως. A new variant spelling, if correctly read; see Rink, *Strassen- und Viertelnamen von Oxy.*, p. 35, cf. 2918 7.

13–16 The exact interpretation of these broken lines is not yet clear, but it seems likely that this applicant claims that he has been listed wrongly by the phylarch in the category of ῥεμβοί or ὁμόλογοι, though he is in fact a citizen who has been successful in the lot.

17 Κλαυδίου. This is not necessarily a Roman *gentilicium*. The most likely pattern is perhaps: 'X, son of Claudius, grandson of Y, mother Z, alias Diogenis(?)'.

18 The traces would permit ]. καὶ Διογεν[; it is perhaps part of the mother's name, e.g. τῆ]ς καὶ Διογεν[ίδος.

29–31 This is different from the phylarch's usual subscription—references in 2927 introd.—and the meaning of it is obscure. The first letter might be ]α or ]ε; after ω perhaps ν or ς.

## 2896

3 1B.77/A(5)a                5·5 × 14 cm.                Sept./Oct., A.D. 268, 269, or 270

.     .     .     .     .     .

τὰ δόξαν]τα τῇ κρατίστ[ῃ βουλῇ
ἐπίλογχος λ]αχὼν χώρα[ς παραπε-
coύcηc εἰcάγ]ω ἐμαυτὸν ἀ[ντὶ . . . .
. . . . . . . . Π]αύλου Cωκρά[τους . . .
5   . . . . . . . . . .] μητρὸς Παυ[. . . . . . .
ἐπὶ τοῦ αὐτ]οῦ ἀμφόδου τ[ετελευ-
τηκότος κα]ὶ ἀξιῶ ἐνταγ[ῆναι πρὸς

τὸ κἀμὲ μετα]cχεῖν τῆc τ[οῦ
cιτηρεcίου δ]ωρεᾶc. (vac.) [
10 (ἔτουc) . Αὐτοκ]ράτοροc Καίcα[ροc
Μάρκου Αὐρηλίο]υ Κλαυδίου Ε[ὐcεβοῦc
Εὐτυχοῦc Cεβαc]τοῦ Φαῶφι [(day).
(m. 2) . . . . . . . . . . .] .άμμωνοc ἐπ[ιδέδωκα
. . . . . . . . . . .] .άμμων ἔγρα[ψα
15 ὑπὲρ αὐτοῦ μὴ] εἰτότ(οc) γράμματα [
(m. 3) . . . . . . . . . . .] ἐπικ(ριτήc)· οὗτόc ἐcτιν
ὁ ἐπικριθ(εὶc) ὃc κ]αὶ ἀναγορευθεὶc
ὑπήκουcεν ] (vac.)
(m. 4) . . . . . . . . . . .] .c γενό(μενοc) φύλαρχοc
20 . . . . . . . . . . .] . . . . .ου οὕτωc
. . . . . . . . . . . . . . προ]κίμεγο[c

. . . . .

15 ειτοᵀ, l. εἰδότ(οc)    16 επιᵏ    19 γενο᾿

'(In accordance with?) the decrees of the most excellent council having obtained by lot the succession to a place which had fallen vacant, I enter myself in place of . . . (alias) Paul, son of Socrates, grandson of . . . , mother Pau . . . , of the same quarter, deceased, and ask to be enrolled so that I too may share the gift of the corn dole. Year . . . of Imperator Caesar Marcus Aurelius Claudius Pius Felix Augustus, Phaophi (day). (2nd hand) I, . . . , son of . . . ammon, submitted (this petition). I, . . . ammon, wrote on his behalf because he does not know letters. (3rd hand) . . . , scrutineer: This is the person scrutinized, who also answered when his name was proclaimed. (4th hand) . . . , ex-phylarch: . . . thus . . . aforesaid . . .'

2 ἐπίλογχοc. Cf. 2894 13.

20–1 It looks as if the subscription proper begins with οὕτωc, e.g. οὕτωc ²¹ [ἔχει καί ἐcτιν αὐτὸc ὁ προ]κίμεγο[c κτλ., cf. 2892 i 25. If so, the illegible part before οὕτωc might be part of the phylarch's title even though elsewhere—references in 2927 introd.—there are no additions to (γενόμενοc) φύλαρχοc. It is not τοῦ αὐτοῦ] ἀμφόδου, nor can I read the name of any quarter. Another possibility is δι' ἐμοῦ followed by the name of a deputy.

**2897**

22 3B.15/D(12–13)c          2·5×9 cm.          A.D. 268–70

For the formulas cf. **2894**, **2896**.

. . . .

τ]ῆc λαμπρ[ᾶc
ἀναγρα]φόμενοc[
]ἐπικριθε[ὶc
]stripped[
5 ]stripped[

λαχ]ὼν χώρας [

ἀν]τὶ Cιλβα[νοῦ

Ἀ]φύγχιο[c

το]ῦ αὐτοῦ ἀ[μφόδου

10     ἐ]νταγῆνα[ι

]cιτηρεcί[ου

Καίc]αρος Μά[ρκου

·   ·   ·   ·   ·

8 ]φυγ'χιο[

## 2898

22 3B.14/F(7–8)a       12 × 26 cm.       A.D. 270/1

ii

(m. 2) ἐπεκ(ρίθη ?) (m. 3) ιη

(m. 1)   Καλπουρνίῳ Ὠρίωνι τῷ κρατίcτ[ῳ

ὑπομνηματογράφῳ βουλευτῇ τῆc λαμ-

προτάτηc πόλεωc τῶν Ἀλεξανδρέων

5     παρὰ Αὐρηλίου Μέλανος Ἡρακλείδου

τοῦ Ἀμμωνίου ⟨τοῦ καὶ ?⟩ Διογένους μητρὸς Θαή-

cιος ἀπὸ τῆc λαμπρᾶc Ὀξυρυγχειτῶ[ν

πόλεωc. προcβὰc καὶ ἐπικριθεὶc

ἐπ᾽ ἀμφόδου Μυροβαλάνου καὶ ἐντα-

10     γεὶc τοῖc ἐπιδοθεῖcι πρὸc τὸ ἱερὸν

cιτηρέcιον ὑπὸ τοῦ φυλάρχου κατ᾽ ἄν-

δρα βιβλίοιc, ἐν δὲ τῇ διακρίcει ταc-

cόμενοc οὐ δεδύνημαι τὰc τοῦ γένουc

μου ἀποδείξειc παραcχέcθαι· ἀναγ-

15     καίωc νῦν παρέχων τῆc ἐπικρί-

c[εωc τὸ c]ύμβολον καὶ τοῦ γένουc

τὰ[c ἀ]ποδείξειc ἐπιδίδωμι τάδε

τὰ [βι]β[λ]ία καὶ ἀξιῶ καὶ αὐτὸc

μετα[c]χ[εῖ]ν τῆc τοῦ cίτου δωρεᾶc

20     ἐπικρι[θ]εὶc τῷ ιε (ἔτει) κατὰ τὰ δόξαν-

τα τῇ κ[ρ]ατίcτῃ βουλῇ πρὸc ἴcον

τῶν ὁ[μ]οίων μοι. διευτύχει.

(ἔτουϲ) α [Α]ὐτοκράτοροϲ Καίϲαροϲ

Λουκ[ίου] Δομιττίου Αὐρηλιανοῦ

25      Εὐϲεβο[ῦϲ] Εὐτυχοῦϲ ϲεβα[ϲ]τοῦ καὶ Ἰουλίου

Αὐ[ρηλίου ϲε]πτιμίου Οὐαβαλλάθου

Ἀθηνοδώ]ρου τοῦ λαμπροτάτου βαϲιλέωϲ

ὑπάτου αὐ]τοκράτοροϲ ϲτρα[τ]ηγοῦ Ῥωμ[αίων

(month) (day)] (m. 4) Αὐρήλιο[ϲ] Μέλαϲ Ἡρα-

30      κλείδου ἐπιδέ]δωκα. Αὐρήλιοϲ

. . . . . . . . . . ἔγρα]ψα ὑπὲρ αὐτοῦ μὴ

εἰδότοϲ γράμμ]ατα.

· · · · · ·

1 επεκ′      10 ἴερον      14 αναχ′      20 ιϛ′      21 ϊϲον      23 ↄ α      24 δομιτ′τιου

Col. ii '(2nd hand) He has been scrutinized(?). (3rd hand) No. 18. (1st hand) To Calpurnius Horion, the most excellent *hypomnematographus*, councillor of the most glorious city of the Alexandrians, from Aurelius Melas, son of Heracleides, grandson of Ammonius (son of ?, alias?) Diogenes, mother Thaësis, from the glorious city of the Oxyrhynchites. Having reached (the age of maturity) and been scrutinized in the Myrobalanus quarter and having been enrolled in the individual lists submitted by the phylarch for the imperial corn dole, when I took my place at the examination I was unable to produce the proofs of my descent; now necessarily producing my certificate of scrutiny and the proofs of my descent, I submit this application and I request that I too may share the gift of corn, since I was scrutinized in the 15th year, in conformity with the resolutions of the most excellent council in like measure with my equals. Farewell. Year 1 of Imperator Caesar Lucius Domitius Aurelianus Pius Felix Augustus and Julius Aurelius Septimius Vaballathus Athenodorus, the most glorious king, consul, *imperator*, general of the Romans (month, day). (4th hand) I, Aurelius Melas, son of Heracleides, submitted (the petition). I, Aurelius . . . , wrote on his behalf because he does not know letters.'

Col. ii The traces of the preceding item in the ϲυγκολλήϲιμον are very scanty. After ii 32 there are very meagre traces of perhaps 10 lines of subscriptions on a fairly narrow vertical strip, but nothing of significance can be read. On the back there are other illegible traces, perhaps of further subscriptions, cf. 2908 ii 44–7, iii 42–4.

1 ἐπεκ(ρίθη?). This supplement is suggested by the other applications that have a docket λι(τουργ-), where they are made on grounds of public service.

6 Διογένουϲ. This looks like a patronymic of the grandfather, which would be unusual, though see also 2935 ii 8 n. It may be better to take it as an alias of Ammonius, which is what is implied by the insertion of ⟨τοῦ καὶ?⟩ in the text. The form as it stands in the original may be acceptable as a double name, see P. Mich. v, Introd. p. 15.

8 προϲβάϲ. Sc. ἀπὸ γραφῆϲ ἀφηλίκων, cf., e.g., 2927 4, or εἰϲ τοὺϲ τεϲϲαρεϲκαιδεκαετεῖϲ, cf., e.g., 1028 11, 1202 18.

10 ἱερόν. In the sense of 'imperial', LSJ s.v. ἱερόϲ II, 3, c. Cf. WChr. 425, 9 ff. ϲυνχωρηθέντοϲ ἡμῖν ϲιτηρεϲίου ἐκ τῆϲ μεγαλοδωρίαϲ τῶν κυρίων ἡμῶν . . . ϲεβαϲτῶν; van Berchem, *Les distributions*, pp. 98–9.

13 δεδύνημαι. The grammar could be regularized by emending to δεδυνημένοϲ, but the result is not elegant, and probably it is best simply to recognize that the text is badly drafted.

## 2899

22 3B.15/D(14–15)b       7·5 × 17 cm.       s.d.

ii

.[

Αὐρηλί[ῳ Ἀχιλλεῖ?

νεωκ[όρῳ τοῦ μεγάλου] Ϲα-

ράπιδο[ϲ τῷ κρ(ατίϲτῳ) ὑπομνημ]ατογρά-

φῳ καὶ [τοῖϲ αἱρεθεῖ]ϲι ὑπὸ τῆϲ

κρατίϲτη[ϲ βο]υλῆϲ διακριταῖϲ

παρὰ Αὐρηλ[ί]ου Λογγείν[ο]υ

Θέωνοϲ τοῦ Θέωνος μη-

τρὸϲ Διογενίδοϲ ἀπ' Ὀξυρ[ύ]γ-

χων πόλεωϲ τῆϲ λαμπρᾶϲ. ἐ-

πικριθεὶϲ ἐπ' ἀμφόδο[υ Κρη-

τικοῦ ἐπὶ τοῦ δ (ἔτουϲ) ....[....

Ἀλεξάνδρου βαϲιλείαϲ ἀπ[όδη-

μοϲ τυνχάνων καὶ παρε[ίθην

κατ' ἄγνοιαν ὑπ[ὸ] τοῦ φ[υλάρ-

χου. ἐπὶ οὖν ἔδοξεν ἐν [τῇ κρα-

τίϲτῃ βουλ[ῇ ὥϲτε τοὺϲ ἔχον-

τάϲ τι δίκαιο[ν τοῦτο ἐντὸϲ

τῆϲ τριμήν[ου παραθέϲθαι

πρὸϲ τὸ διακ[ριθέντοϲ τοῦ πρά-

γματοϲ ἐπ[ανορθώϲεωϲ τυ-

χεῖν, ἐπιδίδ[ωμι ταύτην

τὴν ἀξίωϲι[ν ὅπωϲ κελεύϲη-

τε τῷ φυλάρχ[ῳ τοῦ δηλουμέ-

νου ἀμφόδ[ου ἐφ' οὗ καὶ ἐλειτούρ-

γηϲα καὶ τὸ ἡ[μέτερον ὄνομα

ἐν τοῖϲ ἀν[αγορευομένοιϲ

.....].[

        .        .        .        .

5 (line marker)    10   15   20   25

7 λογ'γειν[ο]υ      9 οξυρ[υ]γ'      12 δϟ      15 ϋπ[ο]      16 l. ἐπεί

Col. ii 'To Aurelius (Achilles?), temple servant of the great Sarapis, the most excellent *hypomnematographus*, and to the examiners chosen by the most excellent council, from Aurelius Longinus, son of Theon, grandson of Theon, mother Diogenis, from the glorious city of the Oxyrhynchi. Although I was scrutinized in the Cretan quarter in the fourth year ... of the reign of (Severus) Alexander, because I was away from home I was also mistakenly passed over by the phylarch. So then, since a decree has been passed in the most excellent council that those who have some claim should declare it within three months so that they may obtain redress after the matter has been examined, I submit this petition that you may give orders to the phylarch of the specified quarter, in which I have also done public service, (to submit) my name among those to be proclaimed . . .'

Col. ii 1 ̣[. Trace of an item number or a docket in the top margin. There are very slight traces of the previous item.

2 [Ἀχιλλεῖ? Cf. Introd. p. 31.

6 διακριταῖς. διάκρισις is apparently any sort of *ad hoc* examination, e.g. of goods supplied to the government by way of tax. The other occurrences of the word διακριτής seem not to be connected with this particular process; P. Giss. 58 ii 11, 59 i 7a, BGU 734, 6, 32, SB v 7741, 9.

12 δ (ἔτους) . . . .[. i.e. A.D. 224/5. The traces are hard to reconcile with τῆς ̣[ or θεοῦ[ or Ϲεου[ήρου, any of which might possibly be right; but none is really suitable. The letters look very like προτ[, which seems promising at first sight, as either πρό or πρότερος, but the solution is still to be found.

14 παρε[ίθην. The finite verb is restored in an effort to make grammar, but the καί suggests that the writer actually put παρεθείς and ignored the absence of a main verb.

16 For the restorations compare **2900** 5 seqq.

## 2900

4 1B.75/G(i)            7 × 12 cm.            s.d.

.    .    .    .    .

```
    ]εντ . . .[ . . . .] . .[ . . . .] .[ . .] .̣
    ἐ]πιδοθέντων ὑπὸ τοῦ φυ-
    λά]ρχου ἀμφόδου Μητ[ρ]ώ-
    ου] τῆς δια⟨δό⟩cεωc βιβλίων
5   . .] . . κα[τ]' ἄγνοιαν. ἐπεὶ οὖν
    ἔδο]ξεν ἐν τῇ κρατίϲτῃ βουλῇ
    ὥϲ]τε τοὺς ἔχοντάς τι δί[κ]α[ι]ον
    τοῦτο ἐντὸ]ς τῆς τριμήνου
    πα]ραθέ[ϲ]θαι π[ρ]ὸς τὸ δια-
10  κριθέντος τοῦ πράγματος
    ἐπανορθώϲεωϲ τυχεῖν,
    ὅθεν ἐπιδίδωμι ταύτην
    τὴν ἀξίωϲιν ὅπως κελεύ-
    ϲητε τῷ φυλάρχῃ τοῦ δη-
15  λουμένου ἀμφόδου ἐφ' οὗ καὶ
    ἐλειτούργηϲα [κ]αὶ τὸ ἡμέ-
    τερ]ον ὄνομα ἐν τοῖς ἀναγο-
    ρ[ε]υομένοιϲ ἐπιδοῦναι
    πρὸ]ς τὸ κἀμὲ τῆ[ϲ τ]οῦ [ϲ]ιτη-
20  ρεϲί]ου δόϲεω[ϲ
```

.    .    .    .    .

'(I was passed over in) the records of the distribution submitted by the phylarch of the Metroum quarter (perhaps?) by mistake. So then, since a decree has been passed in the most excellent council that those who have some claim should declare it within three months so as to obtain redress after the matter has been examined, for this reason I submit this petition that you may give orders to the phylarch of the specified quarter, in which I have also done public service, to submit my name among those to be proclaimed so that I too (may share) the gift of the corn dole . . .'

1 The sense requires something like παρε]ίθ[ην δι]ὰ [τῶ]ν here, but the traces are minute.

3 Μητ[ρ]ῴ-. The remains are very scanty, but the only other possibility is Μυρoβ[αλ]ά[[νου], which would be cramped in both lines.

5 Perhaps ἴc]ως, cf. 2110 5, 14, 32, 1202 22. Or this place might suit παρ⟨ε?⟩ί]θ[η]ν, but the space is very short.

8 τοῦτο ἐντό]c e.g.; ἐντὸc ταύτη]c perhaps.

9 πα]ραθέ[c]θαι. Cf. WB s.v. παρατίθημι (4), citing, e.g., WChr. 26, 35.

13 κελεύcητε. For the plural compare 2899 23, where the addressees are a *hypomnematographus* and διακριταί.

20 Supply μεταcχεῖν but not necessarily in this line, i.e. κατ᾽ ἴcον τῶν ὁμοίων μου *vel sim.* might intervene.

## 2901

23 3B.11/D(19–20)a          8 × 10 cm.          30 Dec., A.D. 268

.    .    .    .

τ . . [
κελεύcητ[ε τῷ] φ[υλάρχῳ
τοῦ προκειμένου ἀ[μφόδου
καὶ τὸ ἡμέτερον ὄν[ομα
5    ἐν τοῖc ἀναγορευομένο[ιc
ἄνδραcι Ἀλεξανδρέων
ἐπιδοῦναι πρ[ὸc τὸ] κἀμὲ
τὸν λελειτουργηκότα
τῆc τοῦ cιτηρεc[ίο]υ δόcεω[c
10    μεταλαμβάνειν. (ἔτουc) α′
Αὐτοκράτοροc Καίcαροc Μάρκου Αὐρηλίου
Κλαυδίου Εὐcεβοῦc Εὐτυχοῦc
Cεβαcτοῦ, Τῦβι δ‾.

(m. 2)   Αὐρήλ[ιοc
15      . . .] . [

.    .    .    .

10 L a′

'. . . that you may give orders to the phylarch of the aforesaid quarter to submit my name too among those men of Alexandrian citizenship whose names are to be proclaimed, so that I too, who have performed a public service, may receive a share of the gift of the corn dole. Year 1 of Imperator Caesar Marcus Aurelius Claudius Pius Felix Augustus, Tybi 4. (2nd hand) I, Aurelius . . .'

10–13 This is the earliest dated document in the archive, 30 December, A.D. 268. See Introd. p. 24 for the chronology adopted.

## 2902

22 3B.15/E(8–10)c  12 × 26 cm.  24 June, A.D. 272

ii

.  .  .  .  .

(traces of lines 1–3)

```
    καὶ ἐπικριθεὶς τῷ α (ἔτει) ........ ἐτῶν ἐκκαιδ[εκα
5   ταγεὶς τε διὰ τοῦ ἐπιδοθέντος ὑπὸ τοῦ τοῦ προκειμέ-
    νου ἀμφόδου φυλάρχου πρὸς τὴν τῶν ἐκκαιδ[ε]κ[α-
    ετῶν σιτοδοσίαν ἐν τῇ τῶν ἐπικεκριμένων
    τάξει καὶ μέχρι δεῦρο μὴ ὑπακούσας τῷ ἐπὶ τῆ[ς
    ἀλλοδαπῆς ἀναγκαίας χρείας χ[ά]ριν παρεστρα-
10  τεῦσθαι, νῦν ἀφειγμένος καὶ ἐπιδικνὺς τήν τε
    ἐπίκρισίν μου καὶ δηλῶν τὸ ἐντετάχθαι με διὰ
    τῶν βιβλίων ὡς προεῖπον, ἀξιῶ καὶ αὐτὸς πολείτη[ς
    ὢν καὶ αὐθιγενής, ἐπιδιδοὺς ἅμα τάδε τὰ βιβλία,
    καθ' ὁμοιότητα τῶν ἀπὸ τοῦ τῶν ἐπικεκριμέ-
15  νων τάγματος ⟨μετασχεῖν⟩ τῆ⟨ς⟩ τοῦ σιτηρεσίου δωρεᾶς.
         διευτύχει.
    (ἔτους) γ´´ Αὐτοκράτορος Καίσαρος Λουκίου Δομιττίου
    Αὐρηλιανοῦ Γουνθικοῦ Μεγίστου Εὐσεβοῦς Εὐτυχοῦς
    Σεβαστοῦ. Παῦνι λ¯.
         (vac.)
20 (m. 2) Αὐρ(ήλιος) Σερῆνος ἐπικ(ριτής)· οὗτός ἐστιν ὁ ἐπικριθείς,
    ὃς καὶ ἀναγορευθεὶς ὑπήκουσεν.
   (m. 3) Αὐρήλ(ιος) Σιλβανὸς γνωστήρ· γνωρίζω
    τὸν προκ(είμενον) οὕτ(ως) ἔχοντα καὶ αὐτ(ός) ἐστιν
    ὁ διακριθ(εὶς) καὶ ἐπὶ τῆς ἀναγορ(ίας) ὑπήκ(ουσεν).
```

4 αϛ    9 αναγ'καιας    17 δομιτ'τιου    20 αυρ', επι<sup>κ</sup>    22 αυρηλ    23 προ<sup>κ</sup>ουτ, αυτ
24 διακριθ, αναγορ'υπη<sup>κ</sup>?

Col. ii '. . . and scrutinized in the first year (and having reached the age?) of 16 years and been enrolled in the (register?) submitted by the phylarch of the aforesaid quarter for the distribution of corn to 16-year-olds in the category of scrutinized persons, and up to now not having answered to my name because of having been away from home on unavoidable duty following the army, now, having come home and shown my certificate of scrutiny, and explaining that I have been enrolled in the records, as I said before, I ask that I too, being a citizen and of local birth, submitting also this petition, (may share?) the gift of the corn dole on the same terms as those in the category of scrutinized persons. Farewell. Year 3 of the Imperator Caesar Lucius Domitius Aurelianus, Gothicus Maximus, Pius Felix Augustus, Payni 30. (2nd hand) Aurelius Serenus, scrutineer: This is the scrutinized person, who also answered when his name was proclaimed. (3rd hand) Aurelius Silvanus, witness of identity: I identify the aforesaid person, who is as described, and he is the same person who was examined and answered to his name at the muster.'

Col. ii 1–3 Traces of these lines remain on fibres that are too loose and confused for any coherent account of them to be given, even though we know that the form of it was roughly: 'To X, (plus title), from Y, son of Z, grandson of A, whose mother is B, listed in the C quarter . . .'

At the top left there are also traces of the previous item in the file.

4 a (ἔτει) = A.D. 269/70, cf. Introd. p. 24 for the chronology adopted. Perhaps read καὶ γενο῾μ΄-(ενος), cf. 2893 9.

5 The word qualified by ἐπιδοθέντος has been omitted. Supply it—say βιβλίου or κατ' ἄνδρα—after φυλάρχου (6) or perhaps better after cιτοδοcίαν (7).

8 seq. τῷ . . . παρεcτρατεῦcθαι. Possibly during the recapture of Egypt for Aurelian, cf. Introd. pp. 24–5. παραcτρατεύομαι is a rare word known only from a quotation in the *Suda*, s.v. λεῖξαι.

15 Certainly τη not τῆc was written, but δωρεᾶc looks probable and a verb has been omitted. The common form suggests supplying ⟨μεταcχεῖν⟩ and τῆ⟨c⟩.

17–19 Compare Introd. pp. 24–5 for the interpretation of this date, which is equivalent to 24 June, A.D. 272, according to the chronology adopted here.

Γουνθικοῦ. The SHA says that Aurelian defeated the Goths on his way to face Zenobia (*Aur.* 22, 1–2), but even if this is reliable no argument about the date can be based on the absence of a title referring to the defeat of the Palmyrenes, e.g. *Parthicus, Persicus, Palmyrenicus*, because no such title is yet attested in Egyptian documents. The only other title mentioned at all is *Carpicus Maximus* (Bureth, *Titulatures*, p. 123).

## 2903

23 3B.11/D(16)a           13 × 15 cm.           c. A.D. 271–2

Καλπ[ουρ]νίῳ Ὡρί[ωνι τῷ κρατίcτῳ
ὑπομνημα[τογράφῳ
παρὰ Αὐρηλίου Cαραπί[ω]νος [. . . . . το]ῦ
Πτολεμαίου μητρὸς Θαήcιο[c ἀπὸ τῆ]c
5    λαμπρᾶc Ὀξυρυγχειτῶν πόλ[ε]ω[c. π]ροcβὰc
καὶ ἐπικριθεὶc ἐπ' ἀμφόδου Ἑρμαίου
τῷ ιγ (ἔτει)″ τῆc Γαλλιηνοῦ βαc[ι]λείαc τα[γ]ε[ί]c τε
διὰ τοῦ ἐπιδοθέντοc ὑπὸ [τοῦ] τ[ο]ῦ π[ροκε]ιμέ-
νου ἀμφόδου φυλάρχου βιβλίου [κ]αὶ ἐν τῇ
10    γενομένῃ τότε τῶν ὁμοίων μ[ο]υ ἀναγορείᾳ
ἐτύγχανον ἐν ἀποδημίᾳ ὤν, νῦν γοῦν
παραγενόμενοc cημαίνω ἐμαυτὸν κ[αὶ ἀξιῶ
μεταcχεῖν καὶ αὐτ[ὸ]c τῆc τοῦ cιτηρεcίου
δωρεᾶc κατ' ἴcον τῶν ὁμοίων μου κ[ατὰ τ]ὰ

15    δό[ξα]ντα τῇ [κρατίς]τῃ βουλῇ. διευ[τύ]χει.

     (ἔτους) [ . Αὐ]τοκράτορ[ος Καίσα]ρος

     Λουκίου Δομιτ]τίου Αὐρ[ηλιανοῦ Εὐσεβοῦς

     Εὐτυχοῦς Σεβα]στοῦ [

     .   .   .   .   .

2 ὑπομνημα[     5 οξυρυγ'χειτων     7 ιγϛ″     16 ∟[

'To Calpurnius Horion, the most excellent *hypomnematographus*, from Aurelius Sarapion, son of . . . , grandson of Ptolemaeus, mother Thaësis, from the glorious city of the Oxyrhynchites. Having reached (the age of maturity) and undergone scrutiny in the Hermaeum quarter in the 13th year of the reign of Gallienus and having been enrolled in the list submitted by the phylarch of the aforesaid quarter, on the occasion of the muster of persons of the same condition as myself that took place then I happened to be away from home; now however that I have arrived (home) I declare myself and ask that I too may share the gift of the corn dole on equal terms with persons of the same condition as myself in accordance with the decree of the most excellent council. Farewell. Year . . . of the Imperator Caesar Lucius Domitius Aurelianus Pius Felix Augustus (and Vaballathus? month, day).'

    1 The top margin is almost entirely lost and with it any docket or item number. The joins at either side show that this too is from a roll file, but only a few spots of ink remain from the flanking items.

    7 ιγ (ἔτει) etc. = A.D. 265/6.

    10 τότε. This ἀναγορία took place in A.D. 265/6. Though the possibility can be envisaged that these roll calls may not have been specifically concerned with the corn dole, see Introd. p. 6, the wording of 2913 14–16—ἀξιῶ ἐνταγῆναι ἐν τοῖς ἀναγορευομένοις πρὸς διάδοσιν τοῦ σιτηρεσίου ὀνόμασι—seems to show that they were. Consequently it is probable that the dole was being issued in A.D. 265/6 and this is the earliest date for which there is evidence from Oxyrhynchus. In Hermopolis and Alexandria there were doles in or around A.D. 261, see Introd. pp. 1–2.

## 2904

22 3B.15/D(1–3)a           10 × 23 cm.           17 April, A.D. 272

         (m. 5) λι(τουργ-)

     Αὐρηλίῳ Εὐδαίμονι τῷ καὶ Ἑλλαδίῳ ἄρξ(αντι)

     βουλ(ευτῇ) Ἀλεξανδρείας καὶ ὡς χρηματίζει

     παρὰ Αὐρηλίου Ἀπολλωνίου καὶ ὡς χρημ(ατίζω)

5      μητρὸς Ταμόιτος· δόξαντος ἐν τῇ κρ(ατίστῃ)

     βουλῇ ὥστε τοὺς λελειτουργηκότας με-

     τασχεῖν τῆς τοῦ σείτου δωρεᾶς καὶ αὐ-

     τὸς λειτουργῶν ἐπὶ τοῦ λειτουργοῦν-

     τος τῷ ἐνεστῶτι β (ἔτει) καὶ ε (ἔτει) ἀμφόδου

10      Ποιμενικῆς δημοσίαν ὀνηλασίαν

     τῆς μητροπόλεως ἀξιῶ καὶ ἐπ' ἐμοῦ

     τὰ δεδογμένα φυλαχθῆναι καὶ τῆς

1 λ     2 αρξ′     3 βοῠᴧ     4 χρημ)     5 κρϛ     8 ων corr. ex ουντ?     9 βϛ, εϛ

τοῦ [ϲεί]του δόϲεωϲ ἐν τῇ τῶν [ὁ]μοίων

τάξ[ει] μεταϲχεῖν. διευτύχει.

15 (m. 2)  (ἔτουϲ) β″ Αὐτοκρᾱτ[οροϲ

Καίϲαροϲ Λουκίου̣ Δομι[τίου

Αὐρηλιανοῦ Εὐϲεβοῦ[ϲ

Εὐτυχοῦϲ Ϲεβαϲτοῦ

καὶ (ἔτουϲ) ε″ Ἰουλίου

20        Αὐρηλίου Ϲεπτιμίου Οὐαβαλάθου

Ἀθηνοδώρου τοῦ λαμπροτάτου

βαϲιλέωϲ ὑπάτου αὐτοκράτοροϲ

ϲτρατηγοῦ Ῥωμαί[ων

Φαρμοῦθι κβ‾.

25 (m. 3)  Αὐρήλιοϲ Ἀπολλώνιοϲ ἐπιδέδω[κα. Αὐ-

ρήλιοϲ Διοϲκουρίδηϲ ἔγραψα ὑπ[ὲ]ρ̣[ αὐτοῦ

μὴ εἰδότοϲ γράμματα.

Verso, across the fibres: (m. 4) .. Φαρμοῦθι

15 Ⳑ β″        19 Ⳑ ε″ ϊουλιου

'(5th hand) Liturg-. (1st hand) To Aurelius Eudaemon, alias Helladius, ex-magistrate, councillor of Alexandria and however he is officially described, from Aurelius Apollonius, and however I am officially described, mother Tamois. Whereas it was decreed in the most excellent council that those who have performed a liturgy should share the gift of corn and since I too am performing a liturgy, the public donkey service of the nome capital, in the Shepherds' quarter, which is providing the public service in the present second and fifth year, I ask that the provisions of the decree be observed in my case also and that I may share the distribution of corn in the category of persons of the same condition. Farewell. (2nd hand) Year 2 of Imperator Caesar Lucius Domitius Aurelianus Pius Felix Augustus and year 5 of Julius Aurelius Septimius Vaballathus Athenodorus the most glorious king, consul, *imperator*, general of the Romans, Pharmouthi 22. (3rd hand) I, Aurelius Apollonius, submitted (the petition). I, Aurelius Dioscurides, wrote on his behalf since he does not know letters.'

8–10 λειτουργοῦντοϲ... ἀμφόδου Ποιμενικῆϲ. Cf. Introd. pp. 6 seq. If my conclusions about the tribes are correct this is a short way of referring to a tribe that probably included more than one ἄμφοδον and provided public servants for a year at a time. The tribe could probably have been described as the φυλὴ Ποιμενικῆϲ καὶ ἄλλων ἀμφόδων, cf. 1116 5–6, 2715 5–6, P. Flor. 39, 4.

27 Below this line is *c*. 1 cm. of blank papyrus, but the edge is broken and it may be that other subscriptions followed.

28 ..Φαρμοῦθι. The traces are perhaps to be read (π)ρ(οϲ)γί(νεται) in the form ρ̣˙χ˙ (see 2915 20 n.). Another appropriate possibility is λˌ = λει(τουργ-), but the abbreviation usual in this archive for this word has the *iota* underneath the *lambda* (cf. 1) and the final traces here are a probable *iota* cut across by a horizontal.

If (π)ρ(οϲ)γί(νεται), 'he joins the recipients', is right, it is perhaps of significance for the interpretation of the council's decree that the λελειτουργηκότεϲ—past tense—should share the dole. One might have supposed that admission to the dole would depend on serving the full term of a public service satisfactorily. This man uses the present tense (8), which suggests that the decree was interpreted generously, but the possibility remains that he finished his term of service satisfactorily between 22 Pharmouthi and the end of the month.

## 2905

22 3B.15/D(14–15)b        6·5 × 10 cm.        s.d.

```
                                    . .
       (m. 2)  ι.  (m. 3)  εξε . . [
       (m. 1)  Αὐρηλίῳ Πλ[ο]υτί[ωνι
               γραμματῖ ⟨τ⟩οῦ ϲιτηρε[ϲίου
     5         παρὰ Αὐρηλίου Διδύ[μου
               Ἑρμίου μητρὸϲ Θαῆϲι[οϲ
               ἀπὸ τῆϲ λαμπρᾶϲ Ὀξυρύ[γ]χ(ων)
               πόλεωϲ. ἀναγραφόμενοϲ
               ἐπ' ἀμφόδου Ἡρῴου
    10         ἐφ' οὗ καὶ ἐλειτούργηϲα
               ἐπεὶ παρείθην ὑπὸ τοῦ
               τοῦ ἀμφόδου φυλάρχου
               ἐν τοῖϲ ἐπιδοθεῖϲι ὑπ' αὐτοῦ
               βιβλί[ο]ι[ϲ] τοῦ ϲιτηρεϲίου ἀξι-
    15         ῶ .[. . . . . . . . .] . ναιων
                  .      .      .      .      .
```

7 οξυρυ[γ]χ

'(2nd hand) No. 13 (?). (3rd hand) ... (1st hand) To Aurelius Plution, secretary of the corn dole, from Aurelius Didymus, son of Hermias, mother Thaësis, from the glorious city of the Oxyrhynchi. Being listed in the Heroum quarter, in which I have also done public service, since I was passed over by the phylarch of the quarter in the records of the corn dole submitted by him, I ask ...'

1 Very faint traces, perhaps accidental ink.

2 Perhaps ιχ = 13; otherwise ι = 10 followed by a stroke indicating a numeral.

Above and to the right of the second *epsilon* of εξε..[ there is a stroke rising upwards to the right. It might be part of yet another line above, but the ink looks the same, so it is best taken as a letter written above the line or a mark of abbreviation coming rather far back; ε is linked to the following letter which looks like τ.[ or π[. Since this is the only petition addressed to Aurelius Plution that concerns an omitted person, it may be that the docket indicates that it was out of order, see Introd. p. 32. Part of ἐξετάζειν might be appropriate, or perhaps ἐξετά[γη, but it is difficult to identify the letter or mark above the line. All this is very doubtful.

## 2906

23 3B.11/D(9)     17·5 × 23·5 cm.     A.D. 270/1?;
2 Nov., A.D. 270

i

(m. 5) κγ

Καλπουρνίῳ Ὠρείωνι τῷ κ[ρατ]ίςτῳ ὑπομνηματογράφῳ     (vac.)
παρὰ Αὐρηλίου Ἀνεικήτου Ϲα[ρα]πάμμωνος
5     μη]τρὸϲ Ἰϲιδώραϲ ἀπὸ τῆϲ λαμπρᾶϲ Ὀξυ-
ρυ]γχειτῶν πόλεωϲ.
ἐ]πειδὴ ἔδοξεν [ἐν τ]ῇ κρατίϲτῃ βουλῇ
ὥϲτε τοὺϲ λε]λ[ει]τουργηκόταϲ μεταϲχεῖν
τῆ]ϲ τοῦ ϲιτηρεϲίου δόϲεωϲ καὶ αὐτὸϲ
10     λειτουργ]ῶ νῦν ἐπ᾽ ἀμφόδου Ἑρμαίου
. . . . . . . . . μ]ητροπόλεωϲ, ὁ δὲ τοῦ ἡμετέρου ἀ]μφ[ό]δου φύλαρχοϲ ἐκ τῶν ἐπι-
δοθέ]ν[τ]ων ὑπ᾽ αὐτοῦ τῶν ὁμοίων μοι
κατ᾽ ἄν]δρα βιβλίῳ[ν] παρεῖκ[ε]ν τὸ ἡμέ-
15     τε]ρον ὄνο[μ]α, ἀνα[γκαίωϲ] τῶνδε
τῶν β]ιβλ[ίω]ν ἐ[πίδοϲιν ποιοῦ]μαι ἀξιῶ-
ν ταγῆναί με πρὸϲ τὸ δύναϲθαί μ]αι μεταϲχεῖν τῆϲ τοῦ ϲιτηρεϲίου δόϲεω]ϲ κα[τὰ] τὰ
δόξαντα τῇ] κρα[τίϲτῃ βουλῇ κατ᾽ ἴϲ]ον
20     τῶν ὁμοίω]ν μοι. δ[ι]ευτύ[χει.
(ἔτουϲ) α᾽ Αὐτο]κράτοροϲ Καίϲαρ[οϲ Λουκίου
Δομιττίου Αὐρ]ηλιανοῦ Εὐϲεβ[ῦϲ] Εὐτυχ[ο]ῦϲ
Ϲεβαϲτοῦ καὶ] Ἰουλίου Αὐρηλίου Ϲεπτιμίου
Οὐαβαλλάθου] Ἀθηνοδώρου τοῦ λαμπροτάτου
25     βαϲιλέωϲ ὑπάτου αὐ]τοκράτοροϲ ϲτρατηγοῦ
Ῥωμαίων . . . . . . . . .]. κϲ̄
(m. 2)     . . . . . . . . . . . . . .] λιτουργεῖ εανου
. . . . . . . . . . . . .]υρηϲ ἐν οἰκ᾽ε᾽ίᾳ
τάξει . . . . . . . . .]λαβε αὐτόν.

(vac.)

30 (m. 3) . . . . . . . . . . . . . .]... ὁ προκ(είμενος) λιτ[

 . . . . . . . . . . . . . ].... ὑπακ[ου-

(m. 4) . . . . . . . . . . . . .]. .[

2 ὗπο-    5 ἵcιδωραc    6 ρυ]χʹχειτων    13 ὕπαυτου    17 l. μ]ε

ii

(m. 4) κδ

Αὐρηλίῳ Πλουτίω[νι γραμματεῖ cιτηρεcίου [
παρὰ Αὐρηλίου Εὐφρ[οcύνου . . . . .

5      ...ου Διογένουc ἐξηγ[. . . . . . . . .
τῆc λαμπρᾶc Ὀξυρ[υγχιτῶν πόλε-
ωc. ἀναγραφόμε[νος ἐπ' ἀμφόδου Ἑρμαίου ἐφ' οὗ καὶ [. . . . . . . . .
δημοcίαν ὀνηλ[αcίαν . . . . .

10      . . . . . . . .[. . . . . . . . . . .
...τηρ.[. . . . . . . . . . . . . .
οὐκ ὑπήκο[υcα τυγχάνων ἐν ἀποδημίᾳ ὤ[ν, νῦν γοῦν παραγεν]όμ[ε-
ν]οc καὶ το.[. . .].... ἐπ[ιδί-

15      δωμι τὰ βιβλία ἀ̣ξιῶν μ[ετα-
cχεῖν τοῦ cιτηρεcίου ἀκολού-
θωc τοῖc περὶ το̣ύ̣τ̣ο̣υ δόξαcι
τῇ κρατίcτῃ [βου]λῇ.
ἐπὶ ὑπάτων τοῦ ἐνεcτῶτο̣c

20      ἔτουc Ἁθὺρ ϛ.
(m. 2) Αὐρήλιο[c] Εὐφ[ρ]οcύνηc
ἐπιδέδωκα.
(m. 3) εἰ ἐνετάγη τῷ ἐπιδοθ(έντι) βιβλίῳ
καὶ ἐν..αγ.[.]...[....]εν

25      ..[. . . . . . . . . . . . . . . . .]ει

12 ουκʹ    23 επιδοθ

Col. i '(5th hand) No. 23. (1st hand) To Calpurnius Horion, the most excellent *hypomnematographus*, from Aurelius Anicetus, son of Sarapammon, mother Isidora, from the glorious city of the Oxyrhynchites. Whereas it has been decreed in the most excellent council that persons who have performed a public service shall share the gift of the corn dole and I myself am now performing in the Hermaeum quarter the public service of the . . . of the nome capital, but the phylarch of our quarter has omitted my name from the records of individuals submitted by him of persons of the same condition as myself, I necessarily make submission of this petition asking that I be enrolled, so that I may be able to share in the distribution of the corn dole, in accordance with the resolutions of the most excellent council, on equal terms with persons of the same condition as myself. Farewell. Year 1(?) of Imperator Caesar Lucius Domitius Aurelianus Pius Felix Augustus and Julius Aurelius Septimius Vaballathus Athenodorus, most glorious king, consul, *imperator*, general of the Romans, (month) 26 . . .'

Col. ii '(4th hand) No. 24. (1st hand) To Aurelius Plution, secretary of the corn dole, from Aurelius Euphrosynes, (freedman?) of Diogenes, (ex-?)*exegetes* (. . .?) of the glorious city of the Oxyrhynchites. Being listed in the Hermaeum quarter in which also I (have performed? am performing?) the public donkey driving service . . . I did not answer to my name, since I happened to be abroad, now however having arrived (home) and (learnt this?), I submit the petition asking to share the corn dole in accordance with the resolutions of the most excellent council on the matter. Under the consuls of the present year, Hathyr 6. (2nd hand) I, Aurelius Euphrosynes, submitted (the petition). (3rd hand) If he was enrolled in the list submitted . . .'

Col. i 11 Supply the name of the liturgy, e.g. ὀνηλασίαν, φυλακίαν, ἐπιδρομήν, cf. N. Lewis, *Inventory of Compulsory Services*, s.vv.

21 (ἔτους) α. Restored on the basis of the length of the gap in line 23, which is long enough for Cεβαστοῦ καί] only. If it was late in 1 Aur. 4 Vab. or in 2 Aur. 5 Vab., there would be a figure as well, (ἔτους) δ or (ἔτους) ε. Weight is added to this argument by col. ii, which is dated ἐπὶ ὑπάτων τοῦ ἐνεστῶτος ἔτους, i.e. early in the same Graeco-Egyptian year as 1 Aur. (4) Vab.

26 Since there was probably a space between 'Ρωμαίων and the month name there is no way of estimating the latter's length. The trace is a mere dot.

27 seqq. For the sense restore something like [ὁ προκείμενος, ὥς φησι,] λιτουργεῖ. ἐὰν οὖ[ν ἀληθεύοντα ε]ὕρῃς, ἐν ⟨τῇ⟩ οἰκείᾳ [τάξει (εὐθέως?) ἀνά]λαβε αὐτόν. 'The aforesaid, as he claims, is performing a public service. So then, if you find that he speaks the truth, enrol him (immediately?) in the proper category.'

Col. ii 5 . . .ου. The traces suit ἀπελευ]⁵θέρου. This is at least consistent with the name Euphrosynes, since there are two slaves called Euphrosynus in P. Mich. v 326, 7, 28 and 9, 18 and another in **1451** [6], [8], 32, whose name appears in the genitive as Εὐφροςύνου. If ἀπελευ]⁵θέρου is correct, this is the only recognizable application from a freedman in the archive.

8 Restore part of λειτουργεῖν—ἐλειτούργηςα or λειτουργῶ.

10 This is illegible because of the rapidity of the writing, which is not much damaged.

11 ϛειτηρε[ϲι- would be suitable, but in 3 and 16 the word is written without iotacism and the conventional spelling would not suit these traces.

14 Perhaps τοῦ[το μ]αθών, but this is not in the other petitions from returned absentees and would have to refer to the illegible passage in 10–11.

23 It seems that in 10–11 he must have claimed that he had been registered as properly entitled to the dole.

24 One might expect καὶ ἐνταγῆ[τ]ῳ, but it seems not consistent with the traces.

25 ]ει seems likely to be τάξ]ει. Just possibly restore ἐν ²⁵ τῇ [τῶν ἀπελευθέρων τάξ]ει.

## 2907

23 3B.11/D(7)c                    12 × 13 cm.                    1 Nov. (?), A.D. 270;
                                                                Oct./Nov., A.D. 270

i

.    .    .    .

ἡμέτ[ε]ρ[ο]ν ὄ[νο]μα πρὸς
τὸ κἀμὲ μετέχειν [τῆς
τοῦ cειτηρεcίου δω-
ρεᾶc καθ᾽ ἴcον τῶν
5    ὁμοίων. ἐπὶ ὑπ[ά-
τ̣ων τοῦ ἐνεcτῶτ̣[οc
ἔτ̣[ουc], Ἀθὺρ [[.]]ε′
(m. 2)   Αὐ̣[ρή]λιοc Θέων
ἐ̣[πι]δέδωκα.
10   Αὐ̣[ρ]ήλι̣ο̣ς Ἀγαθὸc Δα̣ί̣-
μω̣ν̣ ἔγραψα ὑπὲρ αὐτοῦ
μὴ] ε̣ἰδότοc γράμμα̣τ̣α.
(m. 3)   . .].. . λιτ̣ουρ( ) εν̣τα
. . . . . . .]. τῇ οἰκείᾳ
15   . . . . .] τάξει.
(m. 4)   . . . . . .]. . . . . . . .[

.    .    .    .    .

4 l. κατ᾽ ἴcον      13 λιτ̣ουρ̣

ii

.    .    .    .

. .].[
ἀ]ν̣αγκα̣[ίω]ς [τῶνδε τῶν
βιβλίω̣ν̣ [ἐ]πί̣δοcιν ποιού[μ]ε̣-
νοc ἀξιῶ ταγῆναί μαι ἀν̣τ̣[ὶ
5      (vac.)

4 l. με

ὄντος ἐπὶ τοῦ αὐτοῦ ἀμφόδου
τετελευτηκότος πρὸς τὸ δ[ύ-
νασθαί μαι μετασχεῖν τῆς
τοῦ ϲείτου δωρεᾶς κατ' ἴϲον
τῶν ὁμοίων μου κατὰ τὰ
δόξαντα τῇ κρατίϲτῃ βουλῇ.
ἐπὶ ὑπάτων τ[οῦ ἐ]νεϲτῶτ[ο]ς
ἔτους, Ἀθὺρ ⟦ . ⟧ . .

(m. 2)  λιτουργήϲας κατ' ἄγνοι-
        α]ν παρείθη. ἀντειϲαχθή-
        τ]ω τῇ οἰκείᾳ τάξε[ι] ἀ-
        ναλημφθεὶς  .[ . . . . .
        .οιϲεν . . .[ . ] . ι[ . . . . .

(m. 3)  Αὐρήλιος Ἄϲκλ . . [γ]ενόμ(ενος) [φύλ(αρχος)· ἐλειτούρ-
        γηϲεν ὁ προκείμενος καὶ [οὕτως ἔχει ἐν
        τῇ βιβλιοθήκῃ.

                ·    ·    ·    ·    ·

8 l. με          19 [γ]ενομ[

Col. i '. . . my name so that I too may share the gift of the corn dole on equal terms with persons
of the same condition. Under the consuls of the current year, Hathyr . . . (2nd hand) I, Aurelius
Theon, submitted (the petition). I, Aurelius Agathus Daemon, wrote on his behalf because he does
not know letters.'

Col. ii '. . . necessarily making submission of this petition, I ask to be enrolled in place of [*left
blank*], of the same quarter, deceased, so that I may be able to share the gift of the corn dole on equal
terms with persons of the same condition as myself in accordance with the decree of the most excellent
council. Under the consuls of the current year, Hathyr . . . (2nd hand) Having performed a public
service he was passed over in error; let him be entered for a vacant place in the proper category, having
been included (among the? . . .). (3rd hand) I, Aurelius Ascl . . ., former phylarch. The aforesaid
person has performed a public service and (is so registered?) in the record office.'

Col. i 13–14 One might expect ἐντα¹⁴[χθήτ]ω, cf. ii 16?, but the trace appears to be the tip of
a descender. It may be just a stray dot of ink.

15 Elsewhere nothing intervenes between οἰκείᾳ and τάξει. It could be that τάξει was the only
word in the line, placed centrally.

Col. ii 19 Ἀϲκλᾶς or an abbreviation of an Asclepius name.

## 2908

22 3B.15/D(19)a       15×28 cm.       Dec./Jan., A.D. 270/1;
A.D. 270/1

ii

(m. 7) ιγ. ἐπεκ(ρίθη?)

(m. 1) Καλπουρνίῳ Ὠρίωνι ⟨τῷ⟩ κρατίστῳ ὑπομνηματογράφῳ
παρὰ Αὐρηλίου Ἀπίωνος Πλουτί-
5 ωνος τοῦ καὶ Ὠρείωνος Διογένους μητρὸς Χαιρημονίδος ἀπὸ
τῆς λαμπρᾶς Ὀξυρυγχειτῶν πόλεως.
ἀναγραφόμενος ἐπ' ἀμφόδου Νότου Κρηπεῖδος καὶ ἐπικριθεὶς
10 τῷ ιγ (ἔτει), ὡς εἶ-
ναί με πρὸς τὸ ἐνεστὸς α (ἔτος) (ἐτῶν) ιθ,
οὐχ ὑπήκουσα ἐν τῇ γενο-
μένῃ ἀναγορείᾳ διὰ τὸ [ε]ἶναί
με ἐπὶ τῆς ἀλλοδαπῆς. νῦν δὲ
15 ἐπιδημήσας ἐπιδίδωμι
τάδε τὰ βιβλία καὶ ἀξιῶ μετασχεῖν ἅμα τοῖς ἄλλοις τῆς
δωρεᾶς τοῦ σειτηρεσίου.
διευτύχει.
20 (ἔτους) α″ Αὐτοκράτορος Καίσαρος
Λουκίου Δομιττίου Αὐρηλιανοῦ Εὐσεβοῦς
Εὐτυχοῦς Σεβαστοῦ καὶ Ἰουλίου
Αὐρηλίου Σεπτιμίου Οὐαβαλάθου
Ἀθηνοδώρου τοῦ λαμπροτάτου βασιλέως
25 ὑπάτου αὐτοκράτορος στρατηγοῦ Ῥωμαίω(ν)
Τῦβι      (vac.)

(m. 2) Αὐρήλιος Ἀπίων Πλουτίωνος ἐπιδέδωκα. Αὐρήλιος Πλουτίων ἔγραψα ὑπὲρ αὐτοῦ μὴ εἰ-

1 επεκ′    2 καλ'πουρνιω    3 ὑπομνηματογραφω    10 ιγ𐅵̄    11 α𐅵 L ιθ    12 ὑπηκουσα
20 L α″    21 δομιτ'τιου    22 ϊουλιου    25 ὑπατου, ρωμαιω̄

30  δότος γρά(μματα).

(m. 3) παρόντων τῶν φυλάρχ(ων) καὶ τῶ(ν)

  γνωστήρων παρεχέτω τὰ

  ςύμβολα τῆς πολειτείας ἵνα

  τῇ [ο]ἰκείᾳ τάξει παραδεχθῇ.

35 (m. 4) παρεδεξάμην ἐν τῇ τά-

  ξε[ι τ]ῶν ἐπικριθέντων.

(m. 5) Αὐρήλιος Πλουτίων ὁ καὶ ........

  ............απιων[.]......

  .....[.]...........[

40  επικ[....].... ἐν [τῇ] ἀναγορείᾳ

  ὑπακου...........[.] (vac.)

(m. 6) Αὐ]ρ(ήλιος) Ζωίλ(ος) γεν[όμ(ενος)] φύλ(αρχος)· οὗτος[

  ..]........[

  • • • • • • •

Verso (m. 8) Αὐρήλ(ιος) Cερῆ(νος) γνωστήρ· γνω-

45  στεύω τὸν προκ(είμενον) ὄντα

  τὸν προκ(είμενον) ὡς πρόκ(ειται)

  καὶ αὐτός ἐστιν ὁ ὑπακούων.

30 γραϚ  31 φυλαρχ, τω⁻  33 ϊνα  42 αυ]ρ'.?, ζωϊ γεν[ομ?], φυλ  44 αυρηλ ϲερη⁻  45 προκ

46 προκ, προκ'

iii

(m. 7) λι(τουργ- ). ιδ

(m. 1) Καλπουρνίῳ Ὡρείωνι τῷ [κρατί-

  στῳ ὑπομνηματογρά[φῳ.

  παρὰ Αὐρηλίου Cαραπιάδου ['Ο-

5  φελλίου μητρὸς Διδύμης ἀ[πὸ

  τῆς λαμπρᾶς 'Οξυρύγχων π[όλε-

  ως. ὁ τρόφιμός μου ἀδε[λφός,

  Αὐρήλιος Ἀφύγχις Διοσκόρ[ου μη-

  τρὸς Φιλήτης ἀπὸ τῆς α[ὐτῆς

10  πόλεως, ἀναγραφόμεν[ος ἐ-

  π' ἀμφόδου Νότου Κρηπεῖδ[ος

  μ..ος ὢν καὶ ἀνεπίκριτο[ς

  ....ως κατὰ πλάνην .[

διὰ τοῦ προμεταδοθέντ[ος κα-
15 τ' ἄνδρα τῶν τὰς ἐννα[κοςίας
ἀρτάβας τοῦ ςειτηρεςίου [λαμβα-
νόντων διαρι.[ *c.* 10–15
τ. δεδόςθαι .[ *c.* 10–15
του προ....[ *c.* 10–15
20 του ἐν τοῖς τ.[ *c.* 10–15
.]..λουςι ο.δε.[.]..οις.[ *c.* 5–10
......].... λειτουργια..[ *c.* 5–10
...]. δα τὴν περὶ αὐτὸν .[ *c.* 2–5
ἐπιδιδοὺς οὖν τὰ βιβλία ἀ[ξιῶ
25 κἂν νῦν ἐνταγῆναι αὐτὸ[ν ἐν
τοῖς (ἐννακοςίοις) πρὸς [τὸ] μεταςχε[ῖν τῆς
κοινῆς τοῦ ςειτηρεςίο[υ δω-
ρεᾶς. διευτύχει.
(m. 2) (ἔτους) α' Αὐτοκράτορος Καίςαρος Λουκ[ίου
30 Δομιττίου Αὐρηλιανοῦ Εὐςεβοῦς Εὐ[τυχοῦς
Сεβαςτοῦ καὶ Ἰουλίου Αὐρηλίου Сεπτιμίου [Οὐαβαλλάθου
Ἀθηνοδώρου τοῦ λαμπροτάτου βαςιλέω[ς ὑπάτου
αὐτοκράτορος ςτρατηγοῦ Ῥωμαίων[ (month, day.)
(m. 3) Αὐρήλιος Сαραπιάδης Ὀ[φελλίου
35 ἐπιδέδωκα.
(m. 4) παρεδεξάμην ἐν [τῇ τάξει τῶν ῥεμβῶν. [
(m. 5) Αὐρήλιος Ζωίλ(ος) γενόμ(ενος) φύλαρχ(ος)· οὗτο[ς
ὅ[ς] καὶ ἐπὶ τῆ[ς] ἀναγορίας ὑπ[.]κου [[..]].[
40 [.]....ρος ἔγραψα ὑ[(πὲρ)] τοῦ πατρός μου βρ[αδέως γρά-
(φοντος)?
(vac.?)
(m. 6) ].. του[
. . . . .
Verso (m. 8) Αὐρήλ(ιος) Сερῆνος γνωςτήρ· γνω-
ςτεύω τὸν προκ(είμενον) ὄντα
τοῦτον καὶ ὑπακούοντα.

1 ί  26 τ  29 Ḻ α'  30 δομιτ'τιου  38 ζωιˡ γενομϚ φυλαρχ'  40 υ[' ?]  42 αυρή
43 προκ

Col. ii '(7th hand) No. 13. (He has been?) scrutinized. (1st hand) To Calpurnius Horion (the) most excellent *hypomnematographus*, from Aurelius Apion, son of Plution alias Horion, grandson of Diogenes, mother Chaeremonis, from the glorious city of the Oxyrhynchites. Being listed in the South Bank quarter and having been scrutinized in the 13th year, so that I am in the present 1st year 19 years old, I did not answer at the last (?) roll call because I was elsewhere, but now that I am here I submit this petition and I ask that I may share the gift of the corn dole along with the others. Farewell. Year 1 of Imperator Caesar Lucius Domitius Aurelianus Pius Felix Augustus, and Julius Aurelius Septimius Vaballathus Athenodorus the most glorious king, consul, *imperator*, general of the Romans. Tybi (day omitted). (2nd hand) I, Aurelius Apion, son of Plution, submitted (the petition). I, Aurelius Plution, wrote for him because he does not know letters. (3rd hand) In the presence of the phylarchs and the witnesses of identity let him provide the proofs of citizenship that he may be admitted in the proper category. (4th hand?) I admitted him in the category of scrutinized persons. (5th hand) Aurelius Plution, alias . . . , . . . at the roll call . . . answer . . . (6th hand) Aurelius Zoilus, ex-phylarch: . . .'

Verso. '(8th hand) Aurelius Serenus, witness of identity: I identify the aforesaid as being the aforesaid as is aforesaid and he is the same person who answers to his name.'

Col. iii '(7th hand) Public service(?). No. 14. (1st hand) To Calpurnius Horion the most excellent *hypomnematographus* from Aurelius Sarapiades, son of Ophellius and Didyme, from the glorious city of the Oxyrhynchi. My foster-brother Aurelius Aphynchis, son of Dioscorus and Philete, from the same city, listed in the South Bank quarter, being of weak mind(?) and unscrutinized . . . by mistake (was omitted?) in the last-registered individual list of those who receive the 900 artabas of the corn dole . . . Therefore I submit the petition and request that he be enrolled among the 900 so as to share the common gift of the corn dole. Farewell. (2nd hand) Year 1 of Imperator Caesar Lucius Domitius Aurelianus Pius Felix Augustus, and Julius Aurelius Septimius Vaballathus Athenodorus the most glorious king, consul, *imperator*, general of the Romans (month, day?). (3rd hand) I, Aurelius Sarapiades, son of Ophellius, submitted (the petition). (4th hand) I admitted him in the 'sundry' category. (5th hand) Aurelius Zoilus, ex-phylarch: This (is the aforesaid person, . . .?) who also answers to his name at the roll call. I, . . . , wrote on behalf of my father who writes haltingly. (6th hand) . . . .'

Verso. '(8th hand) Aurelius Serenus, witness of identity: I identify the aforesaid as being this person and the one who answers to his name.'

Col. i The remains are of the ends of lines only. The item was addressed to a *hypomnematographus*, referred to the council's resolutions about public servants, and was dated by Aurelian and Vaballathus.

Col. ii 9–11 Cf. Introd. p. 21, for the chronology and the significance of this passage.

12–14 From the present tenses of ὑπακούω employed in the formulary (**2927**) I have concluded that the ἀναγορία was an event regularly repeated, see ibid. 19 n., but no details of it are known (Introd. pp. 5–6), so that the precise meaning of τῇ γενομένῃ is doubtful; perhaps he means the roll call '(last) past', or perhaps the one 'that took place' when he was first qualified to draw the dole, cf. **2903** 9–10 τῇ γενομένῃ τότε . . . ἀναγορείᾳ.

20–6 The date falls between 27 December, A.D. 270 and 25 January, A.D. 271 inclusive, according to the chronology adopted in the Introduction, pp. 15–26. The figure for the day was omitted.

31 τῶν φυλάρχ(ων). The significance of the plural is uncertain. If the phylarchs could act as a college this is the first indication of it at Oxyrhynchus, but perhaps it need not be doubted in view of the common action of four phylarchs in SB 7375, perhaps from Hermopolis (Mertens, *L'état civil*, pp. 22–4), and in view of the activity of the 'former' phylarchs that we find in this archive, see Introd. pp. 7–8. There is a possibility, however, that τῶν is a mistake for τοῦ.

31–7 The purport of these two subscriptions is reasonably clear, but their relationship to each other and to the one in iii 36–7 is less so. The two beginning παρεδεξάμην (ii 35–6; iii 36–7) are in the same ink, which is lighter than that in ii 31–4, and are very probably by the same hand, though the first is written smaller than the second for lack of space. The blacker ink of the other produces initially the impression that it is by a different hand, but the shapes of the letters are very similar and I am inclined to think that all three are in the same hand. I take it that all three represent the words and decisions of Calpurnius Horion. By the first he postpones a decision in order to allow the petitioner to produce documentary proofs. By the second he agrees to the petition of col. ii and by the third, written at much the same time as the second, he agrees to the petition of col. iii. It is not necessary that it should be the personal handwriting of Calpurnius Horion rather than that of a clerk, but it may be.

37–41 The remains of this subscription are more substantial than the text would suggest. It is the rapidity of the writing as much as the damage which renders it illegible. It is suggested by ἐπικ (40), whether it represents ἐπικ(ριτής) or ἐπικ(ριθ-), that this is the subscription of an ἐπικριτής, cf. **2892** i 23, ii 25, **2894** ii 34, iii 31, **2895** i 22, **2896** 16, **2902** ii 20. None of these parallels appears to have the same wording as here, nor can I find the name of Aurelius Serenus, who is scrutineer in every place where a name survives.

40 ἐν [τῇ] ἀναγορείᾳ. More usual is ἐπὶ τῆς ἀναγορείας, but cf. 12 here.

Col. iii 12 μ . . ος. Because of the appearance in a fragmentary context of the phrase ᾽Ρωμαίων καὶ ἀνεπικρίτων (597), ᾽Ρω]¹²μαῖος must be considered a possibility here, in default of a thoroughly satisfactory reading. *Mu* is practically certain because of the characteristic course of its first stroke, which begins below the base line and swells outwards to the left before sloping up to the right. The next letter could possibly be an *alpha* or an *omega* with the last part missing; only the bottom of it survives. The next letter has a long descender, but it has considerable traces to the right of the upright which suggest ρ or perhaps φ rather than ι. On the whole I prefer μωρός to ᾽Ρω]¹²μαῖος, though the *omega* will have lost its last curve or been conflated with the *mu*. If right, it explains why the petition is not submitted by the person who is to benefit by its success. His foster-brother may have been his *curator*. Compare P. Bouriant 20 (= P. Abinnaeus 63), where a young person has his brother as *curator* διὰ τὸ μὴ ἔχειν παρακολουθήσειс 'because he has not got the faculty of consecutive thought' (26). He is not merely a child, though he is referred to as ὁ παῖс (27, 36); the opposition alleges that he ought not to have a *curator* because he is ἐρρωμένον τὴν διάνοιαν (43–4).

13 . [. Apparently π[ or τ[. Numerous parallels suggest π[αρείθη or π[αρεθείς or the like. At the beginning of the line the traces are: (1) a right angle top left—γ or τ or π or ς? (2) one dot at top level, perhaps not a separate letter. (3) a probable ν or η. (4) is obscured by the tail of ρ or ι from the line above, so that it is difficult to see where the ensuing series of loops begins; κως or μος or μας look possible. λελειτουρ]/γηκώς might suit the sense, but it seems much too long.

14 προμεταδοθέντος. This seems to refer to the transfer to the corn-dole officials of the list compiled by the phylarch. Elsewhere the expression is usually ἐπιδοθέντων βιβλίων.

15 ἐννα[κοσίας. Cf. 24–6 ἀ[ξιῶ] ²⁵κἂν νῦν ἐνταγῆναι αὐτὸ[ν ἐν] ²⁶τοῖς (ἐννακοσίοις) and 36–7 παρεδεξάμην ἐν [τῇ τά]³⁷ξει τῶν ῥεμβῶν. In spite of the damage to the document it is an inevitable conclusion that the number of ῥεμβοί was ideally fixed at 900 and that they received an individual ration of 1 artaba, presumably for each month. For the significance of this amount, see Introd. p. 6.

17 διαρι . [. The loop of *rho* is very small but *iota* is hard to articulate. The final trace is a horizontal at top level extending back to ι; besides τ and π, θ is a possibility—διαριθ[? For ι . [, *eta* is possible, but the upright seems too long and straight.

33 The date was probably in or near Tybi, see ii 26, and the absence of a figure before Vaballathus' titles is probably another indication that it was in the first half of the year. The earliest papyrus with a regnal year for Vaballathus is P. Strasb. inv. gr. 1238 (*Recherches* iii pp. 62–3), of Phamenoth 18, with the exception of the retrospective CPR i 9, 8.

38–9 The formula is not identical with any other but resembles **2892** i 25, **2894** ii 36. Instead of ὁ[ς] καὶ . . . , ὁ καί is possible, and the deleted letters could have been [[ων]].

39–40 Αὐρή-]⁴⁰λιος ῟Ωρος is a possible reading. Below 40 the papyrus is slightly damaged, but there appears to be no writing in the space. βρ[αδέως γράφοντος may have been abbreviated in some way. It is surprising to find a person who was illiterate occupying the phylarchy, which was very much concerned with the compiling of records. The best parallel is the *comogrammateus* of P. Petaus, see *CÉ* xli (1966), pp. 127–43, *GRBS* xii (1971) pp. 239–61. The phylarch, however, was a superior official, a metropolitan, though not a councillor (**2664** 15). Even for a *comogrammateus* illiteracy was officially undesirable (P. Petaus 11, 9).

41 The remains are in a large cursive. It may have been simply a note of the quarter, ] Νότου [ Κρηπῖδος, rather than another subscription, which is not known to be wanted.

## 2909

22 3B.15/E(3–4)b 5·5 × 13 cm. s.d.

Καλπουρνίῳ ['Ωρίωνι νεωκόρῳ τοῦ
μεγάλου Ϲαράπιδ[ος τῷ κρατίϲτῳ
ὑπομνηματογράφ[ῳ
παρὰ Αὐρηλίου .[................

5 Θαήϲιος ἀπὸ τῆϲ λαμ[πρᾶϲ 'Οξυρυγχιτῶν πόλεωϲ. ἐπειδ[ὴ] ἔδοξ[εν ἐν τῇ κρατίϲτῃ βουλῇ ὥϲτε τοὺϲ λελ[ειτουργηκότας μεταϲχεῖν τῆ[ϲ το]ῦ ϲί[του δωρεᾶϲ καὶ αὐτὸϲ λειτουργήϲ[αϲ ἐπ' ἀμφόδου ......
10 δημοϲίαν ὀνη[λαϲίαν, ταγεὶϲ τε διὰ
τῶν ἐπιδοθέν[των ὑπὸ τοῦ ἡμετέρου φυλάρχο[υ βιβλίων, πρὸϲ δὲ
τὴν τῆϲ η....[......... ἐτύγχανον ἐν ἀπ[οδημίᾳ ὤν, νῦν
15 γοῦν παραγ[ενόμενοϲ ϲημαίνω
ἐμαυτ[ὸ]ν κ[αὶ ἀξιῶ καὶ αὐτὸϲ
μεταϲχεῖν τῆ[ϲ τοῦ ϲίτου δωρεᾶϲ
κ[ατ]ὰ τὰ δόξ[αντα τῇ κρατίϲτῃ βουλῇ
καθ' ἴϲον τῶ[ν ὁμοίων μου.
20 διευτύ[χει.

· · · · · ·

19 l. κατ' ἴϲον

'To Calpurnius Horion, temple attendant of the great Sarapis, the most excellent *hypomnemato-graphus*, from Aurelius . . . , son of . . . , (grandson of . . . ?), mother Thaësis, from the glorious city of the Oxyrhynchites. Whereas a decree has been passed in the most excellent council that those who have performed public service should share the gift of corn; I myself have performed in the . . . quarter the service of public donkey driving and have been enrolled in the records submitted by our phylarch, but at the muster of the . . . I happened to be away from home; now, however, that I have arrived (home) I declare myself and ask that I too may share the gift of corn in accordance with the decree of the most excellent council on equal terms with those of the same condition as myself. Farewell.'

12–13 We must supply ἀναγορίαν from 2910 ii 10, and this will very nearly fill the gap, to judge from the neighbouring lines. For η....[, ἡμέρα[ϲ is a palaeographical possibility. If right, it probably means that the proclamation of names was made at least partly to arrange the day for collecting each issue of corn. ἡμετέρα[ϲ e.g. τάξεωϲ is less good palaeographically and is obviously too long both here and in 2910 ii 9–10, though it would correspond very well with τῇ . . . τῶν ὁμοίων μου ἀναγορείᾳ in 2903 9–10.

## 2910

23 3B.11/D(16)a        8·5 × 10·5 cm.            s.d.

i

.    .    .    .    .

ἐτύγχανον ἐν ἀποδ]ημίᾳ ὤν.
νῦν γοῦν παραγενόμε]νος cημαίνω ἐμαυτὸν καὶ ἀξι]ῶ μεταcχεῖν
τῆc τοῦ cίτου διαδόc]εωc
5       κατὰ τὰ δόξαντα τῇ κ]ρατίcτῃ
βουλῇ κατ᾽ ἴcον τῶν ὁ]μοι-

.    .    .    .    .

ii

.    .    .    .    .

. . . .].．.[
. . . . . . .[. . . .].．.[
λελει[το]υργηκότας μ[εταcχεῖν
τῆc τ[οῦ cι]τηρεcίου [δωρεᾶc, καὶ αὐ-
5       τὸc λειτ[ο]υργήcαc ἐ[π᾽ ἀμφόδου
Δρόμου Θοήριδοc τα[γείc τε διὰ τῶν
ἐπιδοθέντων ὑπ̣[ὸ τοῦ τοῦ προκειμένου ἀμφόδου φυλάρχο̣υ̣ [. . . . . . . . . . .
βιβλίων, πρὸc δὲ τὴν [τῆc . . . . . . . .
10      ἀ̣ναγορείαν ἐτύγχα̣[νον ἐν ἀποδημί-
ᾳ ὤ[ν,] ν̣ῦν γο[ῦν παραγενόμενος
c̣η[μαί]νω ἐ[μαυτὸν καὶ ἀξιῶ
μεταc[χε]ῖ̣ν τ̣[ῆc τοῦ cίτου διαδόcεωc
κατὰ [τὰ δό]ξαν[τα τῇ κρατίcτῃ βου-
15      λῇ[

.    .    .    .    .

10 ε̣τυγ̓χα̣[

Col. i As for col. ii 10–14.
Col. ii '(Whereas a decree has been passed in the most excellent council that) those who have performed a public service should share the gift of the corn dole; I myself, having performed public

service in the Thoëris Street quarter and having been enrolled in the records . . . submitted by the phylarch of the aforesaid quarter, happened to be away from home at the muster of the . . . ; now, however, having arrived (home) I declare myself and ask to share the distribution of the corn in accordance with the decree of the most excellent council . . .'

## 2911

22 3B.15/D(11)b                    9·5 × 10·5 cm.                    s.d.

ii

(m. 2) λι(τουργ-) (m. 3) λα

(m. 1)  Αὐρηλίῳ Πλουτίωνι
        γραμματεῖ cιτηρεcίου
        παρὰ Αὐρηλίου Διονυcίου Cαρα-
5       πίωνος καὶ ὡς χρημ(ατίζω)
        Ἀ[λ]θαιέωc. δόξαντός τε
        τ]ῇ κρατίcτῃ βου[λ]ῇ ὥcτε τοὺc
        λε]λειτουργηκότας μετέχειν
        τ]ῆc τοῦ cιτηρεc[ίου] δωρεᾶc
10      κ]αὶ αὐτὸc ..[. λειτου]ργήcαc
        ἐπ'] ἀμ[φόδου .......]. ου 'φυλακία[ν]' καὶ ἐν-
        ταγεὶc διὰ τῶν ἐπιδοθέν]των ὑπὸ
        τοῦ τοῦ δηλουμένου ἀμφό]δου φυλάρ-
        χου ..................]ων

· · · · ·

1 λ̣        5 χρημ𝈍′        12 ὕπο

Col. ii '(2nd hand) Li(turg-). (3rd hand) No. 31. (1st hand) To Aurelius Plution, secretary of the corn dole, from Aurelius Dionysius, son of Sarapion, and however I am styled, of the Althaean deme. Whereas a decree has been passed by the most excellent council that those who have performed public service should share the gift of the corn dole; I myself, having performed a public service as guard in the . . . quarter and having been enrolled in the (records) submitted by the phylarch of the specified quarter . . .'

Col. ii There are scanty traces of the flanking items of the roll file.

10..[.. Perhaps ἐχ̣[ώ is the most likely, though the first letter looks more like omicron. ο̣ὖ[ν upsets the syntax, but is not for that reason impossible.

11 Μυροβαλά]ϝου is the most likely possibility.

14 Supply βιβλίων somewhere in this line or further on.

## 2912

23 3B.11/D(3)a                    8 × 11·5 cm.                    s.d.

(m. 2) κε [

(m. 1) Καλπουρνίῳ Ὠ[ρίωνι τῷ κρατίστῳ
        ὑπομνημα[τογράφῳ
        παρὰ Αὐρηλίου .[ . . . . . . . . . . . . .
5       Τεχώσιος ἀπὸ τῆ[c λαμπρᾶς Ὀξυρυγ-
        χειτῶν πόλεως. ἀνα[γ]ρ[α]φό[μενος
        ἐπ' ἀμφόδου Ἡρακλέους τόπων, [ἀπο-
        γραφεὶς καὶ προσβὰς ἀπὸ ἀπογρ[αφῆς
        ἀφηλίκων, ταγεὶς [τ]ε καὶ διὰ [τῶν
10      ἐπιδοθέντων ὑπ[ὸ] τοῦ φυ[λάρχου
        ἐν τῇ τάξε[ι τῶν ὁ]μολόγ[ων κατ' ἄν-
        δρα βιβλί[ω]ν, ἐτύγχανον ἐπὶ [τῆς
        ἀλ]λοδαπῆς ὤ[ν, ν]ῦν γοῦν παρα[γενό-
        με]νος σημα[ί]νω ἐμαυτὸν [καὶ
15      ἀ]ξ[ιῶ] καὶ α[ὐ]τὸς μετασχε[ῖν τῆς
        τοῦ ceίτου δ[ω]ρεᾶς κατὰ [τὰ δόξαν-
        τα τῇ κρατίς[τ]ῃ βουλῇ κ[ατ' ἴcον
        τ]ῷ[ν] ὁμοίων μου. [

                .     .     .     .

(2nd hand) No. 25. (1st hand) To Calpurnius Horion, the most excellent *hypomnematographus*, from Aurelius . . . , mother Techosis, from the glorious city of the Oxyrhynchites. Being registered in the District of Heracles quarter, listed and having come forward from the list of minors, and enrolled also in the records of individuals submitted by the phylarch in the category of ὁμόλογοι, I happened to be away from home. Now, however, having arrived (home), I declare myself and ask that I too may share the gift of corn in accordance with the decree of the most excellent council on equal terms with those of the same condition as myself . . .'

4 Comparing **2913** ii 2, where the applicant is also probably in the category of the ὁμόλογοι, one might expect this man to be illegitimate, and therefore officially known by the name of his mother, cf. Introd. p. 5. The space here is not enough for a name plus χρηματίζοντος μητρός as there, nor is it enough for the usual complete nomenclature, i.e. name, patronymic, and grandfather's name, plus μητρός. I incline to think that an abbreviation of χρηματίζοντος μητρός is more likely, say χρη^μ μη᾽. Also possible is a nomenclature not including the grandfather's name, such as Θ[έωνος Θέωνος μη(τρός).

7 ἀπογραφείς. This probably refers either to a declaration of birth or to a census return, though the word is used also for other sorts of registration.

8 Usually ἀπὸ γραφῆς ἀφηλίκων. Probably there is dittography of ἀπό here, but a variant is possible.

**2913**

23 3B.11/D(14–15)a         17 × 19 cm.         19 Feb., A.D. 269;
                                                        Jan./Feb., A.D. 269

ii

(m. 3) ..
τοῖϲ διακρειταῖϲ ἄρχουϲι ϲιτηρεϲ[ίου
παρὰ Αὐρηλίου Ἡρακλέωνοϲ χρη-
ματίζοντοϲ μητρὸϲ Ἴϲειτοϲ Ἀχιλλέωϲ
5     ἀπὸ τῆϲ λαμπρᾶϲ Ὀξυρυγχειτῶν
πόλεωϲ ἀναγραφομένου ἐπ' ἀμφόδου
Νότ[ο]υ Δρόμου. ἀπογραφεὶϲ καὶ προϲβ(ὰϲ)
ἀπὸ γραφῆϲ ἀφηλίκων τῷ α (ἔτει)
Δεκίων ἀκολούθωϲ τοῖϲ ἐν κα-
10    ταχωριϲμῷ βιβλίοιϲ, παρεθεὶϲ
δὲ ἐν τοῖϲ ἐπιδοθεῖϲι βιβλίοιϲ
ὑπὸ τοῦ τοῦ ἀμφόδου φυλάρχου,
δεικνὺϲ τὰ περὶ ἐμοῦ οὕτωϲ
ἔχοντα, ἀξιῶ ἐνταγῆναι ἐν
15    τοῖϲ ἀναγορευομένοιϲ πρὸϲ διάδοϲιν τοῦ ϲιτηρεϲίου ὀνόμαϲι,
ἵνα κἀγὼ τῆϲ δωρεᾶϲ μεταλάβω.
(ἔτουϲ) αʹʹ Αὐτοκράτοροϲ Καίϲαροϲ
Μάρκου Αὐρηλίου Κλαυδίου
20    Εὐϲεβοῦϲ Εὐτυχοῦϲ Ϲεβαϲτοῦ,
Μεχεὶρ κε‾.

(m. 2)   Αὐρήλιοϲ Ἡρ]ακλέων ἐπιδέδωκα.
Αὐρήλιοϲ . . . .] ἄμμων ἔγραψα
ὑπὲρ αὐτοῦ διὰ τὸ] μὴ εἰ[δέν]αι
25    αὐτὸν γράμματα. ] vac.

.    .    .    .

4 ϊϲειτοϲ     5 οξυρυγʼχειτων     7 προϲβʹ     8 αϛʹ     17 ϊνα     18 Ⳑ αʹʹ

iii

> . . . . . .
>
> .[                                      ἀναγρα-
>
> φόμε[νος ἐπ᾽ ἀμφόδου . . . . . .
>
> Παρεμβο[λῆς, ἐπικριθεὶς τῷ x (ἔτει) Μάρκων
>
> Ἰουλίων κα[ὶ γενόμενος πρὸς
>
> 5  τὸ ἐνεσ[τὸ]ς α (ἔτος) [(ἐτῶν) . .
>
> παρεθ[εὶ]ς δὲ ἐ[ν το]ῖ̣[ς ἐπιδοθεῖ-
>
> σι βιβλίο̣[ι]ς ὑπὸ τοῦ τ[οῦ ἀμφόδου
>
> φυλάρχ[ου], δ̣ε̣ικνὺς τὰ [περὶ ἐμοῦ
>
> ἐν ἐκτ[ά]κτῳ οὕτω[ς ἔχοντα,
>
> 10  ἀξιῶ ἐνταγῆναι [ἐν τοῖς
>
> ἀναγορευομένοις [πρὸς διά-
>
> δοσιν τοῦ σιτηρε[σίου ὀνό-
>
> μασι, ἵνα κἀγὼ τ̣[ῆς δωρε-
>
> ᾶς μετα̣[λ]ά̣βω. (ἔτους) [α′
>
> 15  Αὐτοκρά[τ]ορος Κα[ίσαρος
>
> Μάρκου Αὐρηλίου Κ̣[λαυδίου
>
> Εὐσεβοῦ[ς] Εὐτυχ[οῦς
>
> Σεβαστοῦ, Μεχ[εὶ]ρ̣ [
>
> (m. 2)  Αὐρήλιος Παυσ[          ἐπιδέδω-
>
> 20  κα. Αὐρήλι[ος
>
> ἔγραψα ὑ[πὲρ
>
> (m. 3)  Αὐρ(ήλιος) Θε[
>
> ο.[
>
> ο.[
>
> 25  ..[
>
> . . . . . .

4 ϊουλιων    5 αϛ′    7 ϋπο    13 ϊνα    14 L    22 αυρ′

Col. ii '(3rd hand) No. . . . (1st hand) To the examiners in charge of the corn dole from Aurelius Heracleon, officially described as the son of his mother Isis, daughter of Achilles, from the glorious city of the Oxyrhynchites, listed in the South Street quarter. Being registered and having come forward from the list of minors in the first year of the Decii according to records in official custody, but omitted in the records submitted by the phylarch of the quarter, having proved that the facts about me are as stated, I ask to be enrolled among the names to be proclaimed for the distribution of the corn dole so that I too may share in the gift. Year 1 of Imperator Caesar Marcus Aurelius Claudius Pius

Felix Augustus, Mecheir 25. (2nd hand) I, Aurelius Heracleon, submitted (the petition). I, Aurelius
... ammon wrote on his behalf because he does not know letters.'

Col. iii '. . . listed in the Cavalry (or Lycian?) Camp quarter, scrutinized in the . . . th year of
the Marci Julii (Philippi), and being in the present first year . . . years old, but omitted in the records
submitted by the phylarch of the quarter, having proved that the facts about me—on a separate
sheet—are as stated I ask to be enrolled among the names to be proclaimed for the distribution of the
corn dole, so that I too may share in the gift. (2nd hand) I, Aurelius Paus . . . , submitted (the petition).
I, Aurelius . . . wrote on his behalf . . . (3rd hand) Aurelius The . . .'

Col. i The much damaged remains of this item are interesting because they do not conform to the
known formulas, but little can be made of them. The most extensive traces are near the foot, as follows:
*c.* 18 π]ρος το . . . . (perhaps κ̣α̣ὶ ἢ/[μᾶς corrected from κ̣ᾀ̣μέ?)[19]ϲμετατηντου [20] μ]ητροπόλει εις [21]ξετελεϲ
. . . . αυ [22] . . . . ιαϲμετε (φιλαν]θρωπίαϲ μετέ/χειν?) [23]]διευτυχεῖτε.
Col. iii 1–5 For the restorations in general compare **2894** ii 7–10.
2–3 Restore either Λυκίων] Παρεμβολῆϲ or Ἱππέων] Π.
3–4 Μάρκων] Ἰουλίων (sc. Φιλίππων). Cf. **1119** 22, 24, 28; P. Grenf. ii 69, 16; SB vi 9298 (= 1010),
21. They reigned from A.D. 244 to A.D. 249. The applicant's age in 1 Claudius = A.D. 268/9 would
probably be between 32 and 38.

# 2914

23 3B.11/D(10–11)c　　　　　　　11 × 24 cm.　　　　　　　Jan./Feb., A.D. 269

i

```
           •    •    •    •    •
.....................].ϲα.
.............λει]τουρ-
γ-      ἀκολούθωϲ τοῖϲ] ἐν
καταχωριϲ]μῷ βιβλίοιϲ
```
```
5      καὶ τοῖϲ] ὑπομνηματιϲθεῖ-
ϲιν ἐν τῇ κρ]ατίϲτῃ ἡμῶν
βουλῇ π]ερὶ τῶν δημοϲίω(ν)
.......] ἐπιδίδωμι τά-
δε τὰ βιβ]λία ἀξιῶν κα-
```
```
10     ταταγῆ]ναι ἐν τοῖϲ ἀ̣ν̣α-
γορευομέν]οιϲ πρὸϲ διάδο-
ϲιν τοῦ ϲιτη]ρεϲίο̣[υ ὀ]νόμα[ϲ]ι̣
.....................].
```
```
.........] ἵνα κ̣[ἀ̣]γὼ τῆϲ
15     δωρεᾶϲ μετ]αλάβω. εἶναι
δέ με πρὸ]ϲ τὸ ἐνεϲτὸϲ
α (ἔτοϲ)] (ἐτῶν) . .
(m. 2) Αὐρήλιοϲ] Νεμεϲιαν̣ὸϲ
```

γνωστήρ·] οὗτός ἐστιν

20 ὁ διακρι]θεὶς ὁ προκ(είμενος),

ὃν καὶ γν]ωρίζω.

(m. 1) (ἔτους) α Αὐτ]οκράτορος

Καίσαρος Μ]άρκου Αὐρηλίου

Κλαυδίου] Εὐϲεβοῦϲ Εὐτυχοῦς

25 Ϲεβαϲτοῦ, Μ]εχεὶρ [...

. . . . . .

7 δημοσιῶ    17 ʟ..    20 προᵏ    21 l. γνωρίζω

ii

. . . . .

.....].[

τὰ περὶ ἐμο[ῦ ἐν ἐκτάκτῳ

οὕτως ἔχοντα ἀξιῶ [ἐντα-

γῆναι ἐν τοῖς ἀναγορε[υο-

5 μένοις πρὸς διάδοσι[ν

τοῦ ϲιτηρεϲίου ὀνόμ[αϲι

ἵ]να κἀγὼ [τῆϲ] δωρεᾶς [με-

ταλάβ[ω. ..].. (ἔτους) α′ Αὐτοκρ[άτορος

Καίϲα[ρ]ο[ϲ] Μάρκου Αὐ[ρηλίου

10 Κλαυδίου Εὐϲεβοῦϲ [Εὐτυχοῦς

Ϲεβαϲτοῦ, Μεχεὶρ [

(m. 2) Αὐρήλιος .[

ἐπιδέδω[κα.

(vac.)

(m. 3) Αὐρ(ήλιος) Ἀπολλοδίδυμος

15 φύλ(αρχος)· ϲυνφω(νῶ) καί ἐϲτιν

οὗτος ὁ προκ(είμενος)

(m. 4) Αὐρ(ήλιος) Ἄρειος γνωστήρ· οὗτός

ἐϲτιν ὁ προκ(είμενος) ὁ διακριθ(είς),

ὃν καὶ γνω(ρίζω).

8 ʟα′    14, 17 αυρ⁻    15 φυλʲϲυνφῶ    16 προᵏ    18 προᵏ, διακριθ    19 γνω⁻

Col. i '... public service ... in accordance with the records in official custody and the minutes of proceedings in our most excellent council about public (services?), I submit this petition asking to be enrolled among the names to be proclaimed for distribution of the corn dole . . . so that I too may get a share of the gift. (Sc. I declare that) I am in the present first year . . . years old. (2nd hand) Aurelius Nemesianus, witness of identity: This is the person aforesaid who was examined, whom I also identify. (1st hand) Year 1 of Imperator Caesar Marcus Aurelius Claudius Pius Felix Augustus, Mecheir . . .'

Col. ii '. . . (having proved) that the facts about me—on a separate sheet—are as stated, I ask to be enrolled among the names to be proclaimed for the distribution of the corn dole so that I too may get a share of the gift . . . Year 1 of Imperator Caesar Marcus Aurelius Claudius Pius Felix Augustus, Mecheir . . . (2nd hand) I, Aurelius . . ., submitted (the petition). (3rd hand) Aurelius Apollodidymus, phylarch: I concur and this person is the aforesaid. (4th hand) Aurelius Areius, witness of identity: This person is the aforesaid, who was examined, whom I also identify.'

Col. i 8 In view of λει]τουρ/[γ- (2), λειτουργιῶν] seems a possible restoration, but the space is rather short for it. An alternative would be χρειῶν], which would have virtually the same sense.

13 In the parallels, col. ii and 2913 ii and iii, there is nothing between ὀνόμασι and ἵνα. He might have specified the category in which he wished to be enrolled, and/or something like κατ' ἀκολουθίαν (κατ' ἴσον?) τῶν ὁμοίων μου.

15 εἶναι κτλ. This clause stating the applicant's age seems to have been added as an afterthought in the accusative and infinitive in the manner of official declarations where a verb of saying is understood.

Col. ii 8 . . ] . . Possibly (ἐτῶν) . ] . . Compare col. i 15–17, where the applicant's age is declared at greater length in the same place.

17 Ἄρειος. The fact that the γνωστήρ is different in i 18 does not necessarily imply that these items concern different quarters, because there were at least two γνωστῆρες per quarter (or tribe?), cf. 2892 i, ii.

Col. iii There are traces of beginnings, first of the applicant's subscription—2 lines, the second ἐπιδέδω]/κα—and then of 3 more lines much nearer the foot; the middle one is Αὐρ.[ .

## 2915

22 3B.14/F(10–12)b                    11 × 17·5 cm.                    s.d.

τῷ κρ]ατίϲτῳ Ἀχιλλεῖ
παρὰ Α]ὐρηλίου Κερδάμμωνος
Ἀμμ]ωνίου Νεοκοϲμίου τοῦ καὶ
Ἀλθ]αιέωϲ. λειτουργήϲαϲ
5      ἐν] τῷ ιγ (ἔτει) ἐπ' ἀμφόδου
Μυροβαλάνου ἀξιῶ καὶ αὐ-
τ[ὸ]ϲ εὐεργετηθῆναι καὶ ἐνταγῆναι τῇ τοῦ ϲιτηρ⟨εϲ⟩ίου
γραφῇ κατ' ἴϲον τῶν ὁμοί-
10     ων καὶ ὑπὸ ϲοῦ εὐεργετηθέ(ν)-
των. ἔϲτι δέ· ἐκ προϲαγ-
γέλματοϲ ιγ (ἔτουϲ) Ἀμυντιανοῦ
τοῦ καὶ Ἀπίωνοϲ εἰϲ ὀνη-
λαϲίαν ἀντὶ Εὐδαίμονοϲ

15    Cαραπίωνος Κερδάμμω(ν)

Ἀμμωνίου Νεοκόσμιο[ς

ὁ καὶ Ἀλθαιεὺς εἰς χώρ(ας) (τρίτον).

καὶ ἐ[κ γ]ραφῆς Ῥωμαίων καὶ Ἀλεξ(ανδρέων)

τοῦ αὐτοῦ ιγ (ἔτους) οὕτως·

20    (π)ρ(ος)γί(νεται?) τῷ ιγ (ἔτει) Μυροβαλάνου

Κερδάμμων Ἀμμωνίου

Νεοκόσμιος ὁ κ]αὶ Ἀλθαιεύς.

διευτύχει.

5 ιγ⟋    10 ευεργετηθε‾    11 προσαγ'    12 ιγ⟋    15 κερδαμμω‾    17 χωρ′. χ′.
18 αλεξ′    19 ιγ⟋    20 ℗ γι, ιγ⟋

'To the most excellent Achilles, from Aurelius Cerdammon, son of Ammonius, of the Neocosmian tribe and the Althaean deme. Having performed a public service in the 13th year in the Myrobalanus quarter I ask that I too should enjoy the benefit and be enrolled in the list for the corn dole on equal terms with persons of the same condition likewise benefited by you. Viz.: (extract) from a nomination list (submitted by ?) Amyntianus alias Apion—to donkey transport service in place of Eudaemon, son of Sarapion, Cerdammon, son of Ammonius, of the Neocosmian tribe and the Althaean deme: to ⅓ of a place. (Extract) from the list of Romans and Alexandrians of the same 13th year as follows: There acceded in the 13th year, Myrobalanus quarter, Cerdammon, son of Ammonius, of the Neocosmian tribe and the Althaean deme. Farewell.'

1–4 A detached scrap appears to contain the beginnings of these lines, but it is so badly abraded that, apart from Ἀλθ- in line 4, it is very difficult to decide what letters the scattered traces of ink represent.

17 εἰς χώρ(ας) (τρίτον). Cf. 2940 9. Here, however, the reading is somewhat doubtful.

20 (π)ρ(ος)γι(νεται?). Other parts of the same verb are possible. This is apparently the same abbreviation that Wilcken discovered and expanded in P. Flor. 4, 18, see *Archiv* iv (1907–8), p. 426, and it occurs elsewhere in the registers of this archive, e.g. 2935 19, 21, 23, 2936 ii 1, 4, 6. π(ρ)ο(ς) is represented by a *rho* with, in this instance, a circle described around the loop leaving space only for the tail to pass through. In the registers the arc is not so complete and looks more like the right upper quadrant of a circle. The same abbreviation of πρός in compounds occurs elsewhere, e.g. PSI 202, 23 (π)ρ(ος)φωνοῦμεν, PSI 1230, 1, 5 (π)ρ(ος)β( ) for parts of προσβαίνειν. In γι( ) the *iota* cuts the crossbar of *gamma* and usually has a longish descender.

# 2916

22 3B.15/E(5–7)b      18·5 × 8·5 cm.      A.D. 270/1?

ii

..[ . . . .]δ′

Αὐρηλίωι Πλουτί[ω]νι γραμματεῖ ςιτηρεςίου

παρὰ Αὐρηλίου Ἀπ[ο]λλωνίου τοῦ καὶ Νεμεςι[. .]..

Cαραπίωνος καὶ ὡ[ς] χρηματίζω· Ἀλεξανδρεὺς τυγχ[άνω]ν

4 τυγ′χ[ανω]ν

5    καὶ ἐφέϲτιον α̣...[..]...ο̣ϲ οἰκί[αν] ἐνταῦθα ἐν τῇ λαμπρᾷ

      καὶ λαμπροτάτῃ Ὀξ[υρ]ύγχων πόλει καὶ δεδογμένου ἐν τῇ αὐτῇ

      ἐνταῦθα κρατίϲτῃ [βο]υλῇ ὥϲτε τοὺϲ Ἀλεξανδρεῖϲ μεταλαβεῖν τῆϲ

      τοῦ ϲίτου δωρεᾶϲ [καὶ] αὐτὸϲ τὴν ἑϲτίαν ἔχων ἐπ' ἀμφόδου Βορρᾶ

      Δρό]μου τὴν ἀξίω[ϲιν τ]αύτην προϲάγω ὑποτάξαϲ ἅμα καὶ τοῦ ἐφεϲτί-

10   ου] τὸ ἀντίγραφο[ν ἵνα] κατ' ἀκολουθίαν τῶν ὁμοίων μοι καὶ αὐτὸϲ

      μεταλάβω τῆϲ τοῦ ϲι]τηρεϲίου δωρεᾶϲ. διευτύχει.

      (ἔτουϲ) . Αὐτοκράτοροϲ Καίϲαροϲ Λουκίου Δομι]ττίου Αὐρηλιανοῦ

      Εὐϲεβοῦϲ Εὐτυχοῦϲ Ϲεβαϲτοῦ καὶ Ἰουλίου Αὐρη]λίου

•   •   •   •   •

6 οξ[υρ]υγ'χων, πόλει corr. e πόλεωϲ     12 δομι]τ'τιου

Col. ii '(2nd hand?) . . . (3rd hand?) No. [?]4. (1st hand) To Aurelius Plution, secretary of the corn dole, from Aurelius Apollonius, alias Nemesi . . . , son of Sarapion, and however I am officially described. Since I am an Alexandrian and (have successfully claimed?) as a residence a house here in the glorious and most glorious city of the Oxyrhynchi and since it has been decreed in the same excellent council here that the Alexandrians share the gift of corn, I too, having my hearth in the North Street quarter, bring forward this request, subjoining at the same time the copy (of the certificate?) of residence, so that in conformity with my equals I too may take my share of the gift of the corn dole. Farewell. Year 1? of Imperator Caesar Lucius Domitius Aurelianus Pius Felix Augustus and of Julius Aurelius Septimius Vaballathus etc.'

1 ..[....]δ'. The item number is preceded by some sort of docket. The remains of the previous item are negligible, the longest being ]υπεταξα, c. line 4, cf. ii. 9.

5 α̣...[..]...ο̣ϲ. Perhaps αἰτη[ϲά]μενοϲ, meaning that he had petitioned for permission to have an official residence in Oxyrhynchus, but something meaning just ἔχων would be easiest, cf. τὴν ἑϲτίαν ἔχων (8) and likewise 1206 3; P. Oslo III, 235; SB 9897, 2. On ἐφέϲτιον see most lately Braunert, *Binnenwanderung*, p. 25 n. 39, taking a view different from that of Hombert–Préaux, *Recensement*, p. 67.

One might suggest the possibility that the persons of whom it is said in P. Mil. Vogl. iv 254 that they were put in charge of (the) ἑϲτία—προεχειρίϲθηϲαν ἐπὶ τῆϲ ἑϲτίαϲ—were commissioners to investigate the claims of foreigners to residence. The religious interpretation given by the editor may be correct, of course, and would be supported if the reference to a temple of the Dioscuri were certain (16 seq. Διοϲκου/ρ[είο]υ). The plate (VII) however reveals that the papyrus is badly damaged and allows us to doubt it. In particular there is a mark after the supposed final *hypsilon* which suggests an abbreviation; it looks rather like a known form for ὑ(πέρ) or ὑ(πηρέτηϲ). Διοϲκουρ[ may well be part of a personal name.

13 Αὐρη]λίου. The traces are very scanty. If the date is not early in 1 Aur., (ἔτουϲ) δ or ε may have appeared in this line before Ἰουλίου, but all the other dated documents addressed to Plution belong to the reign of Claudius II. On the other hand Professor Turner points out that the earliest dated occurrence of the city's double honorific λαμπρὰ καὶ λαμπροτάτη, which appears here (5–6), is in 1264 of 2 Aur. 5 Vab., Phamenoth 8 = 4 March, A.D. 272; see also *JEA* 38 (1952), p. 78. It occurs only once again in the rest of this archive, in 2923 4, which is undated but not earlier than A.D. 271. The latest date in this archive for the simple titulature λαμπρά is Dec.–Jan. A.D. 270/1 from 2908 ii.

## 2917

3B.11/D(19–20)a            7·5 × 9·5 cm.                              s.d.

Καλπουρ]νίῳ Ὡρίωνι ν[εωκόρῳ
τοῦ μ]εγάλου Cαράπιδος τ[ῷ κρατίcτῳ ὑπ]ομνηματογράφῳ  (vac.) [
παρ]ὰ Αὐρηλίου Ἀντινόου τοῦ [καὶ
5      . . .]αντινόου Ἰ[cι]δώρου C[α]βεινίο[υ
τοῦ] καὶ Ἡρεαίωc. Ἀντινο[εὺc τυγ-
χά]νων καὶ λειτουργήcα[c ἐπ'] ἀμ[-
φό]δου Βορρᾶ Δρόμου ἐλειτούργη[-
cα] ὀνηλαcίαc, δόξαν δὲ ε. .[
10      . . . . . .]τ. . Ἀντινοέων τ.[
. . . . . . . . . .]. .λειτουρ[γ-

.    .    .    .    .

5 ἴcιδωρου        6 l. Ἡραιέωc

'To Calpurnius Horion, temple servant of the great Sarapis, the most excellent *hypomnematographus*, from Aurelius Antinous, alias . . . antinous, son of Isidorus, of the Sabinian tribe and Heraean deme. Though I am an Antinoite and have (before?) performed public service in the North Street quarter, I performed donkey transport services, and since it has been decreed (in the council that those?) of the Antinoites (who have performed?) public service . . .'

5 Νικ]- or Φιλ]αντινόου are the most likely.
9–11 It seems best to see in this damaged sentence a common-form reference to the decree of the Oxyrhynchite council about the eligibility of liturgists for the corn dole. It could be, however, that it refers to a decree of the Antinoite council.

## 2918

22 3B.15/D(9–10)b            10 × 16 cm.                              s.d.

Μάρκῳ Αὐρηλίῳ Ἀχιλλεῖ τῷ καὶ Ἀ[μμωνίῳ (?) τῷ
κρατίcτῳ ὑπομνηματογρά[φῳ
καὶ τοῖc αἱρεθεῖcι ὑπὸ τῆc κρατίcτηc [βουλῆc
δ[ι]άδοcιν ποιήcαcθαι τοῦ cειτηρε[cίου
5      παρὰ Αὐρηλίου Cαραπάμμ[ωνοc . . . . . . . .
τοῦ καὶ [Ἀ]λεξάνδρου [. . . . . ἀνεγράφην
ἐπ' ἀμφόδου Τεμιούθε[ωc ἐφ' οὗ λειτουργῶ καὶ ἐπεκρίθην [τῷ . (ἔτει). νῦν δὲ δι-

3 ὕπο

ἀ τῶν ἐπιδοθέντ[ων πρὸς τὸ cιτηρέcιον
10    βιβλίων ὁ τοῦ ἡμετ[έρου ἀμφόδου φύλαρχοc Ἀμύντας π[αρεῖκέ μου τὸ ὄνομα
κατὰ πλάνην. διὰ τ[αῦτα ἀξιῶ κατὰ τὴν ὑμῖν
προcοῦcαν ἀγαθὴ[ν εὐεργεcίαν διᾱ-
κελεῦcαι ταγῆναί με [ἐν τοῖc τὸ cιτηρέcι-
15    ον λαμβάνουcιν π[ρὸς τὸ κἀμὲ δύνᾱ-
cθαι τῆc κοινῆc φιλα[νθρωπίας μεταcχεῖν.
διευτυχ[εῖτε.

'To Marcus Aurelius Achilles alias A(mmonius?), the most excellent *hypomnematographus* and to the persons appointed by the most excellent council to make distribution of the corn dole, from Aurelius Sarapammon, (son of . . . , grandson of . . .?), alias Alexander, (mother . . .). (I was listed?) in the Temiouthis quarter, in which I am performing a public service, and I underwent scrutiny (in the . . .th year?), but now in the records submitted concerning the corn dole, the phylarch of my quarter, Amyntas, has passed over my name by mistake. For this reason I ask that in your kindly beneficence, you give orders that I be enrolled among those receiving the corn dole, so that I too may be able to share in the common privilege. Farewell.'

1 Ἀ[μμωνίῳ(?). Cf. **2568** 4–5; see Introd. p. 32.
7 Τεμιούθε[ως. Cf. **2895** ii 8 n. for the spelling.
12–16 For the supplements compare **2919** 5 seqq., though the wording is not exactly the same and if we can trust διευτύχει (11), that document is addressed to a single official. εὐεργεcίαν, partly from **2919** 6, is a stop-gap.

## 2919

4 1B.75/G(i)           7·5 × 7 cm.           s.d.

```
          .     .     .     .
. . . . . . . . . . . . . . . . . ].. [
. ] . . . . . . . . . . . βιβλι . . . [
ἀντίγραφον ἐκλαβὼν ἐκ τῆ[c ἐπὶ
τόπων βιβλιοθήκηc ἐπιφ[έρω τὴν
5      ἀπόδειξιν καὶ ἀξιῶ κατ[ὰ τὴν cὴν
περὶ πάντα ἀγαθὴν εὐ[εργεcίαν
διακελεῦcαι καταταγῆναί μ[ε ἐν
τοῖc τὸ cιτηρέcιον λαμβάνου[cι πρὸc
τ]ὸ κἀμὲ δύναcθαι τῆc κοινῆ[c
10     φ]ιλανθρωπ[ί]αc μεταcχεῖν.
          διευτύχει.
          .     .     .     .     .
```

'. . . having obtained a copy . . . from the local record office I bring forward the proof (certificate?) and ask that, in your universal kindly beneficence, you give orders that I be enrolled among those receiving the corn dole so that I too may be able to share the common privilege. Farewell.'

## 2920

22 3B.15/D(1–3)b                    10 × 8·5 cm.                                              s.d.

$$
\begin{array}{l}
Μάρκῳ\ Αὐρηλίῳ\ Ἀχιλλεῖ\ [τῷ \\
\quad κρατίστῳ\ ὑπομνημ[α]τογράφῳ \\
\quad καὶ\ ὡς\ χρημ(ατίζει). \\
δέης[ις]\ παρὰ\ Αὐρηλίου\ [Θ]ώνιος\ [ \\
\quad Ὀφελλ[ίο]υ\ Μαξίμου\ [ \\
\quad μητρὸς\ Διονυσίας\ [ἀπὸ\ τῆς\ λαμ- \\
\quad πρᾶς\ Ὀξυρύγχων\ πόλ[εως.\ παρε- \\
\quad θεὶ[ς]\ διὰ\ τῶν\ ἐπιδ[οθέντων\ βι- \\
\quad βλίων\ ὑπὸ\ τοῦ\ φ[υλάρχου \\
\end{array}
$$

5 (line number at left)

. . . . . .

2 ὑπομνημ[α]τογραφω        3 χρημ⳽        9 ὑπο

'To Marcus Aurelius Achilles, the most excellent *hypomnematographus*, and however he is officially described. Request from Aurelius Thonis, son of Ofellius Maximus, (grandson of . . .), mother Dionysia, from the glorious city of the Oxyrhynchi. Having been passed over in the records submitted by the phylarch . . .'

## 2921

23 3B.11/D(17–18)b                    7 × 10·5 cm.                          7–15 Dec., A.D. 270

. . . . . .

$$
\begin{array}{l}
.].[ \\
....[..].[ \\
τὰ\ βιβλείδια,\ ἀξιῶ[ν\ καὶ\ αὐτὸς\ μετασχεῖν\ τῆς\ φι- \\
λανθρωπίας\ καὶ\ τῆ[ς\ κοινῆς\ τοῦ\ σιτηρεσίου \\
δωρεᾶς\ κατὰ\ τὰ\ δ[όξαντα\ τῇ\ κρατίστῃ\ βουλῇ. \\
(ἔτους)\ α'\ Αὐτοκράτορος\ Καίς[αρος\ Λουκίου \\
Δομιττίου\ Αὐρηλια[νοῦ\ Εὐσεβοῦς\ Εὐτυχοῦς \\
Σεβαστοῦ\ καὶ\ ['Ιο]υλίου\ [Αὐρηλίου\ Σεπτιμίου \\
\end{array}
$$

5 (line number at left)

6 L α'        7 δομιτ'τιου

          Οὐαβαλλάθου Ἀθην[οδώρου τοῦ λαμπροτάτου
10       βασιλέως ὑπάτου αὐ[τοκράτορος cτρατηγοῦ
          Ῥωμαί[ω]ν̣, Χοιὰκ ι̣.[
               (vac.)
(m. 2)     Α]ὐρήλιος ....[
          Αὐρήλ]ι̣ος ..ν[
15       ......] μὴ [εἰ]δότο[c γράμματα
(m. 3)     .......].......[
         ........]..[.].[

       •  •  •  •  •

10 ὑπάτου

'(I submit this) petition, asking that I too may share the privilege and the common gift of the corn dole according to the decree of the most excellent council. Year 1 of Imperator Caesar Lucius Domitius Aurelianus Pius Felix Augustus and of Julius Aurelius Septimius Vaballathus Athenodorus the most glorious king, consul, *imperator*, general of the Romans, Choeac ...'

6–11 This is the earliest papyrological date for Aurelian so far. For its importance see Introd. pp. 20–21.

**2922**

3 1B.77/A(4)a          7·5 × 18·5 cm.          10 Jan., A.D. 271 or
                                                11 Jan., A.D. 272

         •  •  •  •  •

       Εὐτ[υ]χο̣[ῦc Cεβαcτοῦ καὶ
       Ἰουλίου Α[ὐ]ρηλίο̣υ̣ ϲ[επτιμίου
       Οὐαβαλλάθου Ἀθη[νοδώρου
       τοῦ λαμπροτάτου β[αcιλέωc ὑπάτου
5      αὐτοκράτορ[οc cτρατηγοῦ Ῥωμαίων
       Τῦβι ιε‾. [
(m. 2)     Αὐρήλιοc Ζωιλ[. .].[.].[. .].[
       ἐπιδέδωκα.
(m. 3)     Cεπτί(μιοc) Ἀλέξανδροc γενόμ(ενοc)
10      φύλ(αρχοc)· οὗτόc ἐcτιν
       ὁ προκ(είμενοc) καὶ λειτουργή-
       cαc καὶ ἐπὶ τῆc ἀναγορ(ίαc)
       ὑπακ(ούων).

(m. 4) ....λλ.ϲ γνωϲτήρ· γνωρίζω

15    τὸν προκείμενον οὕτωϲ

ἔχοντα.

(vac.)

(m. 5) Ἑρμαίου—

9 ϲεπτι′, γενοᵘ    10 φυλ    11 προᵏ    12 αναγορϛ    13 υπαᵏ

'... Felix Augustus and (year ...?) of Julius Aurelius Septimius Vaballathus Athenodorus the most glorious king, consul, *imperator*, general of the Romans. Tybi 15. (2nd hand) I, Aurelius Zoil ..., (son of ...?), submitted (this petition). (3rd hand) Septimius Alexander, former phylarch. This is the aforesaid person and he has performed public service and answers to his name at the roll call. (4th hand) Gemellas(?), witness of identity. I identify the aforesaid person, who is as described. (5th hand) Hermaeum.'

1–6 If *Ε̣ὐ̣τ̣[υ]χο̣[ῦϲ* (1) is right, and it seems better than any other possibility, the line is rather short. If this, in turn, implies that (ἔτουϲ) δ or (ἔτουϲ) ε appeared before the titles of Vaballathus, (ἔτουϲ) ε is the more likely because in **2908** ii 20–6, of 1 Aur. (4) Vab., Tybi (no day), no regnal year figure is given and the earliest papyrus with a regnal year number for Vaballathus is P. Strasb. inv. gr. 1238 (*Recherches* iii pp. 62–3, no. 8) of Phamenoth, 1 Aur., 4 Vab. The date therefore is more likely to be 11 January, A.D. 272 than 10 January, A.D. 271. However, there is no decisive argument on either side.

9 Here as in 14 the Aurelius part of the name is omitted, unusually for this archive.

14 Perhaps read *Γ̣ε̣μ̣ε̣λλᾶϲ*; less likely is *Π̣έ̣κ̣υ̣λλο̣ϲ*.

## 2923. APPLICATION TO A STRATEGUS

33 4B.79/L(a)              12 × 11·5 cm.              *c.* A.D. 271/2

This applicant submits to a hitherto unknown strategus a copy of a petition to the prefect, of which just enough survives to show that it was a request to share the corn dole in Oxyrhynchus on grounds of public service. It is of interest as the only example of appeal to the prefect in this connection.

Αὐρηλίῳ Τούρβωνι ϲτρα(τηγῷ) Ὀξυ(ρυγχίτου)

πα⟨ρὰ⟩ Αὐρηλίου Ϲτεφάνου Ἀράχθου τοῦ καὶ Ἀγαθείνου

μητρὸϲ Ϲινθώνιοϲ ἀπὸ τῆϲ λαμπρᾶϲ καὶ λαμπρο-

τάτηϲ Ὀξυρυγχειτῶν πόλεωϲ. βιβλειδίου οὗ διε-

5    πεμψάμην [τ]ῷ μεγέθει τῆϲ ἡγεμονίαϲ

καὶ ἧϲ ἔτυχον ὑπ' αὐτοῦ ὑπογραφῆϲ τὸ ἀντίγρα-

φον οὕτω[ϲ ἔ]χει.—

Ϲτατιλίῳ Ἀμμιανῷ τῷ διαϲημοτάτῳ

ἐπάρχῳ    Αἰγύπτου

1 ϲτρϛ οξυ′    6 υπογραφηϲ

10   πα⟨ρὰ⟩ Αὐρηλίου Cτεφάνου Ἀράχθου τοῦ καὶ Ἀγαθείνου
     μητρὸς [Cι]νθώνιος ἀπὸ τῆ[c] λαμ(πρᾶc) κ̣α̣ὶ̣ [λαμ(προτάτηc) Ὀξυρυγχι-
     τ]ῶν πόλεωc. Ὀξυρυγχείτηc καθ̣.[. . . . . . . . . . . ἀνα-
     γραφόμενοc ἐπ' ἀμφόδου Ἱππέω̣ν̣ [. . . . . . . . . . . . .
     λειτουργήcαc τῇ πατρίδ̣[ι . . . . . . . . . . . . . . . .
15   τοc ἐπὶ τὰ λειτουργήματ̣[α . . . . . . . . . . . . . . . . .
     ἐπὶ οὖν τοῦ cειτηρεc̣ί̣[ου . . . . . . . . . . . . . . . . .
     .[

          .        .        .        .        .

    'To Aurelius Turbo, strategus of the Oxyrhynchite nome, from Aurelius Stephanus, son of Hara-
chthes alias Agathinus, mother Sinthonis, from the glorious and most glorious city of the Oxyrhynchites.
The copy of the petition, which I sent up to his highness of the prefecture, and of the subscription which
I received from him runs as follows:
    "To Statilius Ammianus, the most perfect prefect of Egypt, from Aurelius Stephanus, son of
Harachthes alias Agathinus, mother Sinthonis, from the glorious and most glorious city of the Oxyrhynchites. (Being) an Oxyrhynchite . . . (and) registered in the Cavalry (Camp) quarter . . . having
performed public service for my homeland . . . public services . . . Since(?), then, . . . corn dole . . ."'

    1 Τούρβωνι. An approximate date for this new strategus can be deduced from the name of the
prefect, see 8 n.
    8 Cτατιλίῳ Ἀμμιανῷ. See Stein, Die Präfekten, pp. 150–1, BASP iv 121, and for correction of his
place in the list of prefects CÉ xliv (1969), pp. 134–8. He was in office in 2 and 3 Aurelian (P. Wis. 2,
as corrected in CÉ loc. cit.). This means, if my interpretation of the chronology is right and if 'year
2' in P. Wis. 2, 22 is a retrospective date, A.D. 270/1 and A.D. 271/2, see Introd. p. 24, but his term
began after Marcellinus, who was still in office some time in A.D. 271 (PSI 1101).
    10 The initial pi is on a detached scrap, but the fibres suggest that it should be replaced to give
a straight left-hand margin πα⟨ρά⟩, thus repeating the mistake in line 2. It seems less likely that π[αρ]ά
was set out into the margin while the names of the prefect and strategus were not.
    13 Ἱππέων [. The quarter called Ἱππέων Παρεμβολή is sometimes referred to without the addition
of the second word.
    15 ἐπὶ τά. An alternative is ἔπιτα = ἔπειτα. The last letter of the line is uncertain.
    16 ἐπί. Probably understand ἐπεί.


                          **2924. PUBLIC NOTICE?**

4 1B.75/G(c)                      19 × 9·5 cm.                              s.d.

    The magistrates in charge of the corn dole state that they have found it necessary to
give warning that they are going out of office and that holders of *tesserae* issued by them
should collect their corn immediately. For what this implies about the nature of the
*tesserae* see Introd. pp. 6, 9–12.
    Since there is no address, the prescript beginning with παρά, it may be that the
sheet is a public notice, but equally it might be, for instance, instructions to another
official to issue such a notice or to take some other action in connection with the
*tesserae*. The hand is a good clear cursive, but not above a normal size.

παρὰ Cεπτιμίου Ὡρίωνος τοῦ καὶ Διογένους γυμν(αςιαρχήςαντος)
καὶ Ἀππιανοῦ τοῦ καὶ Cεουήρου καὶ τῶν cὺν αὐτοῖς
ἀρχόντων. δι' αὐτῶν ἡμῶν τὸν χρόν[ο]ν τῆς διαδό-
cεως ἀποπεπληρωκότων καὶ ἑτέρων προχειριςθέντων
5 ἐν τῇ κρατίςτῃ βουλῇ, ἀναγκαῖον ἐνομίςαμεν ὑπομνῆ-
cαι τοὺς παρ' ἡμῶν τάβλας μὲν ἐςχηκότας ἐν τῇ δια-
δόςει μηδέπω δὲ τὸν cεῖτον εἰληφότας κἂν νῦν ταύ-
τας π[.].[.].α.[..]. ἡμ[[ε]]ῖν λημψομένους τὸν πυρὸν ο.[
.........................]νεται πρὸς τὸ μὴ α.[
10 ...............................].[
.    .    .    .    .

1 γυμν⳽    5 αναγ᾽καιον, ὑπομνη

'From Septimius Horion alias Diogenes, ex-gymnasiarch, and Appianus alias Severus, and their associate magistrates. Whereas we have in our own persons served in full the term of the distribution and others have been appointed in the most excellent council, we considered it necessary to warn those who have had tokens from us in the distribution but have not yet received the grain, immediately to present(?) these to us so as to receive the wheat ... so that no ...'

1 Ὡρίωνος. Cf. 1416 4, apparently about A.D. 298. The date of this document is unknown, but one would expect it to be *c.* A.D. 268–72. Compare the case of Eudaemon alias Helladius (2904 2, of A.D. 272), known again as late as A.D. 309 (MChr. 196; for the correct date see Lallemand, *L'Administration*, p. 261). In 2925 10 it may be right to restore Cεπτιμίου Διο/[γένους τοῦ καὶ Ὡρίωνος. The order of aliases is not fixed, cf., e.g., Chaeremon alias Spartiates (2560 2) and Spartiates alias Chaeremon (2126 4, P. Princ. 30, 1).

6 τάβλας. Cf. SB i 4514, of which there survive, apart from the significant date (6 March, A.D. 269) only the closing words ἐςτὶν ὥςτε τοὺς λαμβ[ά]νοντας τάβλας καὶ τὸν cῖτον λαμβάνειν.

8 π[α]ρ[α]γαγ[εῖ]ν is a possibility. The traces are doubtful and the spacing also is uncertain. The meaning must be something like 'produce', 'show'.

ο.[. π[ or τ[.

## 2925. OFFICIAL CORRESPONDENCE

22 3B.15/C(4–5)a                    11 × 15·5 cm.                    s.d.

This document concerns the activities of Calpurnius Horion, who was out of office as a *hypomnematographus* when it was written, so that it is later than any other document in the archive which mentions him. The person to whom it is addressed has the new, and probably garbled, title of κανανικλάριος, which appears to refer to the *canon frumentarius*, see van Berchem, *Les Distributions*, pp. 106–8. All that can be guessed from the fragment that remains is that when Horion was in office, he and his assistant, who wrote the papyrus or had it written, brought charges against one Aurelius Heras alias Sarapion, who has now submitted a petition, presumably in protest and in defence of himself.

Αὐρη]λίῳ Ἡρακλειανῷ κανανικλαρίωι

παρὰ] Καλπουρνίου Εὐϲεβίου ἱππικοῦ πραγματευτοῦ Καλπουρ-

νίου Ὡρίωνοϲ τοῦ κρατίϲ]του γενομένου ὑπομνηματογράφου.

. . . . . . . . . . . . . . . . . . . . . . . . ]. Αὐρήλιον Ἡρᾶν τὸν καὶ Cαραπίωνα

5　. . . . . . . . . . . . . . . . . . . . . . . ].ιαου βιβλία ἐπιδεδωκότα περὶ οι-

. . . . . . . . . . . . . . . . . . . . . . . ] ἔτι ἄνωθεν ὁ κράτιϲτοϲ Καλπούρνιοϲ

. . . . . . . . . . . . . . . . . . . . . . . ].. μήπω ἐνκαλεῖται ἐφ' οἷϲ πρώτοιϲ

. . . . . . . . . . . . . . . . . . . . . . . ]. δίκαιον ἦν ἡμᾶϲ αἰτιᾶϲθαι τοῦτον

. . . . . . . . . . . . . . . . . . . . . . . ἔ]τι ἄνωθεν δι' ἐμοῦ ὁ κράτιϲτοϲ Ὡρίων

10　. . . . . . . . . . . . . . . . . . . . . . ]. . . Φιλέαν παρὰ Cεπτιμίου Διο-

. . . . . . . . . . . . . . . . . . . . . . ].....β.... λαμπρᾶϲ Ὀξυρυγχει-

τῶν πόλεωϲ . . . . . . . . . . . τῆϲ λ]αμπροτάτηϲ πόλεωϲ τῶν Ἀλεξανδρέω[ν

. . . . . . . . . . . . . . . . . . . . . . ]αϲ Ἐπιμαχοῦτοϲ τῆϲ καὶ Διεῦτοϲ απ[

. . . . . . . . . . . . . . . . . . . . . . ]. ιν δὲ οὗτοι, ἄνδρεϲ ουκοιτυ

15　. . . . . . . . . . . . . . . . . . . . ]. δ. ριων.. δημοϲίων ἀρχείων γενο-

μεν. . . . . . . . . . . . . . . . . ]. ηϲαμενων παραϲχεῖν. ἐπεὶ δὲ ε.. ω

. . . . . . . . . . . . . . . . . . . . . . ]. . . . . . ν τὴν τούτων ἀναζήτηϲιν

. . . . . . . . . . . . . . . . . . . . . . ].. η.....τεϲ 'αὐτοὺϲ' παρὰ τω[

. . . . . . . . . . . . . . . . . . . . . . ]. . . . . . λάττοντεϲ πε[ρὶ] τῶν

20　. . . . . . . . . . . . . . . . . τοῦ κρα]τίϲτου Καλπουρνίου Ὡρίωνοϲ

. . . . . . . . . . . . . . . . . . . . . ἐ]μαυτοῦ μέτρα μηδ...

. . . . . . . . . . . . . . . . . . . . . ]υθετηϲ. ι εἰϲ τὸ λογι-

ϲτήριον? . . . . . . . . . . . . . . . . . . . . . . . ]...[.]...υτον...[

. . . . . . . . . .

2 ἱππικου　　　14 ουκ'οιτυ

1 κανανικλαρίωι. Perhaps equivalent to *canonicarius*, 'a collector of grain taxes' (read κανονικ{λ}α-ρίωι?); at least *canonicularius* is not attested. An official perhaps called κανονικ(άριος?) may occur in a sixth-century account, P. Masp. i 67057 ii 5, 34, cf. κανονικ(ά?) in 67041, 4 and 67042, 2. It seems obvious that there is a connection with the *canon frumentarius*, see introd.

3 γενομένου. The last dated document addressed to Calpurnius Horion as *hypomnematographus* is **2908** ii, of Dec./Jan., A.D. 270/1.

7 Probably restore Ὡρίων at the beginning of the line, cf. 20, but in 9 he is called ὁ κρ. Ὡρίων and ὁ κρ. Καλπούρνιος is also possible.

10 Perhaps restore Cεπτιμίου Διο-/[γένους τοῦ καὶ Ὡρίωνος, cf. **2924** 1 n.

11 Read perhaps βου[λ](ευτοῦ?) τῆς.

14 Perhaps the writer intended οὗτοι, ἄνδρες οὐχ οἱ τυ/[χόντες etc., cf. **2906** ii 12.

16 Perhaps α]ἰτησαμένων, and ἐν τῷ.

## 2926. Letter of a Shipmaster

23 3B.13/C(4–5)b                     8 × 5·5 cm.                     s.d.

This illiterate letter to Plution, secretary of the corn dole, comes from a ship-master taking a load to Pelusium. The unspecified load is likely to be grain, but the letter breaks off before it makes clear what the traffic between Pelusium and Oxyrhynchus has to do with the corn dole.

Πλουτίωνος γραμματεὺς
cιτηρεcίου 'πολλὰ χαίρειν' παρὰ ῾Ωρίων
κυβερνήτης Ἀρcενίου. οἶδεc
καὶ cύ, κύριέ μου, ὅτι εἰc Πηλού-
5          cιν ὑπάγω μετὰ τοῦ γόμου
῾Ηρακλ . . . ῳου κατάγων
ϟάτω κατὰ τὴν δύν[αμιν
. .] . . .[. .].[.] . .[

·          ·          ·          ·

Verso, along the fibres, upside down to one another
γραμμα]τεὺc cιτηρεcίου
10          π(αρὰ) ῾Ωρίωνοc   Χ[

1 l. Πλουτίωνι γραμματεῖ          2 l. ῾Ωρίωνος          3 l. κυβερνήτου          4–5 l. Πηλούcιον          5 ὕπαγω
9 l. γραμματεῖ          10 ϟ

'To Plution, secretary of the corn dole, many greetings from Horion, shipmaster of Arsenius. You know yourself, my lord, that I am setting out for Pelusium with the load of Heracl . . . bringing it downstream(?) to the best of my ability . . .'
Verso. 'To the secretary of the corn dole. From Horion.'

6 Perhaps ῾Ηρακλαμμῳου for -νοc. καϟάγων is far from certain and ϟάτω (7) might be ϟἀγώ.

## 2927. FORMULARY

22 3B.15/D(20)a　　　　　　　　23·5 × 32·5 cm.　　　　　　　　s.d.

There are eight specimen formulas here. The first three are headings to be pre-fixed by the phylarchs to the lists of the three categories of persons eligible for the corn dole, ἐπικριθέντες, ὁμόλογοι, and ῥεμβοί. We have actual examples of such headings for two of the categories, ἐπικριθέντες (**2931** and **2932**), and ῥεμβοί (**2930**).

The other five formulas are subscriptions to the same lists. They take the form of declarations that the persons named in the lists are qualified to receive the corn dole on the grounds stated and are in fact the persons to whom the documentary proofs apply. The declarers are first an ἐπικριτής, who acts only in the case of ἐπικριθέντες, second a γνωστήρ, whose declaration is the same for all three categories, and third a phylarch, who must use a separate declaration for each class. Only one example of this type of declaration survives in its proper place (**2936** ii 28–9).

Very similar declarations by the same officials appear at the foot of some of the applications (ἐπικριτής **2892** i, ii, **2894** ii, iii, **2895** i, **2902** ii, γνωστῆρες **2892** i, ii, **2894** ii, iii **2895** i, **2902** ii, **2908** ii, iii, **2914** i, ii, **2922**, φύλαρχοι **2892** i, ii, **2894** ii(?), iii(?), **2895** ii, **2896**, **2907** ii, **2908** ii, iii, **2914** ii, **2922**). All these are drawn up in the singular referring to the individuals to whose applications they are appended.

In each of these cases the ἐπικριτής is the same, though we know from other docu-ments that there might be more at any one time (Oertel, *Liturgie*, p. 178). In the WB there are no third-century references to them under this title, but they are presumably the same officials as οἱ πρὸς τῇ ἐπικρίσει, see Mertens, *Les services*, pp. 103, 113, 117.

The phylarchs are the same for different people of the same quarter, as we would expect (**2892** i, ii, **2908** ii, iii).

It is illuminating, however, that the γνωστῆρες are also sometimes the same for different people of the same quarter (**2892** i, ii, **2908** ii, iii), because we might have supposed incautiously that each individual had to find a γνωστήρ as a personal guarantor, sometimes two. In fact it is known that the γνωστῆρες were officials, as is shown by the occurrence of a γνωστὴρ φυλῆς in Hermopolis and a γνωστὴρ ἀμφόδου in Oxyrhynchus (Oertel, *Liturgie*, pp. 177–8).

In the bottom margin and in some spaces near the foot and the right-hand margin there are various jottings, some upside down in relation to the main text. Most of these appear to concern the corn dole, but they are too incomplete and disorganized to be meaningful. The bottom margin is broken and it is clear from a narrow strip originally attached that it was at least 5 cm. deeper and contained more writing of some sort. The top margin is also broken, but it appears from both sides that nothing much can be lost unless there were dockets or headings.

The next item (**2928**) stands on the verso of this one.

ἐπικριθ(έντες) φύλ(αρχος). κατ᾽ ἄνδρα ἐπικριθέντων [[ἀκολουθ]] ὡς ἔχουσι καὶ ἐν τῇ δημ[οσ]ίᾳ βιβλιο-
θ(ήκῃ)

αὐτῶν ὄντων τῶν διακριθέντων καὶ ἐπὶ τῆς ἀναγορείας ὑπακουόντων
ὑφ᾽ οὓς Ῥωμαῖοι καὶ Ἀλεξανδρεῖς.

φύλ(αρχος). κατ᾽ ἄνδρα ὁμολόγων ἀπογραφέντων καὶ ἀπὸ γραφῆς ἀφηλίκων προσ-
βάντων

5 ..........ρ( ) ἀκολούθως τῇ δημοσίᾳ βιβλιοθήκῃ αὐτῶν ὄντων τῶν διακριθέντων
καὶ ἐπὶ τῆς ἀναγορείας ὑπακουόντων.

ῥεμβοί.     κατ᾽ ἄνδρα [[προλελιτουργηκότων καὶ]] λελιτουργηκότων [[ἀκολούθως τῇ
δημοσίᾳ]]

[[βιβλιοθη]] καὶ ἀπελευθέρων λελιτουργηκότων ἀκολούθως τῇ δημοσίᾳ βιβλιοθήκῃ αὐτῶν ὄντων τ[ῶ]ν διακριθέντων καὶ ἐπὶ

10 τῆς ἀναγορείας ὑπακουόντων.

Αὐρήλ(ιός) τις ἐπικριτής. ἐπεκρίθησαν οἱ προκείμενοι καὶ αὐτοί εἰσιν οἱ καὶ διακριθέντες

καὶ ἐπὶ τῆς ἀναγορίας ὑπακούοντες.

Αὐρήλ(ιός) τις γνωστήρ. γνωρίζω τοὺς προκειμένους [[καὶ αὐ]] οὕτως ἔχοντας
καὶ αὐτοὺς ὄντας τοὺς καὶ ἐπὶ τῆς ἀναγορείας ὑπακούοντας.

15        ]φυλ( ) [λ]ειτ

Αὐρήλ(ιός) τις] φύλαρχος. ἐπεκρίθησαν οἱ προκείμενοι καὶ αὐτοί εἰς{τ}ιν οἱ καὶ
διακριθέντες

καὶ ἐπὶ τ]ῆς ἀναγορείας ὑπακούοντες.

Αὐρήλ(ιός) τις φύ]λ(αρχος). εἰσὶν ὁμόλογοι οἱ προκείμενοι καὶ ἀπὸ γραφῆς
ἀφηλ(ίκων) προσβάντες

ὡς ἔ]χουσι καὶ ἐν βιβλιοθήκῃ καὶ αὐτοί εἰσιν οἱ διακριθέντες καὶ ἐπὶ τῆς
ἀναγορ]είας ὑπακούουσι.

20 ῥεμβ(οί). Αὐρήλ(ιός) τις φύλαρχ(ος). ἐλειτούργησαν οἱ προκείμενοι καὶ οὕτως
ἔχουσι

καὶ ἐν βιβλιοθ(ήκῃ) καὶ αὐτοί εἰσιν οἱ διακριθέντες καὶ ἐπὶ τῆς ἀναγορείας ὑπακούοντες.

---

1 επικριθ φυλ, βιβλιοθ      4 φυλ      11, 13 αυρηλ      15 φυλ[λ]ειτ      18 φυλ], αφηλ
21 ρεμβ⁻, αυρηλ, φυλαρχ      22 βιβλιοθ

'Those who have passed the scrutiny. Phylarch. Register of individuals who have passed the
scrutiny as they stand in the public records, being the same persons whose qualifications were examined
and who answer to their names at the muster, beneath whom (are appended) Roman and Alexandrian
citizens.'

'. . . Phylarch. Register of individuals listed without demur and who have been promoted from the list of minors in agreement with the public records, being the same persons whose qualifications were examined and who answer to their names at the muster.'

'Sundries. Register of individuals who have performed a public service and of freedmen who have performed a public service in agreement with the public records, being the same persons whose qualifications were examined and who answer to their names at the muster.'

'Aurelius X, scrutineer. The above-mentioned passed the scrutiny and are the same persons whose qualifications were examined and who answer to their names at the muster.'

'Aurelius X, witness to identity. I identify the above-mentioned as being what they declare and as the same persons who answer to their names at the muster.'

'. . . Phylarch (or tribe?). Lit(urgy?).'

'Aurelius X, phylarch. The above-mentioned passed the scrutiny and are the same persons whose qualifications were examined and who answer to their names at the muster.'

'Aurelius X, phylarch. The above-mentioned are listed without demur and have been promoted from the list of minors as they stand in the records and are the same persons whose qualifications were examined and they answer to their names at the muster.'

'Sundries. Aurelius X, phylarch. The above-mentioned have performed a public service and stand so also in the records and are the same persons whose qualifications were examined and who answer to their names at the muster.'

3 ὑφ' οὕϲ. I take this to mean that there was a separate list of Romans and Alexandrians appended to the list of Oxyrhynchites, first because of the mention in 2915 18 of a list called the γραφὴ Ῥωμαίων καὶ Ἀλεξ(ανδρέων) and secondly because there is a variant ὑφ' ὅ, of which the antecedent is τὸ κατ' ἄνδρα, in 2933 4. Otherwise ὑπό might have been used 'of the logical subordination of things under a class' (LSJ s.v. ὑπό C I 3), and have meant simply 'under whom (i.e. in which class) are included . . .'. For ὑπό meaning 'at the foot of' a document compare, e.g., 1634 1, 2131 5.

4 For ὁμόλογοι cf. Introd. pp. 4–5. The marginal entry under and to the left of φυλ( ) is much blotted or it may have been struck through.

7 ῥεμβοί. Cf. Introd. pp. 3–4.

⟦προλελιτουργηκοτωνκα⟧; struck through, like ⟦ακολουθ⟧ (1).

⟦ακολουθωϲτηδημοϲια⟧; secluded by round brackets.

8 ⟦βιβλιοθη⟧; secluded by round brackets that almost enclose it like a cartouche.

15 These additions are written rather large, perhaps in a different hand, and their expansion is doubtful. φύλ(αρχοϲ) would be relevant, if superfluous. [λ]ειτ does not have the appearance of an abbreviation; perhaps it was just abandoned in the middle as being wrong.

20 ὑπακούουϲι. Undoubtedly one expects ὑπακούοντεϲ, cf. 6, 10, 12, 14, 17, 22, but ὑπακούουϲι can be translated and if it is right it reinforces the implication that is already in the present participle, namely that the muster was a regularly repeated event, which all and not only the newly qualified recipients attended. Otherwise one would expect ὑπακούϲαντεϲ generally and ὑπήκουϲαν here.

## 2928. District Totals of ὁμόλογοι and ῥεμβοί

22 3B.15/D(20)a                    23·5 × 32·5 cm.                    s.d.

This and its companion piece (2929) are chiefly of value for what they reveal of the organization of the quarters of the city and for what they perhaps imply about the tribes, see Introd. pp. 6–7.

Also worth noting is the resemblance between these two pieces and *CIL* vi 10211 = *ILS* 6046:

Numerus tr[ibulium . . . et
  quibus locis [frumentum accipiant

| | | | |
|---|---|---|---|
| Pal(atina) | h(omines) | ꟷꟷꟷ̅IIIICLXXXXI i[n | (4,191) |
| Suc( )[1] | h(omines) | ꟷꟷꟷ̅IIIILXVIII in[ | (4,068) |
| Esq(uilina) | h(omines) | MDCCLXXVII a[d | (1,777) |
| Col(lina) | h(omines) | CCCCLVII i[n | (457) |
| Rom(ilia) | h(omines) | LXVIII[ | c. (68) |
| Vol(tinia) | h(omines) | LXXXV.[ | c. (85) |
| | ] h(omines) | .[ | |

.   .   .   .   .   .   .

The theory of the connection of this text with the corn dole was put forward by Mommsen (*Die röm. Tribus*, p. 196, *Staatsrecht* iii 446 n. 3), who supplied the restorations. The connection is far from sure, as Cardinali pointed out (De Ruggiero, *Diz. Epigr.* iii 269), but the inscription's resemblance to the Oxyrhynchite lists, of which at least **2928** certainly relates to the corn dole, suggests that Mommsen may have been right. The numbers are too low to have produced for the 35 tribes the expected total of about 200,000. Mommsen therefore took the inscription for a list of new entrants (*Staatsrecht* iii 446–7). Comparison with the Oxyrhynchite lists suggests that it may have been a list of a single category of recipients. It is uncertain whether the difference of magnitude between the numbers in the urban tribes, which are the first four in the list, and in the rural ones, which the next two are, reflects the real proportions of the two classes of tribesmen in the total number of citizens resident in Rome (G. E. F. Chilver, *CR* lxiv (1950), pp. 134–5; L. R. Taylor, *Voting Districts*, p. 149). The inscription might be a list of freedmen only, in which case the proportions would be sufficiently explained by the inferior prestige of the urban tribes and the tendency to enrol freedmen and others of low status in them, see L. R. Taylor, op. cit., pp. 11–12, 132–49.

This writing surface, which is the verso of **2927**, also carries, upside down in relation to the two lists, two columns of single- and double-figure numbers, one of 16 and the other of 7 items, a separate figure somewhere in the 200s, possibly the total of the two columns, and a four-line formula: γνωϲτήρ· γνωρίζω τὸν [2] προ᾿κ´(είμενον) οὕτωϲ ἔχοντα [3] τὸν καὶ διακριθέντα καὶ ὑπα[4]κούοντα. The same sense occurs in the declarations of γνωϲτῆρεϲ actually found—list in **2927** introd.—but the precise wording does not recur elsewhere.

---

[1] Suc( ) = Suburana, cf., e.g., L. R. Taylor, *Voting Districts*, p. 12 n. 27.

i

κατ' ἄνδρα ῥεμβῶν

| | | | |
|---|---|---|---|
| [[ρα]] | ʽΗρῴου | ἄνδ(ρες) | ϱγ |
| [[ρα]] | Ποιμενικ(ῆς) | ἄνδ(ρες) | ια |
| | ʽΙππέων | ἄνδ(ρες) | κ[[.]]δ |
| 5 | Βορ(ρᾶ) Δρόμου | ἄνδ(ρες) | ρλβ |
| | Δρόμου Θοή(ριδος) | ἄνδ(ρες) | λη |
| | Βορ(ρᾶ) Κρηπῖδος | ἄνδ(ρες) | ρ[[δ]]ʻγʹ |
| | Νότου Κρη(πῖδος) | ἄνδ(ρες) | λα |
| | ʽΕρμαίου | ἄνδ(ρες) | κδ |
| 10 | Πλατείας | ἄνδ(ρες) | νγ |
| | Κρητικοῦ | ἄνδ(ρες) | λδ |
| | Παμμένους | ἄνδ(ρες) | λδ |
| | Μυροβαλάνου | ἄνδ(ρες) | νη |

χλε

1 αν<sup>δ</sup> passim    2 ποιμενι<sup>κ</sup>    5 βορϚ    6 θο<sup>η</sup>    7 βορϚ    8 κρη¯

ii

[[Γάιος Ἰούλιος
Πτολεμαῖος]]
(ὁμολόγων ρ)

| | | | |
|---|---|---|---|
| | ʽΗρῴου | ἄνδ(ρες) | δ |
| 5 | Ποι(μενικῆς) | ἄνδ(ρες) | γ |
| | ʽΙππέων | ἄνδ(ρες) | ϛ |
| | Βορρᾶ Δρόμ(ου) | ἄνδ(ρες) | ιδʹ |
| | Δρόμου Θοήριδ(ος) | | ζʹ |
| | Βορρᾶ Κρηπῖδ(ος) | | ϛ |
| 10 | Νότου Κρη(πῖδος) | | γ |
| | ʽΕρμαίου | ἄνδ(ρες) | ιβ |
| | Πλατείας | | ιγ |
| | Κρητικοῦ | | θ |
| | Παμμέν(ους) | | ια |
| 15 | Μυροβ(αλάνου) | ἄνδ(ρες) | ε |
| | ἄνδ(ρες) | ϱ[[β]]ʻγ | |

5 πο˙    7 δρομʹ    8 θοηριδʹ    9 κρηπιδʹ    10 κρη¯    14 παμμενʹ (or παμμενο'?)
15 μυροβ

Col. i 'Individual list of the sundry category:

| | | |
|---|---|---:|
| Heroum | men | 93 |
| Shepherds' (Street) | men | 11 |
| Cavalry (Camp) | men | 24 |
| North Street | men | 132 |
| Thoëris Street | men | 38 |
| North Quay | men | 103 |
| South Quay | men | 31 |
| Hermaeum | men | 24 |
| Square | men | 53 |
| Cretan | men | 34 |
| Pammenes' (Garden) | men | 34 |
| Myrobalanus | men | 58 |
| | | 635' |

Col. ii 'Admittedly liable category; 100:

| | | |
|---|---|---:|
| Heroum | men | 4 |
| Shepherds' (Street) | men | 3 |
| Cavalry (Camp) | men | 6 |
| North Street | men | 14 |
| Thoëris Street | | 7 |
| North Quay | | 6 |
| South Quay | | 3 |
| Hermaeum | men | 12 |
| Square | | 13 |
| Cretan | | 9 |
| Pammenes' (Garden) | | 11 |
| Myrobalanus | men | 5 |
| | men | 93' |

Col. i 1 ῥεμβῶν. Cf. Introd. pp. 3–4.

2–3 ⟦ϱα⟧ *bis*. These look like the figure 91 repeated and struck through. Their relevance is not apparent.

14 χλε = 635. It is a little surprising that this category, which from **2908** iii appears to have had an ideal membership of 900, should fall so far below that total, whereas for the ὁμόλογοι the real number is 93 per cent of the total (ii 16) and for the ἐπικριθέντες, whose ideal number was 3,000, one real figure was about 2,904 or *c.* 96 per cent. In **2929** 18 a figure of about 3,750 appears to represent the sum total of all the classes; the total of ἐπικριθέντες there is at least 2,904 (line 16), so if we allow about 93 ὁμόλογοι as here in ii 16 we find that at the date of **2929** there were about 753 ῥεμβοί. This is nearer the proportion we might expect, but at *c.* 84 per cent is still lower than for the other two classes. The most likely explanation is that the number of liturgists that could be found always fell below the number hoped for.

Col. ii The name is ringed for cancellation. The same combination of names occurs in D. Foraboschi, *Onomasticum Alterum Papyrologicum* ii 2 s.v. Γαῖος, but the documents cited are too early to refer to a person of this period.

3 The brackets round the heading are puzzling. Normally they indicate cancellation, which is hardly appropriate here.

## 2929. District Totals of a Restricted Population Group

3 1B.77/A(7)a            11·5 × 26·5 cm.            May/June, A.D. 270

There is nothing explicit to show that this document is part of the corn dole archive, but since it gives district totals of a class of persons restricted to the number of 3,000—presumably for the whole city—and is dated to A.D. 269/70, it seems proper to connect it with the petitions for the dole of that year (**2892** i, ii, **2893** i, ii, **2894** ii, iii, **2895** i, ii, **2896**), which imply by their references to the filling by lot of places left vacant by death that the number of recipients was a fixed one. This is confirmed by comparison with the totals likewise listed by quarter on the back of the corn dole formulary (**2928**).

We can deduce that the class in question is the ἐπικριθέντες, since we have ideal totals of 900 for the ῥεμβοί (**2908** iii) and 100 for the ὁμόλογοι (**2928** ii), and we need not hesitate to accept it as the number of a single class since the present papyrus gives, after its total of 2,904 for the ideal 3,000, a sum total of *c.* 3,750, which is plainly the actual number of all recipients.[1] In fact we can conclude that there were 4,000 places in all (3,000+900+100) and on this occasion *c.* 3,750 were filled. That the discrepancy is so great is largely due to the ῥεμβοί, though there were more of them on this occasion than for the list in **2928** i. I have suggested in **2928** i 14 n. that this was due to the chronic shortage of liturgists.

The fact that the list is designated as 'of the month of Payni' may suggest that a review of the numbers was held every month. The alterations in all the easily legible cases (3, 6, 10, 11, 13, 14) are reductions, suggesting that no lottery had been held recently to admit new applicants. Though not conclusive, this tells against the possibility that the lottery was held more than once in the year, see Introd. p. 3 and **2894** ii 13 n.

The list stands on the verso of a piece apparently cut from a register, of which there remain parts of 35 lines, mostly of personal names with amounts of money and other property.

| | | |
|---|---|---|
| κατ᾿ ἄνδρα τῶν τρισχειλίων τῷ[ν | | |
| μηνὸς Παῦνι β (ἔτους) Κλαυδίου | | |
| Μυρ[ο]βαλάνου    ἄνδ(ρες) | | ϲ⟦η⟧`ε′ |
| Παμμ[έ]νους Παρα(δείϲου) | ἄνδ(ρες) | υ⟦ιθ⟧`.′[ |
| 5   Βορρᾶ Κ[ρ]ηπῖδ(οϲ) | ἄνδ(ρες) | ϲπ .[ |
| ῾Ιπ[πέων] Παρ(εμβολῆϲ) | ἄνδ(ρες) | ρ⟦θ⟧ζ[ |
| Ποιμενι]κῆϲ | ἄνδ(ρες) | ϲ . . [ |
| Νότου Κ]ρηπῖδ(οϲ) | ἄνδ(ρες) | ϲϙ .[ |
| ῾Ηρῴου    ] | ἄνδ(ρες) | ϲι . |

[1] For a recent estimate of the total population of the city at *c.* 30,000 in A.D. 235 see *Archiv* 21 (1971), pp. 113–16.

| | | |
|---|---|---|
| 10 Κρητικοῦ | ἄνδ(ρες) | cλ[[α]] |
| Βορρᾶ Δρόμου | ἄνδ(ρες) | ρ[[ο]]ξθ |
| Πλατείας | ἄνδ(ρες) | cι[[ζ]].[ |
| Ἑρμαίου ἄνδ(ρες) | | ρπ[[δ]]γ |
| Δρόμου Θοήριδος | | τι[[δ]]γ |
| 15 γ(ίνονται) ἄνδ(ρες) 'Bϡ[[με]] [[λ]]`[[.α]]ˆκ[[θ]]η' | | |
| γ(ίνονται) ἄνδ(ρες) 'Bϡδ | | |

(m. 2) εξα . . . . . . . . . . . .

(m. 1) ἐ(πὶ τὸ αὐτὸ) 'Γψν[

2 βϛ′    3 ανδ (passim)    4 παρ^α    5 κ[ρ]ηπι^δ    6 παρ′    8 κ]ρηπι^δ    15, 16 γ    18 εϛ

'Individual list of the 3,000 for the month of Payni, 2nd year of Claudius (II):

| | | |
|---|---|---|
| Myrobalanus | men | 205 |
| Pammenes' Garden | men | 4?? |
| North Quay | men | 28? |
| Cavalry Camp | men | 107(?) |
| Shepherds' | men | 2?? |
| South Quay | men | 29? |
| Heroum | men | 21? |
| Cretan | men | 23? |
| North Street | men | 169 |
| Square | men | 21? |
| Hermaeum | men | 183 |
| Thoëris Street | | 313 |
| Total | men | 2928(?) |
| Total | men | 2904 |

(2nd hand) . . .
(1st hand) Sum total. 3,750(+ ?)'

15–16 It is very difficult to say which total was intended. The one in line 16—2,904—seems to be the least doubtful, though there also seems to be a final version of 2,928 left uncancelled in line 15. It is impossible to check the calculation because probably all of the district totals have been corrected and at least eight of them are now doubtful. They are very close to the right edge, where there has been some slight loss of papyrus.

17 This is written in a large upright cursive of which the ink has greatly faded.

## 2930–2933. Headings of Registers of Recipients

It is plain to see both from the remains of names here and from the formulary in **2927** that these four fragments come from the beginnings of lists of the names of persons eligible to receive the corn dole.

A rough idea of the arrangement of the records can be formed. It seems clear from the numbers involved that there would be at least one roll for each tribe. To take **2931** as an example—the ἐπικριθέντες of the Pammenes' Garden tribe in June, A.D. 270

were about 420 (**2929** 4). Two of the largest fragments of registers (**2934** and **2935**) have respectively 14 and 11 names to the column. It would therefore require a roll of somewhere between 30 and 39 columns to accommodate them. The columns are broad, 15 to 20 cm., so that the roll would be about 4·5 to 7·8 metres long. The roll headed by **2932**, for the Shepherds' Quarter tribe, would have been about half that size, see **2929** 7.

It is not so clear whether there would be separate rolls for the smaller categories. If we take **2930** as the example and accept from **2928** i 6 the figure 38 as a typical number of ῥεμβοί in the Thoëris Street tribe, the space required is only between 2 and 4 columns, 30 to 80 cm. The names of the ὁμόλογοι would only occupy about a single column for any one tribe (**2928** ii).

The only real result of these calculations is the conviction that the fairly numerous fragments of register that survive with this archive, of which besides these headings only the four largest pieces are published as specimens (**2934–2937**), are not likely to come from a very small number of rolls. However the rolls do not seem to have been renewed at very frequent intervals, to judge from the strings of month names indicating issues of corn that appear on **2934–2937**, though there may well have been a monthly revision of them, see **2929** introd.

These four fragments are from separate rolls, since they all have different tribe names and three of them headed lists of ἐπικριθέντες.

## 2930

23 3B.11/D(17–18)b                    12·5 × 15 cm.                              s.d.

(m. 4) Δρ[ό]μ[ου Θο]ήρ[ιδος

(m. 1) παρὰ Αὐρηλίου Διδύμου γενομέ[νου φυλάρχου

φυλῆς Δρόμου Θοήριδος καὶ Λυ[κίων (Παρεμβολῆς?)

κατ' ἄνδρα λελειτουργηκότων κ̣[αὶ ἀπελευ-

5      θέρων λελειτουργη(κότων) ἀκολούθως τῇ [δημοσίᾳ βι-

βλιοθήκῃ αὐτῶν ὄντων τῶν [διακριθέν-

των καὶ ἐπὶ τῆς ἀ⟨να⟩γορείας ὑπακου[όντων.

(m. 2) ].ων προλελε[ι]τουργη(κότων) Δρόμου Θοήριδος [

].c Ἰούστου μητρὸς Κυρίλλης                      [

10 (m. 3) Τ]ῦβι, Φαῶφι, Ἀθύρ, ἐξ ἀξ(ιώσεως) Χοι(άκ), Τῦβι, α (ἥμισυ), Ἐπείφ,

Φαμ(ενώθ), (ἀρτ.) α (ἥμισυ) ...[

Θὼ]θ ὑ(πὲρ) Ἐπείφ (ἀρτ.) α (ἥμισυ)

(m. 2) ]νῶφρις Βηсᾶτος μη(τρὸς) Π[

(m. 2)        ].. μη(τρὸς) Λ..[

(m. 3)                    ]...χ..[· ·]..[

.        .             .           .

15        Verso     Δρόμου Θοή[ριδος
                        λελι(τουργηκότων)

5 λελειτουργ^η          8 προλελε[ι]τουργ^η          10 αξχο⁵, αϚ΄, φαμ –̄ αϚ΄          11 υ᾽, –̄ αϚ΄
12, 13 μη᾽       16 λελ

'(4th hand) Thoëris Street. (1st hand) From Aurelius Didymus formerly phylarch of the tribe of Thoëris Street and Lycians' Camp (...?). Individual list of those who have performed public service and freedmen who have performed public service according to the public records, being the same persons who were examined and answer to their names at the muster. (2nd hand) ... from the Thoëris Street quarter, who have previously performed public service ... of Justus, mother Cyrilla. (3rd hand) (Issued in) Tybi, (the allowances for) Phaophi (and) Hathyr, as a result of an application, (for) Choeac (and) Tybi, one artaba and a half; (issued in) Epeiph (for Mecheir and?) Phamenoth, one artaba and a half, ...; (issued in) Thoth for Epeiph, one artaba and a half. (2nd hand) Onnophris(?), son of Besas, mother P... (2nd hand) ... mother L ...'

Verso. 'Thoëris Street; (list) of those who have performed a liturgy.'

2 Διδύμου. See also the subscriptions of **2892** i, ii.

3 Λυ[κίων Παρεμβολῆς is the only suitable possibility. On palaeographic grounds Τε[μγενούθεως or Δε[κάτης can be rejected, as can λο[ιπῶν ἀμφόδων. On the analogy of the short forms Ἱππέων (sc. Παρεμβολῆς), e.g. **2928** i 4, ii 6, and Παμμένους (sc. Παραδείσου), e.g. **2928** i 12, ii 14, there exists the possibility of Λυ[κίων καὶ followed by another short quarter name or even ἄλλων ἀμφόδων in an abbreviated form.

8 Probably not ]τῶν; there is a dot at the level of the tops of the letters some way to the left of ω and confused traces below the line under the beginning of ω. ἀπελευθέ]ρων, with a *rho* hooked forward, is possible.

10 As in the other fragments of registers, the notes of issues are probably in several small cursive hands, but they are hard to distinguish, see **2934–2937** introd.

The quantities do not fit very well with the monthly allowance of one artaba. See **2934–2937** introd. for the interpretation of the month names.

12 The lines above and below ]νωφρις appear to cancel the entry, since no list of months follows. The reason perhaps was that the entry was out of the usual alphabetical order. Ὀννῶφρις is the commonest of the possibilities, none of which comes very early in the alphabet, except the variant Γοννῶφρις, occurring once only in BGU 1242.

## 2931

22 3B.15/E(1–2)a                    10 × 17·5 cm.                    s.d.

παρὰ Αὐρηλίου [ . . . . . . . . . φυλάρχου
φυλῆς Παμμέ[νους . . . . . . . . . . . . . .
κατ᾽ ἄνδρα ἐπικρι[θέντων ὡς ἔχουσι καὶ ἐν τῇ δημοσίᾳ βιβλιοθή[κῃ αὐτῶν ὄντων τῶν δια-
5        κριθέντων καὶ ἐπ[ὶ τῆς ἀναγορείας ὑπακουόντων                    [
                         (vac.)

.        .           .           .           .

'From Aurelius ... (formerly?) phylarch of the tribe of Pammenes' (Garden? and ...?). Individual list of those who have undergone scrutiny as they stand also in the public records, being the same persons who were examined and answer to their names at the muster.'

1 If γενομένου was present in full there is room only for a very short name, e.g. Ἡρᾶ. But there are two more possibilities: this may have been the tribe in office, in which case the word would have been omitted, or it may have been abbreviated to γενο^μ.

2 If Παραδείcου was here, there is room for only about five letters after it, but it can be left out, see 2928 i 12, ii 14. In the parallel place in 2930 there was something up to fifteen letters in length, and in 2932 there was something about twenty-five letters long. It is likely that the tribe was made up of more than one quarter, see Introd. p. 7, though one quarter name may have designated it well enough.

3 ὡς ἔχουcι. The restoration is derived from the final version of the formulary (2927 1) and supported by 2932 2, but the shortish space in comparison with lines 4 and 5 may indicate that instead of ὡς ἔχουcι καὶ ἐν τῇ δημοcίᾳ βιβλιοθήκῃ there was written ἀκολούθως τῇ δ. β., as in the formulas for the other two classes (2927 5, 8, 2930 5) and in the first version of the formulary.

6 Below this there is blank papyrus for a depth of 9·5 cm. The fragment is made up of two sheets of papyrus pasted together with the fibres running in contrary directions. On this side the left-hand half has vertical fibres and the right half horizontal fibres, so that lines 1 and 3–6 have the first one or two letters written across the fibres. This may well be the so-called *protocollon*, the first sheet of the roll put on as a guard with its vertical fibres inside (Turner, *Greek Papyri*, p. 5). On the other side of the *protocollon*, if it is that, are the initial letters of two lines in a large 'Chancery-style' hand. The first begins π[, which could be Π[αμμένουc, the second is illegible.

## 2932

23 3B.11/D(7)b                7 × 8 cm.                s.d.

παρὰ Αὐρηλίου ............ φ]υλάρχου φυλῆς Ποιμενικῆς
...........................] κατ' ἄνδρα ἐπικριθέντων ὡc
ἔχουcι καὶ ἐν τῇ δημοcίᾳ βιβλιοθήκῃ] αὐτῶν ὄντων τῶν διακριθέντων καὶ ἐπὶ τῆς ἀναγορεία]c ὑπακουόντων ἐφ' οὓc
5        Ῥωμαῖοι καὶ Ἀλεξανδρεῖc.]      εἰcὶ δέ·
(m. 2)                              ]υίου μη(τρὸc) Θερμουθ[
(m. 3)                              Με]χείρ, Παῦνι, ὑ(πὲρ) Φ.....[
(m. 2)                              ]...ουτο.....[
(m. 3)                              ].....[

·       ·       ·       ·

6 μη᾿        7 υ᾿

'From Aurelius ... (formerly?) phylarch of the tribe of the Shepherds' Quarter (and ...). Individual list of persons who have undergone scrutiny as they stand in the public records, being the same persons who were examined and answer to their names at the muster, beneath whom (are appended) Romans and Alexandrians. They are: (2nd hand) ... son of ... nius, mother Thermuth ... (3rd hand) ... Mecheir, Payni for Ph ....'

1 As in 2931 1, the name will be short if γενομένου was written in full, but the same two additional possibilities exist.

2 Supply probably another quarter name, cf. 2930 3 and Introd. p. 7.

4 ἐφ' οὓc. It is perhaps uncharitable to transcribe this as ἐφ' when the formulary shows that ὑφ' is intended (2927 3, cf. 2933 4), but the shape of the letter strongly suggests that *epsilon* was written in error.

**2933**

23 3B.11/D(12)                    7 × 23·5 cm.                    s.d.

·     ·     ·     ·     ·

φυλ[

.....[

κατ' ἄν[δρα

ὑφ' ὃ κ[αὶ

5                αὐτῶν [

Βορρᾶ Δ[ρόμου

Ἀπο[

(m. 2)          Ἀθὺρ .[

(m. 1)          Ἀρθω[

10 (m. 2)          ....[

(m. 1)          Ἀθην[

(m. 2)          Φαρμοῦθ[ι

(m. 1)          Ἀμο[

(m. 2)          Χοι(ὰκ) κ.[

15 (m. 1)          Ἀμμ[

(m. 2)          Παῦνι[

Verso    Βορ[ρᾶ Δρόμου

14 χοˑ

1 φυλ[. This might be best taken as part of φυλῆς or φυλάρχου in the normal introduction παρὰ (Αὐρηλίου?) Χ. (γενομένου?) φυλάρχου φυλῆς (Βορρᾶ Δρόμου καί . . .), but the initial letter is set out into the margin and a trace of the line above ought to be visible. Although it is very clear from the individual elements that this strip comes from the heading and the first five items of a list of persons eligible to receive the dole, the heading as a whole does not conform to the pattern of the other actual headings (2930–2932) or to the models in the formulary (2927).

2 .....[. These traces are very puzzling. I should expect them to be part of the name of a quarter that made up the tribe with Βορρᾶ Δρόμου. The first could be ϛ, or ρ, if the crossbar is illusory; the next group of traces is much broken and could be one letter or two; then perhaps ω or μ; then a descender (ρ, ι, or η)?; then a small round letter (ο, ϛ?). ῥύμης would suit the traces quite well but there is only one attestation, doubtful and late, perhaps sixth century, of a quarter that has this word in its title, i.e. PSI i 75, 12 ἐπὶ ἀμφόδου ῥύμ[ης? Ἀ]κακίου.

4–5 ὑφ' ὃ κ[αί(?). This invites comparison with the other headings for the lists of ἐπικριθέντες, ὑφ' οὓς Ῥωμαῖοι καὶ Ἀλεξανδρεῖς (2927 3, 2932 4 n.). The antecedent of ὅ is presumably (τὸ) κατ' ἄν[δρα (3)—'the individual list . . . beneath which (are appended)' etc. This supports the view that these people were listed separately after the Oxyrhynchites rather than distributed among them (2927 3 n.).

5 αὐτῶν [. This recalls the element common to the formulas for all three classes, αὐτῶν ὄντων τῶν διακριθέντων καὶ ἐπὶ τῆς ἀναγορίας ὑπακουόντων, but it comes before ὑφ' οὓς κτλ. in the examples cited above. However, it seems likely that it gives us a minimum length for the line of c. 45 letters.

6 Βορρᾶ Δ[ρόμου is certainly more suitable than Βορρᾶ Κ[ρηπῖδος.

8 This and the succeeding even-numbered lines appear to be in a smaller cursive. The names in 7 and the succeeding odd-numbered lines appear to be in the same large hand as the heading.

## 2934–2937. FRAGMENTS OF REGISTERS

These items come from rolls like those to which 2930–2933 are the headings. They were prepared by writing out in large cursive the official nomenclature of each recipient, that is, in its fullest form, name, patronymic, grandfather's and mother's names, with the addition in some cases of his age. At this stage a good wide space was left between each entry, later to be filled in part by notations in small and rapid cursives, mostly of month names.

The month names show that the distribution was on a monthly basis. From 2908 iii 15 I have concluded that the allowance was theoretically one artaba per month, probably the exact equivalent of the Roman dole of five *modii* (Introd. p. 6). In the registers the amount is generally specified only when it is different from the regular issue.

On this basis an attempt can be made to understand the very cryptic way in which the actual payments were noted down, and fairly satisfactory results can be obtained, especially for 2934; 2935 is harder to understand and the other two fragments cannot be checked properly because they contain no complete entries (2936, 2937).

A major difficulty is that a month name alone is ambiguous, because it can denote the month in which an issue was made, usually in arrears, or the month for which it was the allowance. So in a sequence which is not that of the chronological succession of months, for example Tybi, Phaophi, Hathyr (roughly January, October, November 2934 2 *et al.*) the first month is the date of an issue, the second and third are the months for which it was the allowance.

Perhaps even more confusing are the different ways in which the same allowances can be noted down, sometimes resulting in a short form that suppresses the names of some of the months for which allowances are made. For example Παῦνι ὑ(πὲρ) Μεχεὶρ (ἀρτ.) γ (2934 2 et al.) turns out to be the equivalent of ἐξ ἀξ(ιώσεως) Χοι(άκ), Τῦβι, Παῦνι ὑ(πὲρ) Μεχεὶρ (2934 5 et al.). Both indicate the normal allowances for Choeac, Tybi, and Mecheir. In the first, the total amount for all three months was paid in Payni, late and all in one sum; in the second, the allowances were paid separately, part on time and part late. In the first, therefore, ὑ(πὲρ) Μεχεὶρ stands for ὑ(πὲρ) ⟨Χοιάκ, Τῦβι,⟩ Μεχεὶρ.

Because of these complications the translation is given in sections, each followed immediately by the relevant commentary.

It seems likely in the circumstances that the notes of payment were made at different times, certainly there are variations in the ink, and it is even probable that they were written by several scribes, but it has not proved possible to distinguish hands with any degree of confidence.

It is clear that **2936** and **2937** concern the category of ῥεμβοί. It is not certain which category is listed in **2934** and **2935**, but the regularity of the nomenclatures suggests that the recipients are ἐπικριθέντες.

**2934**

22 3B.14/F(13)a          25 × 28·5 cm.          s.d.

ii

Ἀπολλώνιος Μέλανος τοῦ Ἀπολλωνίου μητρὸς Ἑρμιόνης      (ἐτῶν) λβ

   Τῦβι, Φαῶφι, Ἁθύρ, ἀλλ( ) (ἀρτ.) α, Παῦνι ὑ(πὲρ) Μεχεὶρ (ἀρτ.) γ, Ἐπείφ,
         Φαμενώθ, (ἀρτ.) β, Ἐπείφ ἐξ {.} ἀξ(ιώσεως) [Παχ(ὼν) β]

   Θὼθ ὑ(πὲρ) Ἐπείφ (ἀρτ.) γ

Ἀπίων Σερήνου Λουκίου Ὀφελλίου Σαραπίωνος μη(τρὸς) Ἀπολλωνίας      (ἐτῶν) [

5    Τῦβι, Φαῶ(φι), Ἁθύρ, ἀλλ( ) (ἀρτ.) α, ἐξ ἀξ(ιώσεως) Χοι(άκ), Τῦβι, Παῦνι ὑ(πὲρ)
         Μεχείρ, Ἐπείφ, Φαμενώθ, (ἀρτ.) β, Ἐπείφ ἐξ ἀξ(ιώσεως) Παχ(ὼν) β[

   Θὼθ ὑ(πὲρ) Ἐπείφ (ἀρτ.) γ

Ἀντεόδωρος Ἰσιδώρου τοῦ Σαραπίωνος μη(τρὸς) Διεῦτος Θέων[ος]      (ἐτῶν) κβ

   Τῦβι, Φαῶ(φι), Ἁθύρ, ἀλλ( ) (ἀρτ.) α, Παῦνι ὑ(πὲρ) Μεχεὶρ (ἀρτ.) ⟨figure⟩, Ἐπείφ,
         Φαμενώθ, (ἀρτ.) β, Ἐπείφ ἐξ ἀξ(ιώσεως) Παχ(ὼν) β

   Μες(ορή), Παῦνι, λημ( ) (ἀρτ.) β, Θὼθ ὑ(πὲρ) Ἐπείφ

10 Ἀπολλώνιος Θέωνος τοῦ Διογένους μη(τρὸς) Στρατονείκης      (ἐτῶν) λ

   Τῦβι, Φαῶφι, Ἁθύρ, ἀλλ( ) (ἀρτ.) α, ἐξ ἀξ(ιώσεως) Χοι(άκ), Τῦβι, Παῦνι ὑ(πὲρ) Μεχείρ,
         Ἐπείφ, Φαμενώθ, (ἀρτ.) β, Ἐπ[ε]ίφ ἐξ ἀξ(ιώσεως) Π[αχ(ὼν) β

   Μες(ορή), Παῦνι, λημ( ) (ἀρτ.) β, Θὼθ ὑ(πὲρ) Ἐπείφ

Α[....].[...]....νος τοῦ Ἀμμωνίου μη(τρὸς) ........      (ἐτῶν) λδ

   Τῦβι, Φα[.]..[.]........[

15 Ἁρποκρατίων Δημητρίου μη(τρὸς) Ταύριος      (ἐτῶν) λδ

   Χοι(άκ), Μες(ορή), Θὼθ, ἀλλ( ) (ἀρτ.) γ, ἐξ ἀξ(ιώσεως) Χοι(άκ), Τῦβι, Ἐπείφ, Φαμενώθ,
         (ἀρτ.) γ, Ἐπείφ ἐξ ἀξ(ιώσεως) Παχ(ὼν) β

   Μες(ορή), Παῦνι, λημ( ) (ἀρτ.) β

---

1 ⳽ λβ    2 αλλ ⳽ α, υʼ, ⳽ γ, ⳽ β    3 υʼ, ⳽ γ    4 μηʼ, ⳽ [    5 φαω, αλλ ⳽ α, αξχοˑ, υʼ, ⳽ ., αξπαχβ    6 υʼ, ⳽ γ    7 l. Ἀνταιόδωρος; ἰσιδωρου, μηʼ, ⳽ κβ    8 φαω, αλλ ⳽ α, υʼ, ⳽ ., ⳽ β, αξπαχβ    9 μες, λημ ⳽ β, υʼ    10 μηʼ, ⳽ λ.    11 αλλ ⳽ α, αξχοˑ, υʼ, ⳽ β, αξπ    12 μες, λημ ⳽ β, υʼ    13 μηʼ, ⳽ λδ    15 μηʼ, ταύριος, ⳽ λδ    16 χοˑ μες, αλλ ⳽ γ, αξχοˑ, ⳽ γ, αξπαχβ    17 μες, λημ ⳽ β

Ἀφύγχις Θώνιος τοῦ Ἀντιόχου μητ(ρὸς) Ἰσιδώρας               (ἐτῶν) λε

    Τῦβι, Φαῶφι, Ἁθύρ, ἀλλ( ) (ἀρτ.) α, ἐξ ἀξ(ιώσεως) Χοι(άκ), Τῦβι, Παῦνι ὑ(πὲρ) Μεχείρ,

          Ἐπείφ, Φαμενώθ, (ἀρτ.) β, Ἐπείφ ἐξ ἀξ(ιώσεως) Παχ(ὼν) [β

20     Μ̣ες(ορή), Παῦνι, λημ( ) (ἀρτ.) β, Θὼθ ὑ(πὲρ) Ἐπείφ

Ἀμόις Σαραπάμμωνος τοῦ Θέωνος μη(τρὸς) Σαραπιάδος           (ἐτῶν) λδ

    Τῦβι, Φαῶφι, Ἁθύρ, ἀλλ( ) (ἀρτ.) α, ἐξ ἀξ(ιώσεως) Χοι(άκ), Τῦβι, Ἐπείφ, Φαμενώθ,

          (ἀρτ.) γ, Ἐπείφ ἐξ ἀξ(ιώσεως) Παχ(ὼν) β

Θὼθ ὑ(πὲρ) Ἐπείφ (ἀρτ.) γ

Ἀμόις Ἀφύγχιος τοῦ Ἀμόιτος μητ(ρὸς) Ἀπολλωνίας            (ἐτῶν) λε

25     Χοι(άκ), Μ̣ες(ορή), Θώθ, ἀλλ( ) (ἀρτ.) γ, Παῦνι ὑ(πὲρ) Μεχείρ (ἀρτ.) γ, Ἐπείφ, Φαμενώθ,

          (ἀρτ.) β, Ἐπείφ ἐξ ἀξ(ιώσεως) Παχ(ὼν) β

    Μ̣ες(ορή), Παῦνι, λημ( ) (ἀρτ.) β, Θὼθ ὑ(πὲρ) Ἐπείφ

Ἀμόις Ῥωμανοῦ τοῦ Σαραπάμμωνος μητ(ρὸς) Θαήσιος          (ἐτῶν) λε

    Τῦβι, Φαῶφι, Ἁθύρ, ἀλλ( ) (ἀρτ.) α, ἐξ ἀξ(ιώσεως) Χοι(άκ), Τῦβι, Παχ(ὼν) ὑ(πὲρ)

          Μεχείρ, Ἐπείφ, Φαμενώθ, (ἀρτ.) β, Ἐπείφ ἐξ ἀξιώ(σεως) Παχ(ὼν) [β

    Μ̣ες(ορή), Παῦνι, λημ( ) (ἀρτ.) β, Θὼθ ὑ(πὲρ) Ἐπείφ

30 Ἀντώνιος Ἀσκλᾶτος τοῦ Ἀσκλᾶτος μητ(ρὸς) Πείνης           (ἐτῶν) λς

    Τῦβι, Φαῶ(φι), Ἀθ[ύ]ρ, ἀλλ() (ἀρτ.) α̣, ἐξ ἀ̣ξ(ιώσεως) Χοι(άκ), Τῦβι, Π̣αῦνι ὑ(πὲρ)

          Μεχείρ, Ἐπείφ, Φαμ̣εν̣ώ̣θ, (ἀρτ.) β

    Ἐπείφ ἐξ ἀξ(ιώσεως) Παχ(ὼν) [β], Μ̣ε̣ς(ορή), Παῦνι̣, λημ( ) (ἀρτ.) β

Ἀγαθὸς Δαίμων ὁ καὶ Θῶνις Δημητρίο[υ] μητ(ρὸς) Διδύμης         [

    Τῦβι, Φαῶφι, Ἁθύρ, ἀλλ( ) (ἀρτ.) α, Παῦνι̣ ὑ(πὲρ) Μεχείρ (ἀρτ.) γ, Ἐπείφ, Φαμενώθ,

          (ἀρτ.) β, Ἐπεὶ[φ ἐξ ἀξ(ιώσεως) Παχ(ὼν) β

35     Μ̣ες(ορή), Παῦνι, λημ( ) (ἀρτ.) β, Θὼθ ὑ(πὲρ) Ἐπείφ

Ἀσκληπιάδης Γερμανοῦ τοῦ Διοσκόρου μη(τρὸς) Ταύρι[ος

    Τῦβι Φαῶ(φι), Ἀθύρ, .. (ἀρτ.) δ, ἀλλ( ) (ἀρτ.) α, ἐξ ἀξ(ιώσεως) Χοι(άκ), Τῦβι, Παῦνι

          ὑ(πὲρ) Μεχείρ, Ἐπείφ, Φ[αμενώθ, (ἀρτ.) β, Ἐπείφ ἐξ ἀξ(ιώσεως) Παχ(ὼν) β

    Μ̣ες(ορή), Παῦνι, λημ( ) (ἀρτ.) β, Θὼθ ὑ(πὲρ) Ἐπείφ

Ἀμμώνιος Ὠρείωνος τοῦ Παυσανίου μη(τρὸς) Ἰσιδώρ[ας

40     Τῦβι, Φαῶ(φι), Ἁθύρ, ἀλλ( ) (ἀρτ.) α, Παῦνι ὑ(πὲρ) Μεχείρ (ἀρτ.) γ, Ἐπείφ, Φαμ̣εν̣ώ̣θ,

          (ἀρτ.) [

18 μητ, Ⳑ λε      19 αλλ ⳥ α, αξχοʹ, υʹ, ⳥ β, αξπαχ[      20 μες, λημ ⳥ β, υʹ      21 μη⳽, Ⳑ λδ
22 αλλ ⳥ α, αξχοʹ, ⳥ γ, αξπαχβ     23 υʹ, ⳥ γ     24 αφυγʹχιος, μητ, Ⳑ λε     25 χοʹ μες, αλλ
⳥ γ, υʹ, ⳥ γ, ⳥ β, αξπαχβ    26 μες, λημ ⳥ β, υʹ    27 μητ, Ⳑ λε    28 αλλ ⳥ α, αξχοʹ, παχυʹ,
⳥ β, αξιωπαχ[    29 μες, λημ ⳥ β, υʹ    30 μητ, Ⳑ λς    31 φαω, αλλ ⳥ α̣, αξχοʹ, υʹ, ⳥ β
32 αξπαχ[.], μες, λημ ⳥ β    33 μητ    34 αλλ ⳥ . , υʹ, ⳥ γ, ⳥ β    35 μες, λημ ⳥ β, υʹ    36 μη⳽
37 φαω, αλ ⳥ δ, αλλ ⳥ α, αξχοʹ, υʹ    38 μες, λημ ⳥ β, υʹ    39 μη⳽    40 φαω, αλλ ⳥ α, υʹ, ⳥ γ, ⳥[

Col. i The remains of this column are too scanty to deserve full transcription, but they show some unusual features. They begin with illegible traces apparently of two line ends near the top opposite ii 1–3. Below this there are no traces for *c.* 5 cm. though the edge follows the same vertical for some distance below. It is a possibility that the top of this column had a heading similar to those in 2930–2933, though the traces at the top are unrecognizable. Below the blank there are traces of ten entries like those in col. ii, reaching probably to the foot of the roll. Of the first five only the ages and very intermittent traces of the account survive. The ages are (4?)2, 62, 22 (entry bracketed), 29, 53. This is an unusual range of ages compared with the predominance of the early thirties in the rest of the document, but I can suggest no convincing explanation. Of each of the last five entries there survive the mother's name in full or in part, the ages, and the end of the second line containing the account. The ages are 30, 36, 31, 31, 32. The other remains are all routine except for the second line of the second Παῦνι ὑ(πὲρ) Μεχείρ, Ἐπείφ ἐξ ἀξ(ιώσεως) Παχ(ὼν) δ. This has a certain value in confirming the scheme of one artaba per month, because comparison with some of the entries in col. ii shows that it is the equivalent of Παῦνι ὑ(πὲρ) Μεχείρ, Ἐπείφ, Φαμενώθ, (ἀρτ.) β, Ἐπείφ ἐξ ἀξ(ιώσεως) Παχ(ὼν) β (ii 2, 5, 8, 11, 19, 25, 28, 31, 34, 37). Consequently the last part of the second entry here means '(issued in) Epeiph, as a result of an application, (for Phamenoth, Pharmouthi,) Pachon, (and Payni,) 4 art.', which is effectively the same as the usual one '(issued in) Epeiph, (for) Phamenoth (and Pharmouthi), 2 art.; (issued in) Epeiph, as a result of an application, (for) Pachon (and Payni), 2 art.'.

Col. ii 1–3 'Apollonius, son of Melas, grandson of Apollonius, mother Hermione, aged 32. (Issued in) Tybi (for) Phaophi (and) Hathyr another(?) 1 artaba; (issued in) Payni for (Choeac, Tybi, and) Mecheir, 3 artabas; (issued in) Epeiph (for) Phamenoth (and Pharmouthi), 2 artabas; (issued in) Epeiph, as a result of an application, (for) Pachon (and Payni), 2 artabas; (issued in) Thoth for Epeiph (etc.), 3 artabas.'

2 Τῦβι, Φαῶφι, Ἁθύρ. See introd.

ἀλλ( ) (ἀρτ.) α. The simplest hypothesis would be that half allowances amounting to 1 art. had been issued for Phaophi and Hathyr, completed by late payment in Tybi of the outstanding 1 art.

Παῦνι ὑ(πὲρ) Μεχείρ (ἀρτ.) γ. See introd.

Ἐπείφ, Φαμενώθ, (ἀρτ.) β. Just as in the previous sequence 'for Mecheir, 3 art.' means '3 artabas for (Choeac, Tybi, and) Mecheir', so here '(for) Phamenoth, 2 art.' means '2 artabas for Phamenoth (and Pharmouthi)'. In this and in every other appearance the writing of the month name of Phamenoth is very rapid and only legible as far as μ or ε. Here and in some other places the result seems long enough to encompass all the letters, in others it seems too short, e.g. 19. I have assumed that the same thing is intended in every case and have written the month name out in full, taking it as 'verschleift' rather than abbreviated.

Ἐπείφ ἐξ {.} ἀξ(ιώσεως) [Παχ(ὼν)] β. There can hardly be any doubt of the wording here, see 5, 8, 11, 16, 19, 22, 25, 28, [34], [37]. The manner of writing is not so certain. It might be ἐξ ἀξιώ(σεως) Π[αχ(ὼν) β] as in 28, rather than what I have preferred to offer in the text.

Again '(for) Pachon 2 art.' apparently means '2 artabas for Pachon (and Payni)'.

The applications referred to in these occurrences of ἐξ ἀξ(ιώσεως)—in full at 2935 24—appear to be different from the ones we have, applications for the payment of overdue allowances and not for admission to the dole. In 2936 ii on the other hand the marginal notations (π)ρ(ος)γί(νεται) ἐξ ἀξ(ιώσεως) Φαρ(μοῦθι) etc. do refer to applications for admission.

3 Θὼθ ὑ(πὲρ) Ἐπείφ (ἀρτ.) γ. Here too the excess of 2 art. is not explained but comparison shows that this sequence in 3, 6, 23, is the equivalent of Μες(ορή), Παῦνι, λημ( ) (ἀρτ.) β, Θὼθ ὑ(πὲρ) Ἐπείφ in 9, 12, 20, 26, 29, 35, 38. The extra 2 artabas are apparently a bonus, see 9 n. In entries of this type the bonus is paid in Thoth along with the allowance for Epeiph; in the other type it is issued in Mesore.

If all the explanations offered are correct the entry records issues of the regulation one artaba per month for the period Choeac to Epeiph, plus a bonus of 2 artabas. There were five actual issues, in Tybi, Payni, twice in Epeiph, and in Thoth. There is an evident connection between this pattern and the harvest time. Rents in grain are usually required to be paid in Payni and Epeiph, after the harvest.

4–6 'Apion, son of Serenus, grandson of Lucius Ofellius Sarapion, mother Apollonia, aged . . . (Issued in) Tybi, (for) Phaophi (and) Hathyr, another(?) 1 art., (and), as a result of an application, (the allowances for) Choeac (and) Tybi; (issued in) Payni (the allowance for) Mecheir; (issued in) Epeiph, for Phamenoth (and Pharmouthi), 2 art.; (issued in) Epeiph, as a result of an application, for Pachon (and Payni), 2 art.; (issued in) Thoth (for) Epeiph (etc.), 3 art.'

5 *Τῦβι*. It is not clear whether this means that the allowance for Tybi was issued on a separate occasion in Tybi or at the same time as the arrears. The translation assumes that all the issues were made on the same occasion in Tybi.

7–9 'Antaeodorus, son of Isidorus, grandson of Sarapion, mother Dieus, daughter of Theon, aged 22. (Issued in) Tybi (for) Phaophi (and) Hathyr, another(?) 1 art.; (issued in) Payni for (Choeac, Tybi, and) Mecheir, ⟨3⟩ art.; (issued in) Epeiph (for) Phamenoth (and Pharmouthi), 2 art.; (issued in) Epeiph, as a result of an application, (for) Pachon (and Payni), 2 art.; (issued in) Mesore (for) Payni, as a bonus(?), 2 art.; (issued in) Thoth (the allowance) for Epeiph.'

8 *Μεχείρ* (*ἀρτ*.) ⟨figure⟩. The figure is evidently omitted only through inadvertence since the sign for artabas is there. Supply ⟨γ⟩ as in 2, 25, 34, 40.

9 *Μεϲ*(*ορή*), *Παῦνι*, *λημ*( ) (*ἀρτ*.) *β*. The form of the expansion of *λημ*( ) is doubtful, perhaps *λήμ*(*ματος*) is best. The sense seems to be 'gain, profit', or as we should say 'a bonus'. The argument is as follows. The succession of months involved runs Pachon, Payni, Epeiph, Mesore, Thoth. The previous issue, namely 2 art. in Epeiph credited to Pachon, seems from all that precedes to cover both Pachon and Payni. The next allowance due was for Epeiph and it was issued in Thoth. This intervening issue of 2 art. in Mesore is credited to Payni, for which the normal issue had apparently been made already, and is marked out by the special notation *λημ*( ). Our word for an extra issue of this kind would be 'bonus'.

This hypothesis seems to fit well enough here, but the similar entries in **2936** and **2937** with *Μεϲ*(*ορή*), *Παῦνι*, *λημ*( ) (*ἀρτ*.) *α* are not very amenable to it. However, there the contexts are less secure than they are here.

10–12 'Apollonius, son of Theon, grandson of Diogenes, mother Stratonice, aged 30+. (Issued in) Tybi, (for) Phaophi (and) Hathyr, another(?) 1 art., (and), as a result of an application, (the allowances for) Choeac (and) Tybi; (issued in) Payni (the allowance) for Mecheir; (issued in) Epeiph, (for) Phamenoth (and Pharmouthi), 2 art.; (issued in) Epeiph, as a result of an application, (for) Pachon (and Payni), 2 art.; (issued in) Mesore (for) Payni, as a bonus(?), 2 art.; (issued in) Thoth (the allowance) for Epeiph.'

13–14 'A . . ., son of . . ., grandson of Ammonius, mother . . ., aged 34. (Issued in) Tybi, (for) Phaophi(?)' etc.

As well as being damaged this entry is also unusually short. The only other not to reach a third line is the last in the column (39–40); this one may be even shorter, though it is not certain whether it finishes where the traces end or whether the line rose a little and more has been lost where a long horizontal strip of papyrus has been pulled away.

15–17 'Harpocration, son of Demetrius, mother Tayris, aged 34. (Issued in) Choeac (for) Mesore (?), Thoth, (Phaophi, and Hathyr), another(?) 3 art., (and), as a result of an application, (the allowances for) Choeac (and) Tybi; (issued in) Epeiph (for Mecheir), Phamenoth, (and Pharmouthi), 3 art.; (issued in) Epeiph, as a result of an application, (for) Pachon (and Payni), 2 art.; (issued in) Mesore (for) Payni, as a bonus(?), 2 art.'

15 The grandfather's name is omitted, which is slightly unusual, but the significance of the omission is not known. In 33 the situation is the same and the father's name is also Demetrius; it is remotely possible that these recipients were half-brothers.

16 *Μεϲ*(*ορή*). The writing between *Χοι*(*άκ*) and *Θώθ* is undamaged but very rapid. The formula recurs in 25, but at that point there is damage to the papyrus. The best solution is to read *Μεϲ*(*ορή*). With this reading half allowances would have been paid for Mesore and Thoth, to be completed by the outstanding 1 artaba paid late, in Choeac, together with the standard allowances for Phaophi and Hathyr—a total of 3 artabas paid in Choeac. The writing is very similar to that in the sequence *Ἀθύρ*, . . . , *Θώθ* recurring in **2935** 2 etc., where also *Μεϲ*(*ορή*) is the best solution to the mathematical problem, and to **2934** ii 9 etc., *Μεϲ*(*ορή*), *Παῦνι*, *λημ*( ) (*ἀρτ*.) *β*.

*Φαμενώθ*, (*ἀρτ*.) *γ*. Comparison shows that this sequence occurs only in entries where there is no specific mention of a payment for Mecheir, i.e. here and in 22, so that the 3 artabas here cover (Mecheir), Phamenoth, (and Pharmouthi).

18–20 'Aphynchis, son of Thonis, grandson of Antiochus, mother Isidora, aged 35. (Issued in) Tybi, (for) Phaophi (and) Hathyr, another(?) 1 art., (and), as a result of an application, (the allowances for) Choeac (and) Tybi; (issued in) Payni (the allowance) for Mecheir; (issued in) Epeiph (for)

Phamenoth (and Pharmouthi), 2 art.; (issued in) Epeiph, as a result of an application, (for) Pachon (and Payni), 2 art.; (issued in) Mesore (for) Payni, as a bonus(?), 2 art.; (issued in) Thoth (the allowance) for Epeiph.'

21–3 'Amois, son of Sarapammon, grandson of Theon, mother Sarapias, aged 34. (Issued in) Tybi (for) Phaophi (and) Hathyr, another(?) 1 art., (and), as a result of an application, (the allowances for) Choeac (and) Tybi; (issued in) Epeiph (for Mecheir), Phamenoth, (and Pharmouthi), 3 art.; (issued in) Epeiph, as a result of an application, (for) Pachon (and Payni), 2 art.; (issued in) Thoth for Epeiph (etc.), 3 art.'

24–6 'Amois, son of Aphynchis, grandson of Amois, mother Apollonia, aged 35. (Issued in) Choeac (for) Mesore(?), Thoth, (Phaophi and Hathyr), another(?) 3 art.; (issued in) Payni for (Choeac, Tybi, and) Mecheir, 3 art.; (issued in) Epeiph (for) Phamenoth (and Pharmouthi) 2 art.; (issued in) Epeiph, as a result of an application, (for) Pachon (and Payni), 2 art.; (issued in) Mesore (for) Payni, as a bonus(?), 2 art.; (issued in) Thoth (the allowance) for Epeiph.'

25 Χοι(άκ), Μεϲ(ορή), Θώθ. See 16 n.

27–9 'Amois, son of Romanus, grandson of Sarapammon, mother Thaësis, aged 35. (Issued in) Tybi (for) Phaophi (and) Hathyr another(?) 1 art., (and), as a result of an application, (the allowances for) Choeac (and) Tybi; (issued in) Pachon (the allowance) for Mecheir; (issued in) Epeiph (for) Phamenoth (and Pharmouthi), 2 art.; (issued in) Epeiph, as a result of an application, (for) Pachon (and Payni), 2 art.; (issued in) Mesore (for) Payni, as a bonus(?), 2 art.; (issued in) Thoth (the allowance) for Epeiph.'

30–2 'Antonius, son of Asclas, grandson of Asclas, mother Peine, aged 36. (Issued in) Tybi (for) Phaophi (and) Hathyr, another(?) 1 art., (and), as a result of an application, (the allowances for) Choeac (and) Tybi; (issued in) Payni (the allowance) for Mecheir; (issued in) Epeiph (for) Phamenoth (and Pharmouthi), 2 art.; (issued in) Epeiph, as a result of an application, (for) Pachon (and Payni), 2 art.; (issued in) Mesore (for) Payni, as a bonus(?), 2 art.'

33–5 'Agathus Daemon alias Thonis, son of Demetrius, mother Didyme, (aged . . .). (Issued in) Tybi (for) Phaophi (and) Hathyr another(?) 1 art.; (issued in) Payni for (Choeac, Tybi and) Mecheir, 3 art.; (issued in) Epeiph (for) Phamenoth (and Pharmouthi), 2 art.; (issued in) Epeiph, as a result of an application, (for) Pachon (and Payni), 2 art.; (issued in) Mesore (for) Payni, as a bonus(?), 2 art.; (issued in) Thoth (the allowance) for Epeiph.'

36–8 'Asclepiades, son of Germanus, grandson of Dioscorus, mother Tayris, (aged . . .). (Issued in) Tybi (for) Phaophi (and) Hathyr, . . . 4 art., another(?) 1 art., (and), as a result of an application, (the allowances for) Choeac (and) Tybi; (issued in) Payni (the allowance) for Mecheir; (issued in) Epeiph (for) Phamenoth (and Pharmouthi), 2 art.; (issued in) Epeiph, as a result of an application, (for) Pachon (and Payni), 2 art.; (issued in) Mesore (for) Payni, as a bonus(?), 2 art.; (issued in) Thoth (the allowance) for Epeiph.'

37 . .(ἀρτ.) δ. If this is an additional payment it will not fit into the regular scheme. The total allowances for Phaophi to Tybi inclusive would be 4 art., so that one might guess for the sense 'to complete the amount owed, i.e. 4 art.', but the position seems wrong. This comment one might expect either at the beginning of the allowances issued in Tybi or at the end of them, but not in the middle. The writing could represent ϵ' = ἐ(πὶ τὸ αὐτό), i.e. 'total', followed by a ligature to the artaba sign, but it would be very uncertain.

39–40 'Ammonius, son of Horion, grandson of Pausanias, mother Isidora, (aged . . .). (Issued in) Tybi (for) Phaophi (and) Hathyr, another(?) 1 art.; (issued in) Payni for (Choeac, Tybi, and) Mecheir, 3 art.; (issued in) Epeiph (for) Phamenoth (and Pharmouthi), 2 art. . . .'

Though unusually short the entry follows a standard pattern as far as it goes, see, e.g., 2.

## 2935

22 3B.15/D(18)a          32·5 × 25·5 cm.          s.d.

It is noticeable that in this item it is not possible to match the issues actually noted with the theoretical allowance of one artaba per month quite so satisfactorily as in **2934**. The explanation of the very different pattern may be that this is a register for a different year, perhaps the year preceding that of **2934**. Here the last entry is generally an issue made in Hathyr to cover Mesore and Thoth, there the first issue is generally one covering the next two months, Phaophi and Hathyr, made in Tybi. This first entry in **2934**, however, is only for half the expected quantity, implying a previous instalment, so that the chronological relationship is far from sure.

ii

Ἀμόις ὁ κ(αὶ) Γεννάδιος Ἰσιδώρου μη(τρὸς) Τερεῦτος       (ἐτῶν) κ[

  Χοι(ὰκ) .. (ἀρτ.) β (ἥμισυ), Τῦβι, Μεχείρ, Φαμ(ενώθ), Παῦνι, Μες(ορή), Φαρμ(οῦθι), (ἀρτ.),

           β, Θὼθ ἐξ ἀξ(ιώσεως) Ἐπείφ, Ἀθύρ Μες(ορή), Θ[ώθ]

Ἀμμωνᾶς [Σ]ι̣[λ]βανοῦ τοῦ Θέωνος μη(τρὸς) Ἡρωδιαίνης       (ἐτῶν) κ[

  Παχώ[ν], Μεχείρ, Φαμ(ενώθ), Παῦνι, Θὼθ λ⁻ (ἀρτ.) δ, Ἀθύρ, Μες(ορή), Θώθ.

5 Α̣[ . . . . . . . . . Σ]αραπίωνος τοῦ Ὡρίωνος μη(τρὸς) Σαραλλιο̣[ ]

  [ . . . . . . . . . . . .]νίου τοῦ κ(αὶ) Σαρα( ) κο{ς}ςμη(τεύσαντος) βουλ(ευτοῦ)       (ἐτῶν) κ

  [ . . . . . . . . . . . .] β, Παῦνι, Μες(ορή), Φαρμ(οῦθι), (ἀρτ.) β, Θὼθ ἐξ ἀξ(ιώσεως)

                                    Ἐπείφ[ ]

  [Α . . . . . . . . . . . . . .]ν Παμβήκιος Ἀπίωνος μη(τρὸς) Ἡρᾶτος       (ἐτῶν) κ

  [ . . . . . . . . . . . . . . . .] Μεχείρ, Φαμ(ενώθ), Παῦνι, Ἀθύρ, Μες(ορή), Θὼθ (ἀρτ.) ς.

10 [Α . . . . . . . . . . .]μονος τοῦ κ(αὶ) Αὐνῆ Πλουτίωνος μη(τρὸς) ..[. .].τος       (ἐτῶν) κ

  [ . . . . . . . . . . .] β, Μεχείρ, Φαμ(ενώθ), Μες(ορή), Φαρμ(οῦθι), (ἀρτ.) γ, Θὼθ λ ἐξ

                          ἀξ(ιώσεως) Ἐπείφ, Ἀθύρ, Μες(ορή), Θώ[θ

  [Α . . . . . . . . .]ου τοῦ Παυσᾶτος μη(τρὸς) Τααποῦτος       (ἐτῶν) ιθ⁻

  [ . . . . . . . . . .]., Τῦβι β, Μεχείρ, Φαμ(ενώθ), Παῦνι, Με[ς(ορή), Φαρ]μ(οῦθι), (ἀρτ.) β,

           Θὼθ λ⁻ ἐξ ἀξ(ιώσεως) Ἐπείφ (ἀρτ.) β, Ἀθύρ, Μες(ορή), Θώθ.

  [Α . . . . .].ιανὸς ὁ κ(αὶ) Ὡρίων Ἀρτεμιδ[ώρο]υ τοῦ κ(αὶ) Χαιρήμονος

15 [ . . . . .].[.]. μη(τρὸς) Θατρῆτος       (ἐτῶν) ιθ

  [ . . . . .] (vac.) Χοι(ὰκ) κ̅ς̅, Τῦβι (ἀρτ.) β, Μεχείρ, Φαμ(ενώθ), Παῦνι, Μες(ορή),

        Φαρμ(οῦθι), (ἀρτ.) β, Θὼθ ἐξ ἀξ(ιώσεως) [Ἐ]πείφ, Ἀθύρ, Μες(ορή), Θώθ.

  [Ἀ]μόις ὁ κ(αὶ) Διονύσιος Σεουήρου τοῦ Παάπιος μη(τρὸς) Ταύριος       (ἐτῶν) ις

  [ . . .](ἀρτ.) α, Χοι(ὰκ) κς, Τῦβι β, Μεχείρ, Φαμ(ενώθ), Παῦνι, Μες(ορή), Φαρμ(οῦθι), (ἀρτ.)

           β, Ἀθύρ, Μες(ορή), Θώθ, ⟦Ἀθύρ, Μες(ορή), Θώθ⟧, δ.

  ──────

(π)ρ(ος)γι(ν-) Ἄλυπις ὁ κ(αὶ) Πλούταρχος τοῦ Ἰσιδώρου τοῦ κ(αὶ) Σερήνου μη(τρὸς) Διογενίδος

                                    (ἐτῶν) ις

20   Χοι(ὰκ) .. (ἀρτ.) α, Χοι(ὰκ) κς, Μεχεὶ⟨ρ⟩ (ἀρτ.) γ, Φαμ(ενώθ), Παῦνι, Μες(ορή),

      Φαρμ(οῦθι), (ἀρτ.) β, Θὼθ ἐξ ἀξ(ιώσεως) Ἐπείφ, ⟦Ἀθύρ, Μες(ορή), Θώθ⟧,

                               Ἀθύρ, Μες(ορή), Θώθ.

(π)ρ(ος)γι(ν-) Ἀσ{σ}κληπιάδης Διδύμου τοῦ Ἀσ{σ}κληπιάδου μη(τρὸς) Βερενίκης Θέωνος (ἐτῶν) κ

  Χοι(ὰκ) α (ἀρτ.) α, Χοι(ὰκ) κς, Τῦβι β, Φαμ(ενὼθ) (ἀρτ.) β, Παῦνι, Μες(ορή), Φαρμ(οῦθι),

      (ἀρτ.) β, Θὼθ ἐξ ἀξ(ιώσεως) Ἐπείφ, Ἀθύρ, Μες(ορή), Θώθ.

(π)ρ(ος)γι(ν-) Ἀρείων Μώρου τοῦ Πανςειρίωνος μη(τρὸς) Θατρῆτος        (ἐτῶν) κε⁻
ἐξ ἀξιώςεως
25    Χοι(ὰκ) α (ἀρτ.) α, Χοι(ὰκ) κϛ, Τῦβι β, Μεχείρ, Φαμ(ενώθ), Παῦνι, Μες(ορή), Φαρμ ....
        (ἀρτ.) β, Θὼθ ἐξ ἀξ(ιώςεως) Ἐπείφ, Ἀθύρ, Μες(ορή), Θώθ.

iii

(opposite ii 4–7)

...[
——[

Χοι(άκ), (π)ρ(ος)γι(ν-) [
        Χοιά[κ
5    Χοι(άκ), (π)ρ(ος)γι(ν-) [

ii 1 αμοϊςο^κ, ϊςιδωρουμη’, ⌐ κ    2 χο⸍ ⸓ βϛ’, φα^μ, μεςφαρμ⸓ β, αξ, μες    3 μη’, ⌐ κ[
4 φα^μ, ⸓ δ, μες    5 μη’    6 τουκ̆ςαρα’κοςςμη ‾βου⌐ κ    7 μεςφαρμ ⸓ β, αξ    8 μη’,
⌐ κ    9 φα^μ, μες, ⸓ ϛ    10 τουκ̆, μη’, ⌐ κ    11 φα^μμεςφαρμ ⸓ γ, αξ, μες    12 μη’, ⌐ ιθ⁻
13 φα^μ, με[ςφαρ]μ⸓ β, αξ, ⸓ β, μες    14 ο^κ, τουκ̆    15 μη’, ⌐ ιθ    16 χο⸍, ⸓ β, φα^μ, μεςφαρμ
⸓ β, αξ, μες    17 [α]μοιςο^κ, μη’ταυριος, ⌐ ιϛ    18 ⸓ αχο⸍, φα^μ, μεςφαρμ ⸓ β, μες, μες
19 ρ’γι, ο^κ, ϊςιδωρου τουκ̆, μη’, ⌐ ιϛ    20 χο⸍, ⸓ α, χο⸍, ⸓ γφα^μ, μεςφαρμ ⸓ β, αξ, μες, μες    21 ρ’γι,
μη’, ⌐ κ    22 χο⸍, ⸓ α, χο⸍, φα^μ ⸓ β, μεςφαρμ ⸓ β, αξ, μες    23 ρ’γι, μη’, ⌐ κε⁻    25 χο⸍,
⸓ αχο⸍, φα^μ, μες[φ]αρμ....⸓ β, αξ, μες
    Col. iii 3, 5 χο⸍, ρ’γι

    Col. i There remain only the ends of two finials near the foot to the left of ii 21 and 23.
    Col. ii 1–2 'Amois alias Gennadius, son of Isidorus, mother Tereus, aged 20[+ ?]. (Issued in) Choeac ... 2½ art., Tybi, Mecheir, Phamenoth, Payni; (issued in) Mesore (for) Pharmouthi (and Pachon), 2 art.; (issued in) Thoth, as a result of an application, (the allowance for) Epeiph; (issued in) Hathyr (the allowances for) Mesore (and) Thoth.'
    This entry fits the scheme of one artaba per month, except that in Choeac an unusually large issue of 2½ art. was made, unless the two or three unread letters before the amount mean something significantly different; see also 20 n. Presumably the extra 1½ art. supply deficiencies in the allowances for previous months.
    2 Παῦνι, Μες(ορή), Φαρμ(οῦθι), (ἀρτ.) β. In this recurring sequence it is anomalous that the issue in Payni apparently counts for that month although the deficiency of the preceding Pharmouthi (and Pachon) remains to be made up two months later in Mesore.
    3–4 'Ammonas, son of Silvanus, grandson of Theon, mother Herodiaena, aged 20[+ ?]. (Issued in) Pachon, (the allowances for) Mecheir (and) Phamenoth; (issued in Payni the allowance for) Payni; (issued on) Thoth 30, 4 art.; (issued in) Hathyr (the allowances for) Mesore (and) Thoth.'
    4 (ἀρτ.) δ. The missing months are Pharmouthi, Pachon, and Epeiph, so that there seems to be one artaba too many. Perhaps it goes right back to Tybi, cf. 7 n., 9 n. but see 18 n. The entry is unusual in beginning as late as the allowance for Mecheir paid in Pachon.
    5–8 'A . . ., son of Sarapion, grandson of Horion, mother Sarallium(?), daughter of . . . nius alias Sara(pion?), (former?) *cosmetes*, councillor, aged 20. . . . (Tybi?), 2 art., Payni, (issued in) Mesore (for) Pharmouthi (and Pachon), 2 art.; (issued in) Thoth, as a result of an application, (the allowance for) Epeiph.'
    5 Cαραλλιο[.]. Cf. PSI 713, 7 κληρ(ονόμοι) Cαραλλίου. Probably this is the same name, a woman's name in a neuter form, Cαράλλιον, and is to be supplemented here as Cαραλλίο[υ]. Cf. Cεράλλιον, P. Mil. Vogl. I 26 3, 5, 11, 15, 16, 17; SB VI 9370 iv 23(?).
    6 At the beginning restore probably θυγατρός but it may have been abbreviated. The mark of abbreviation in Cαρα probably implies a following *pi* and Cαρα(πίωνος) is by far the likeliest name to be shortened so drastically.

7 Restore probably $T\hat{v}\beta\iota$] $\beta$, cf. 13, 16, 18, 22, 25. It seems to be normal in this piece for two artabas to be issued in Tybi. The extra artaba should probably be counted back to the earlier months of the year. In the only case where Tybi appears but lacks the double allowance (2), Choeac has an unusually large allowance. In another case Tybi does not appear, but Mecheir has a triple allowance evidently to make up what was not paid in Tybi (20).

This is also the only entry to lack the final sequence $Å\theta\acute{v}\rho$, $M\epsilon c(\text{ορή})$, $\Theta\acute{\omega}\theta$, and there are no amounts that can be assigned to Mecheir or Phamenoth.

8–9 'A . . . , son of . . . , grandson of Pambechis (son of?) Apion, mother Heras, aged 20. . . . , Mecheir, Phamenoth, Payni; (issued in) Hathyr (for) Mesore (and) Thoth, 6 art.'

8 ]$v$ $\Pi\alpha\mu\beta\acute{\eta}\kappa\iota o c$ $Å\pi\acute{\iota}\omega\nu o c$. It is unusual for the grandfather's name to be followed by a patronymic, if that is the case here, cf. **2898** 6 n. Perhaps we should emend to $\tau o]\hat{v}$ $\langle\kappa\alpha\grave{\iota}\rangle$ $\Pi\alpha\mu\beta\acute{\eta}\kappa\iota o c$, cf. 10.

9 ($\dot{\alpha}\rho\tau.$) $\varsigma$. This unusually large issue seems to indicate a situation very like that in 3–4. There $\Theta\acute{\omega}\theta$ $\lambda$ ($\dot{\alpha}\rho\tau.$) $\delta$, $Å\theta\acute{v}\rho$, $M\epsilon c(\text{ορή})$, $\Theta\acute{\omega}\theta$ comes to a total of 6 art. for 5 months, unless we carry the extra artaba back at least to Tybi, cf. 18 n.

10–11 'A . . . , son of . . . mon alias Aunes, grandson of Plution, mother . . . , aged 20. (. . . Tybi?), 2 art., Mecheir, Phamenoth; (issued in) Mesore (for) Pharmouthi, (Pachon, and Payni), 3 art.; (issued on) Thoth 30, as a result of an application, (the allowance for) Epeiph; (issued in) Hathyr, (the allowances for) Mesore (and) Thoth.'

11 $T\hat{v}\beta\iota$] $\beta$. Cf. 7 n.

12–13 'A . . . , son of . . . us, grandson of Pausas, mother Taapous, aged 19. . . . Tybi, 2 art., Mecheir, Phamenoth, Payni; (issued in) Mesore (for) Pharmouthi (and Pachon), 2 art.; (issued on) Thoth 30, as a result of an application, (for Payni and) Epeiph, 2 art.; (issued in) Hathyr (the allowances for) Mesore (and) Thoth.'

12 $T\alpha\alpha\pi o\hat{v}\tau o c$. Perhaps a variant of the known name $T\alpha\pi o\hat{v}c$; only tops of the first few letters survive.

14–16 'A . . . alias Horion, son of Artemidorus alias Chaeremon, grandson of . . . , mother Thatres, aged 19. . . . Choeac 26, Tybi, 2 art., Mecheir, Phamenoth, Payni; (issued in) Mesore, (for) Pharmouthi (and Pachon), 2 art.; (issued in) Thoth, as a result of an application, (the allowance for) Epeiph; (issued in) Hathyr (the allowances for) Mesore (and) Thoth.'

14 Perhaps [$Å\gamma\rho\iota\pi$]$\pi\iota\alpha\nu\acute{o}c$.

16 [. . . . .] (vac.). In spite of the blank the gap at the beginning is wide enough to have contained another entry for Choeac, as in 20, 22, 25, and probably 18.

17–18 'Amois alias Dionysius, son of Severus, grandson of Paapis, mother Tayris, aged 16. (Choeac?), 1 art., Choeac 26, Tybi, 2 art.; Mecheir, Phamenoth, Payni; (issued in) Mesore (for) Pharmouthi (and Pachon), 2 art.; (issued in) Hathyr (for) Mesore and Thoth, 4 art.'

18 [. . .] ($\dot{\alpha}\rho\tau.$) $\alpha$. The space probably contained another entry for Choeac as in 20, 22, 25, (and perhaps 16), though it seems just slightly too narrow for more than $\chi o^{\iota}$. If these places are to fit the hypothesis of the monthly allowance of one artaba, part of them and part of the double allowance for Tybi must be counted back towards the months before Choeac, cf. 7 n.

$\delta$. This issue of 4 art. produces the same sort of surplus of 1 art. that is encountered in the entries of 2–4 and 8–9, see 4 n. Here where the entry is relatively complete it seems unlikely that the extra artaba should be counted backwards. Perhaps it was part of a bonus, cf. **2934** 9 n.

19–20 'New entry. Alypis alias Plutarch, son of Isidorus alias Serenus, mother Diogenis, aged 16. Choeac . . . 1 art., Choeac 26, Mecheir, 3 art., Phamenoth, Payni; (issued in) Mesore (for) Pharmouthi (and Pachon), 2 art.; (issued in) Thoth, as a result of an application, (the allowance for) Epeiph; (issued in) Hathyr (the allowances for) Mesore (and) Thoth.'

19 ($\pi$)$\rho$($o c$)$\gamma\iota$($\nu$-). For the abbreviation, see **2915** 20 n. Note that the paragraphus under 18 separates these new entrants from the preceding established ones.

$Å\lambda\hat{v}\pi\iota c$ = $Å\lambda\acute{v}\pi\iota o c$. Cf. *Class. Phil.* 43 (1948), pp. 243–60.

20 $Xo\iota(\dot{\alpha}\kappa)$ . . ($\dot{\alpha}\rho\tau.$) $\alpha$. The legible parallels (22, 25) have $Xo\iota(\dot{\alpha}\kappa)$ $\alpha$ ($\dot{\alpha}\rho\tau.$) $\alpha$. Here and in 2 the illegible and damaged writing may simply be a day number; if so, it is probably a number in the twenties, $\kappa$ . .

$M\epsilon\chi\epsilon\grave{\iota}\langle\rho\rangle$ ($\dot{\alpha}\rho\tau.$) $\gamma$. Evidently the equivalent of $T\hat{v}\beta\iota$ ($\dot{\alpha}\rho\tau.$) $\beta$, $M\epsilon\chi\epsilon\acute{\iota}\rho$ in (9, 11?), 13, 16, 18, 22, 25, cf. 7 n.

21–2 'New entry. Asclepiades, son of Didymus, grandson of Asclepiades, mother Berenice, daughter of Theon, aged 20. Choeac 1, 1 art., Choeac 26, Tybi, 2 art.; (for Mecheir and) Phamenoth, 2 art.; (issued in Payni the allowance for) Payni; (issued in) Mesore (for) Pharmouthi (and Pachon), 2 art.; (issued in) Thoth, as a result of an application, (the allowance for) Epeiph; (issued in) Hathyr (the allowances for) Mesore (and) Thoth.'

22 $\Phi\alpha\mu(\epsilon\nu\dot{\omega}\theta)$ ($\dot{\alpha}\rho\tau.$) $\beta$. The equivalent of $M\epsilon\chi\epsilon\dot{\iota}\rho$, $\Phi\alpha\mu(\epsilon\nu\dot{\omega}\theta)$ in 2, 4, 9, 11, 13, 16, 18, 25.

23–5 'New entry. Arion, son of Morus, grandson of Pausirion, mother Thatres, aged 25. As a result of an application. Choeac 1, 1 art., Choeac 26, Tybi, 2 art., Mecheir, Phamenoth, Payni; (issued in) Mesore (for) Pharmouthi (and Pachon) . . . 2 art.; (issued in) Thoth, as a result of an application, (the allowance for) Epeiph; issued in Hathyr (the allowances for) Mesore (and) Thoth.'

24 $\dot{\epsilon}\xi$ $\dot{\alpha}\xi\iota\dot{\omega}\epsilon\epsilon\omega\epsilon$ is written in a small hand below 23 but appears from the spacing to have been in place before 25 was written. The significance is doubtful but probably it is to be compared with the marginal notations $\dot{\epsilon}\xi$ $\dot{\alpha}\xi(\iota\dot{\omega}\epsilon\epsilon\omega\epsilon)$ $\Phi\alpha\rho(\mu o\hat{v}\theta\iota)$ etc. in **2936** ii 1–2 *et al.* as referring to applications for admissions to the dole rather than with the other occurrences of $\dot{\epsilon}\xi$ $\dot{\alpha}\xi(\iota\dot{\omega}\epsilon\epsilon\omega\epsilon)$ in the main parts of **2934** and **2935**, see **2934** ii 2 n.

25 $\Phi\alpha\rho\mu$ . . . . This illegible passage does not seem to have $\Phi\alpha\rho\mu o\hat{v}\theta\iota$ in full nor $\Phi\alpha\rho\mu($ $)$ $\Pi\alpha\chi($ $)$. Remotely possible is $\dot{\epsilon}\xi$ $\dot{\alpha}\xi\iota(\dot{\omega}\epsilon\epsilon\omega\epsilon)$.

Col. iii A large blank space about 11 × 17 cm. at the bottom right of this piece shows that col. iii was short, containing perhaps four entries, which may indicate that it was the end of the section for *alpha*.

## 2936

23 3B.11/D(12) and (13)     15·5 × 28 cm.     Dec./Jan., A.D. 271/2

### i

```
].ικης                    (ἐτῶν) κβ
  ]. Ἐπείφ
  ] (vac.)    τελ
'Ε]πείφ                    (ἐτῶν) νε
5 ] (vac.)       τελ
  ] (vac.)       τελ
  ] (vac.)       τελ
]'Επείφ, Φαμ(ενὼθ) (ἀρτ.) ạ
  ] (vac.)
10 ]. ϲ          τελ
  ]. Ἐπείφ, Φαμ(ενὼθ) (ἀρτ.) α
  ] (vac.)
  ].             τελ
'Ε]πείφ, Φαμ(ενὼθ) α (ἥμιϲυ)
```

. . . . .

1 L κβ     4 L νε     8 φαμ ⨤ ạ     11 φαμ ⨤ α     14 φαμ αϛ′

ii

(π)ρ(ος)γί(νεται) ἐξ ἀξ(ιώσεως)   Ἀτρῆς ὁ καὶ Δίδυμος Coντώουτος [

    Φαρ(μοῦθι)            ....χ....., Παῦνι ὑ(πὲρ) Μεχείρ, Ἐπείφ, ...[

                Μ̣ε̣ς(ορὴ) ἐξ ἀξ(ιώσεως) Παχ(ὼν) (ἀρτ.) α, Μ̣ε̣ς(ορή), Παῦνι,

                     λημ( ) (ἀρτ.) α, Θὼθ ὑ(πὲρ) Ἐπ[είφ

(π)ρ(ος)γί(νεται) ἐξ ἀξ(ιώσεως)   Α....εινος ̣μηειτος μη(τρὸς) Ταν̣.[

5    Φαρ(μοῦθι)            .........., Ἐπ[εί]φ, Φαμ(ενὼθ) α (ἥμισυ), Μ̣ε̣ς(ορὴ) ἐξ

                     ἀξ(ιώσεως) Παχ(ὼν) (ἀρτ.) α [

(π)ρ(ος)γί(νεται) ἐξ ἀξ(ιώσεως)   Ἀμόις Cύρου μη(τρὸς) Ταυσείριος [

    Παῦνι            Παῦνι ὑ(πὲρ) Μεχείρ, Μ̣ε̣ς(ορή), Παῦνι, λημ( ) (ἀρτ.)

                            [[α]] γ [

(π)ρ(οσγίνεται) ἐξ (ἀξιώσεως)   Ἄμμων χρηματίζων μη(τρὸς) Ἐλέγ[ης

    Ἐπείφ           ἐνετάγη ὑπ᾽ ἐμοῦ Cερήνου χιρ(οτονητοῦ) νοσοῦν[τος

10           (vac.)   Μ̣ε̣ς(ορὴ) ἐξ ἀξ(ιώσεως) Παχ(ὼν) (ἀρτ.) α,

                     Μ̣ε̣ς(ορή), Παῦνι, λημ( ) (ἀρτ.) α [

(π)ρ(οσγίνεται) ἐξ (ἀξιώσεως)   ζ[ο]ντώους Ὥρου μη(τρὸς) Θατρῆτος     [

    Ἐπείφ           ἐνετάγη ὑπ᾽ ἐμοῦ Cερήνου χιρ(οτονητοῦ) νοσοῦντο[ς

          (vac.)   Μ̣ε̣ς(ορὴ) ἐξ ἀξ(ιώσεως) Παχ(ὼν) (ἀρτ.) α,

                     Μ̣ε̣ς(ορή), Παῦνι, λημ( ) (ἀρτ.) α .[

(π)ρ(οσγίνεται) ἐξ (ἀξιώσεως)   Πράκτικος ὁ κὲ Cεραπιακὸς ἀ(πελεύθερος) Δημητρί[ο]υ̣

                            το̣ῦ̣.[

15    Ἐπ̣ε̣ί̣φ          ἐ̣ν̣ετάγη{ς} ὑπ᾽ ἐμοῦ Cερήνου χιρ(οτονητοῦ) νοσοῦ̣ν̣τ̣ο̣[ς

          (vac.)   Μ̣έ̣ς(ορὴ) ἐξ ἀ̣ξ(ιώσεως) Παχ(ὼν) (ἀρτ.) α,

                     Μ̣ε̣ς(ορή), Παῦνι, λημ( ) [

(π)ρ(οσγίνεται) ἐξ (ἀξιώσεως)   Ἐπαφρόζειτος ἀπε(λεύθερος) Δημητρίου τοῦ [

    Ἐπείφ?         ἐ]ν̣ετάγη ὑπ᾽ ἐμοῦ Cερήνου χιρ(οτονητοῦ) νοσοῦντ[ος

          Ἐπείφ, ... (ἀρτ.) α, Μ̣ε̣ς(ορὴ) ἐξ ἀξ(ιώσεως) Παχ(ὼν)

                     (ἀρτ.) α, Μ̣ε̣ς(ορή), Παῦ[νι

20   (π)ρ(οσγίνεται) ἐξ (ἀξιώσεως)]   Διονύcιος ἀπε(λεύθερος) Θέωνος τοῦ καὶ Διδ[

    Ἐπεί]φ         ἐνετάγη ὑπ᾽ ἐμοῦ Cερήνου χιρ(οτονητοῦ) νοc[ο]ῦντο[ς

          Ἐπείφ, ... (ἀρτ.) α, Θὼθ ὑ(πὲρ) Ἐπείφ β (ἥμιcυ) [

(π)ρ(οσγίνεται)] ἐξ (ἀξιώcεως)   Καλαντίων χρηματίζων μη(τρὸς) [

    Μ]εσορὴ β      Μ̣ε̣ς(ορὴ) ἐξ ἀξ(ιώσεως) Παχ(ὼν) (ἀρτ.) α, Θὼθ ὑ(πὲρ)

                        Ἐπείφ α (ἥμιcυ) [

25   (ἔτους) β᾽ Αὐτοκράτορος Καίcαρος Λ[ο]υκίου Δομι[ττίου Αὐρηλιανοῦ Εὐcεβοῦc

Εὐτυχοῦς Cεβαστοῦ καὶ (ἔτους) ε′ Ἰουλίου Αὐρηλίο̣[υ Cεπτιμίου Οὐαβαλλάθου
τ]ο̣ῦ λαμπροτάτου βασιλέως ὑπάτου αὐτοκρ[άτορος cτρατηγοῦ Ῥωμαίων
Τῦ]βι [?]. Αὐρήλ(ιος) Πανάρης διοικ(ῶν) τὰ κατὰ τὴν [

δι]ακ(ριθέντες) [κ]αὶ ἐπὶ τῆς ἀναγορ(ίας) ὑπακ(ούοντες). Αὐρ[
30    .....]. Cερήνου. ἐλιτούργηcαν οἱ προκ(είμενοι) κ̣α̣ὶ [
καὶ ἐπὶ] τῆς ἀναγωρίας ὑπακο[ύ]ο̣ν̣τες[

                              (vac.)
              ]        traces        [
              ]        traces        [
        .        .        .        .        .

1 ρ̕γι⁻ εξ αξ′    2 φαρ⁻, α̣ξ̣χο̣ι?, υ̕    3 μες εξ αξ παχ ⸗ α, μες, λημ ⸗ α, υ̕       4 ρ̕γι⁻
εξ αξ′, μη̕    5 φαρ⁻, χο̣ι?, φαμ α̣ς, μες εξ αξ παχ ⸗ α[    6 ρ̕γι⁻ εξ αξ′, μη̕    7 υ̕, μες, λημ ⸗
α (struck through) γ    8 ρ̕ εξ′, μη̕    9 χιρ̕ l. χειρ(οτονητοῦ)    10 μες εξ αξ παχ ⸗ α, μες, λημ ⸗ α
11 ρ̕ εξ′, μη̕    12 χιρ̕    13 μες εξ αξ παχ ⸗ α, μες, λημ ⸗ α    14 ρ̕ εξ′, κε = καί, α̕    15 χιρ̕
16 μες εξ αξ παχ ⸗ α, μες, λημ[    17 ρ̕ εξ′, l. Ἐπαφρόδιτος, απε̕    18 χιρ̕    19 φαμ? ⸗ α,
μες εξ αξ παχ ⸗ α μες    20 απε̕    21 χιρ̕    22 φαμ? ⸗ α, υ̕, βς    23 εξ (no oblique stroke),
μη̕    24 μες εξ αξ παχ ⸗ α, υ̕, ας̕    25 Ⳑ β′    26 Ⳑ ε′    28 αυρη λ, διοι κ    29 δι]ακ̕,
αναγορ̕υπακ̕    30 προκ̕.    31 l. ἀναγορίας

Col. i 3 τελ. Possibly τελ(ευτηθείς) in the sense of 'dead', or more probably part of τελειοῦν (τελειω-
θέν?), indicating that the entry was superseded since all the issues due under it had been made.

5–7 The spacing suggests that there were three entries in three lines. If so, they were much shorter
than usual.

10 ].ς. Just possibly this should be read ].ϛ, i.e. an age number. It looks just like the end of 1,
which seems to be a mother's name, but the ages below 4 were either omitted entirely or occurred much
further to the left. So too the finial in 13 could be a figure or a letter.

Col. ii There are three separate illegible patches of ink in the top margin. The right hand one is
clearly a blot; the other two might have significance, e.g. one might be a column number.

1 (π)ρ(ος)γί(νεται). See 2915 20 n.

2 Perhaps read ἐξ ἀξ(ιώσεως) Χο̣ι(άκ), Τῦβι.

3 Μ̣ες(ορή) ἐξ ἀξ(ιώσεως). Here and in every other case (5, 10, 13, 16, 24 and 2937 i, 2, 9) the
writing is very cursive. The entry of similar layout, Ἐπεὶφ ἐξ ἀξ(ιώσεως) Παχ(ὼν) β, which occurs so
frequently in 2934, suggests that Μ̣ες(ορή), which is a plausible reading and the month after Epeiph,
is the right interpretation.

4 After Α, ς or ϛ or perhaps a rounded γ; Ἀγγλεῖνος is the only possibility that I have thought of
which is not excluded, but it is not specially suitable.

.μηειτος. Apparently not in Dornseiff–Hansen, *Rückläufiges Wb. d. gr. Eigennamen*. Perhaps .[.]μηειτος,
if the second letter is thin. Ἑρμήεις is not in NB nor in Foraboschi, *Onomasticon*.

8 From this point the standard abbreviation (π)ρ(ος)γί(νεται) ἐξ ἀξ(ιώσεως) is reduced to (π)ρ(ος-
γίνεται) ἐξ (ἀξιώσεως), i.e. to ρ̕εξ′ in place of ρ̕γι⁻εξαξ′.

9 χ⟨ε⟩ιρ(οτονητοῦ). See 2894 ii 37 n. The line is to be supplemented νοcοῦν̣[τος (X.?) τοῦ φυλάρχου,
and the whole line translated 'He was enrolled by me, Serenus, nominator, because of the illness of
(X.?) the phylarch.'

14 Possibly τοῦ κ̣[αί .... Generally the patronymic occurs without the article in this archive and
this is the usual Oxyrhynchite practice, but there are exceptions. Demetrius may or may not be the
same patron as the one in 17; see also 2937 ii 2.

17 Ἐπαφρό̣ζειτος. ζ for δ, cf. 1069 *passim*, for confusion between the two.

18 Ἐπεὶφ is the only possible restoration if the months follow in order of time, as they appear to
do throughout.

19 Ἐπείφ, . . . (ἀρτ.) α. Perhaps Φαμ(ενώθ), which seems to suit the traces here and in 22. The sequence Ἐπείφ, Φαμενώθ (ἀρτ.) α may be compared with **2934** 2, 5, 8 etc.

20 Διδ[ύμου is most probable, but there are several less likely possibilities in NB.

24 Μεσορὴ β. The figure is undamaged; κ seems less likely but possible.

28 Τῦ]βι[?]. The gap is narrow. Probably no day was given. The significance of the date is a puzzle. One might imagine perhaps that it is the date when the register as first compiled by the phylarch's deputies, that is, containing the names only, was delivered to persons responsible for keeping a record of actual issues of corn. But in that case the names in col. ii were added after the transfer, i.e. in 1 the new entrant was added in the Pharmouthi two to three months after the Tybi in this line. This is possible, but the layout of the page does not suggest that the date at the foot was written first and that the names in col. ii were added in a space left blank for them. More probably, then, the phylarchs— or their deputies, as in this case—had the lists of names compiled, supervised or checked the entries made against the names, added new names from time to time, and finally, when the registers were complete for a specified period, subscribed them as in these lines and had them filed in whatever the appropriate repository was. If this is right, the Pharmouthi of the marginal note to line 1 is the Pharmouthi of A.D. 270/1, nearly a year earlier than the Tybi of this date. This seems to fit best. The last of these additional entrants was added in Mesore, the last month of the Graeco-Egyptian year. Supposing that the register covers the official year A.D. 270/1, Tybi (Dec./Jan.) A.D. 271/2 is a reasonable time for the register to be closed after arrears had been paid off.

28-31 These subscriptions do not quite conform to what we might expect from the formulary in **2927**. First of all there is none by a γνωστήρ. However, this may have followed below, because though the papyrus is blank beneath 31 for a depth of about 2·5 cm., there are very faint traces of two or perhaps three lines on the frayed and rubbed fibres at the foot. Lines 29-31 appear to be the equivalent for the circumstances of the phylarch's subscription **2927** 21-2, from which they might be reconstructed as follows: Αὐρ[ήλιός τις (γενόμενος?) φύλαρχος δι᾽ ³⁰ ἐμο]ῦ Cερήνου. ἐλειτούργηcαν οἱ προκείμενοι καὶ [οὕτωc ἔχουcι καὶ ἐν βιβλιοθήκῃ καὶ αὐτοί εἰcιν οἱ διακριθέντεc ³¹ καὶ ἐπὶ] τῆc ἀναγορείαc ὑπακούοντεc. Certainty about abbreviations and line division cannot, of course, be reached. Nevertheless line 30 appears to be too long, even with drastic abbreviation, and it is probable that a shorter version was used. One may compare in a general way the phylarch's short subscriptions to individual applications (references listed in **2927** introd.).

A problem remains in the first subscription, lines 28-9. Probably we should restore the title of Panares as διοικ(ῶν) τὰ κατὰ τὴν [φυλαρχίαν, even though φυλαρχία has not yet occurred in the papyri. The remains of the subscription in 29 conform to the phylarch's subscription in **2927** 21-2 and to line 31 here. If this is right it would appear that the duties of the indisposed phylarch were taken over by a committee of χειροτονηταί, cf. **2894** ii 37, whose chairman could describe himself as διοικῶν τὰ κατὰ τὴν φυλαρχίαν. In the absence of the phylarch two persons were required to subscribe in the same sense as he would have done had he been able to act.

**2937**

| 23 3B.11/D(13) | frag. 1 15·5 × 16 cm. | s.d. |
| | frag. 2 12·5 × 11·5 cm. | |
| | frag. 3 7·5 × 15 cm. | |

Fragment 1 contains the ends of col. i and the beginnings of col. ii; fragment 2 the ends of col. ii. The position of fragment 3 is uncertain. It appears to come from the foot of the roll, but it might come from either of the two columns here or from a different place altogether.

Fr. 1                i

] Δ[ι]οϲκόρου μη(τρὸϲ) Θερμουθίου

     ].... (ἥμιϲυ), ἐξ ἀξ(ιώϲεωϲ) Χοι(άκ), Τῦβι, Ἐπείφ, Φαμενὼθ a (ἥμιϲυ), Μεϲ(ορὴ) ἐξ
                          ἀξ(ιώϲεωϲ) Παχ(ὼν) (ἀρτ.) a

     ].

     ] Τιθοῆτοϲ μη(τρὸϲ) Ϲοήριοϲ

5     ἐ]ξ ἀξ(ιώϲεωϲ) Χοι(άκ), Τῦβι (ἀρτ.) β (ἥμιϲυ), Παῦνι ὑ(πὲρ) Μεχείρ, Ἐπείφ, Φαμενὼθ
                                    (ἀρτ.) a

     ]Μεϲ(ορή), Παῦνι, ληµ( ) (ἀρτ.) a

] ..     (vac.)

   ].ων Διοϲκόρου μη(τρὸϲ) Ϲαραπιάδοϲ

    ]Ἀθὺρ ... (ἥμιϲυ), ἐξ ἀξ(ιώϲεωϲ) Χοι(άκ), Τῦβι, Ἐπείφ, Φαμενὼθ (ἀρτ.) a (ἥμιϲυ),
                       Μεϲ(ορὴ) ἐξ ἀξ(ιώϲεωϲ) Παχ(ὼν) (ἀρτ.) a

10   Παῦν]ι, ληµ( ) (ἀρτ.) a

     ]     (vac.)

       ] Δημητρίου μη(τρὸϲ) Ταφίλωνοϲ

         ]Παῦνι ὑ(πὲρ) Μεχεὶρ a (ἥμιϲυ), Ἐπείφ, Φαμενὼθ (ἀρτ.) a, Μεϲ(ορὴ) ἐξ ἀξ(ιώϲεωϲ)
                               Παχ(ων) (ἀρτ.) a

     Θ]ὼθ ὑ(πὲρ) Ἐπείφ

15     ]ιοϲ μη(τρὸϲ) Διονυϲίαϲ

     ]..[.] Μ[ε]χεὶρ (ἀρτ.) β, Μεϲ(ορὴ) ἐξ ἀξ(ιώϲεωϲ) Παχ(ὼν) (ἀρτ.) β, Θὼ[θ ὑ(πὲρ)]
                                  Ἐπεὶ⟨φ⟩ a (ἥμιϲυ)

     ]     (vac.)

     μ]η(τρὸϲ) Ἑλένηϲ

      ] ἐξ ἀξ(ιώϲεωϲ) Χοι(άκ), Τῦβι        )

20      ]     (vac.)

     ].θου [μ]η(τρὸϲ) Ϲαρα[

        ]..[

     .    .    .    .    .

1 μη᾽    2 ]αλλα ϛ′ ?, αξχο·, aϛ′, μεϲεξαξπαχ ⸗ a    4 μη᾽    5 αξχο·, ⸗ βϛ′, υ᾽, ⸗ a    6 μεϲ, ληµ
⸗ a       8 μη᾽      9 αλαϛ′ ?, αξχο·, ⸗ aϛ′, μεϲεξαξπαχ ⸗ a        10 ]ιληµ ⸗ a       12 μη᾽
13 υ᾽, aϛ′, ⸗ a, μεϲεξαξ (a corr.) παχ ⸗ a       14 υ᾽       15 μη᾽       16 ⸗ βμεϲεξαξπαχ ⸗ β,
επειαϛ′      18 μ]η᾽      19 ]εξαξχο·      21 [μ]η᾽

Frr. 1+2                  ii

ἀπελεύθ(εροι) [λελει]τουργ(ηκότες)

Ἀκύλας [ἀπελ(εύθερος) Δη]μητρίου τοῦ κ(αὶ) Ἀλεξάνδρου

Χοι(άκ) ‥, Τῦβι, Φ[αῶ]φι, Ἀθύρ, ἀλλ( ) (ἥμισυ), ἐξ ἀξ(ιώσεως) Χοι(άκ), Τῦβι, Παῦνι

            ὑ(πὲρ) Μεχ(είρ), Ἐπεί⟨φ⟩, Φαμενὼθ (ἀρτ.) α̣ [

Μ̣ες(ορὴ) ἐξ ἀξ(ιώσεως) Παχ(ὼν) (ἀρτ.) α, [Μεσ(ορή), Παῦνι, λ]ημ( ) (ἀρτ.) α, Θὼθ

                ὑ(πὲρ) Ἐπείφ

5   Ἀρητίων ἀ̣[πελ(εύθερος) ?Διο]γένους Θώνιος

    Τῦβι, Φαῶφι, Ἀθύρ, α̣[‥‥‥‥‥] Τῦβι, Παῦνι ὑ(πὲρ) Μεχείρ, Ἐπείφ, Φαμενὼ̣θ

                                              (ἀρτ.) α

    Μ̣[ες(ορὴ)] ἐξ ἀξ(ιώσεως) Παχ(ὼν) (ἀρτ.) α, [Μες(ορή), Παῦνι, λη]μ( ) (ἀρτ.) α

    Ἀβάσκαντ[ος ἐπι]κεκλ(ημένος) Καλότυχος ἀπελ(εύθερος) Στεφάνου

    Τῦβ[ι], Φαῶφι, Ἀθύρ, [‥‥ ἐ]ξ ἀξ(ιώσεως) Χοι(άκ), Τῦβι, Παῦνι ὑ(πὲρ) Μεχείρ, Ἐπείφ,

                                        Φαμενὼ̣θ (ἀρτ.) α

10  . ες(ορὴ) ἐξ ἀξ(ιώσεως) Παχ(ὼν) (ἀρτ.) . [Μες(ορή), Παῦ]νι, λ[η]μ( ) (ἀρτ.) α, Θὼθ

                             ὑ(πὲρ) Ἐπείφ

    Διόσκορος ἀ̣[πελ(εύθερος)] Τανεντή[ριος] ἱερίσσης

    Τῦβι, Φαῶφι, Ἀ[θ]ύρ [‥‥](ἥμισυ), ἐξ ἀξ(ιώσεως) Χοι̣(άκ), Τῦβι̣, [‥‥‥‥]. α (ἥμισυ),

                           Μ̣ες(ορὴ) ἐξ ἀξ(ιώσεως) Παχ(ὼν) (ἀρτ.) α

    Μ̣ες(ορή), Παῦνι, λημ( ) [(ἀρτ.)] α, Θὼθ ὑ(πὲρ) Ἐπ̣[είφ          ]

    Εὐτυχι . [. ο]ὐινδικτ[‥‥‥]ειλου βουλ(ευτοῦ) Ἀλεξ(ανδρείας)

15     Τῦβι, Φαῶφι, Ἀθύρ, α̣[‥‥] (ἥμισυ) ἐξ ἀξ(ιώσεως) [Χοι(άκ) ‥‥‥‥‥‥]. α

                                 (ἥμισυ), Θὼθ ὑ(πὲρ) Ἐπείφ α (ἥμισυ)

    Ἥλεις ἀπ[ε]λ[(εύθερος) ‥‥].[

    Τῦβι, Φαῶφι, Ἀ[θύρ

           .     .     .     .     .

1 απελευθ [λελει]τουργ**ϛ**      2 τουᵏ     3 χοˢ, αλλϛ´, αξχοˢ, υˀμεχ.επειφαμενωθ ⸓ α̣[      4 μες
εξαξπαχ ⸓ α, ]ημ ⸓ α, υˀ     6 υˀ, ⸓ α     7 μ̣[εϲ]εξαξπαχ ⸓ α, ]μ ⸓ α     8 ]κεκλ, απελ
9 αξχοˢ, υˀ, ⸓ α     10 μεϲεξαξπαχ ⸓ . , λ[η]μ ⸓ α, υˀ     12 ]ϛ´, αξχοˢ, αϛ´μεϲεξαξπαχ ⸓ α
13 μες, λημ[⸓]α, υˀ     14 βουλ αλεξ´     15 ]´ αξ[, ]. αϛ´, υˀ, αϛ´     16 απ[ε]λ[

Fr. 3

. . . . . .

...]‚‚ ουϲ χρημ[

...]‚...‚ Θώθ, ἀλλ( ) α (ἥμιϲυ) [.]....[

Θ[ὼ]θ ὑ(πὲρ) Ἐπεὶφ α (ἥμιϲυ)         [

(vac.)

πρώτωϲ λελειτουργηκ[ότεϲ

5    Ἄμμων Ὀννώφρ[ιοϲ

   .......  Θώθ, ἐξ ἀξ(ιώϲεωϲ) Χοι(άκ), Τῦβι, [

   ἐξ ἀξ(ιώϲεωϲ) Παχ(ὼν) (ἀρτ.) α       [

   Ἀμ[μ]ώνιοϲ .....[

   ........ Ἀ]θύρ, ἐξ ἀξ(ιώϲεωϲ) Χοι(άκ), Τῦβι α (ἥμιϲυ) [

10   ....] Διοϲκόρου [

  ..........] ἀλλ( ) (ἀρτ.) ᾳ ...[

      ].

      ].

2 αλλαϲ['?]    3 υ', αϲ'    6 αξχο·    7 αξπαχ ∸ α    9 αξχο·, αϲ' [    11 ᾳλλ ∸ α

Col. i 1 Θερμουθίου seems best; other possibilities, e.g. -ος, -ας, are hardly excluded.

2 To begin with ]ᾳλλᾳϲ' = ἀλλ( ) ᾳ (ἥμιϲυ) is perhaps the best in view of **2934** ii 2 etc. ἀλλ( ) (ἀρτ.) α; other possibilities are ].ᾳλ( ) ᾳϲ', ].ᾳλλϲ'.

*Φαμενώθ*: verschleift.

7 ]‚‚‚ These traces are slightly puzzling since the preceding line is so short and since none of the other entries reaches a fourth line. Perhaps the ink is accidental.

9 ἀλλ( ) (ἥμιϲυ) or ᾳλ( ) α (ἥμιϲυ), cf. 2 n.

Μεϛ(ορή). Cf. **2936** ii 3 n.

12 Ταφίλωνος. New; Egyptian feminine article plus *Φίλων*.

16 ]‚‚[.]. Παῦ]ψι [ὑ(πὲρ)] Μ[ε]χείρ is probable.

18–19 This entry is bracketed. Perhaps it was misplaced, cf. **2930** 12 n., or the person was dead.

Col. ii 1 Possibly the heading should be expanded in the genitive rather than the nominative.

3 Possibly ἀλ( ) ᾳ (ἥμιϲυ), cf. i 2 n., but λ looks far preferable.

Μεχ. seems to have been botched in some way now not clear, but cf. 6, 9.

επειφαμενωθ ∸ α. Haplography of *phi*.

5 Διο]γένουϲ is the commonest possibility: Θεα]γένουϲ, Ϲω]γένουϲ, etc., are not excluded.

6 Cf. 3 and restore, e.g., ἀ[λλ( ) (ἥμιϲυ) ἐξ ἀξ(ιώϲεωϲ) Χοι(άκ)].

9 Cf. 3 and restore, e.g., [ἀλλ( ) (ἥμιϲυ).

12 [ἀλλ ( )] or [ἀλλ( ) α] (ἥμιϲυ), cf. 3; probably [Ἐπείφ, Φα]μένωθ α (ἥμιϲυ), cf. 6.

14 Εὐτυχι.[. Also possible is Εὐτυχι[.].[; Εὐτύχιο[ϲ seems best.

ο]ὐινδικτ[.....]ειλου. Ν]ειλου is almost certain. The meaning of ο]ὐινδικτ[ is obviously that the slave had been freed by *vindicta* and so became a full Roman citizen and not a *Latinus*.[1] The form of the restoration is slightly doubtful. The best-attested possibility is ο]ὐινδικτ[άριοϲ, see LSJ Suppl. s.v., referring to *IGRom.* 3. 801, 20; 802, 25. In *SPP* xx 48, 6 the reading is reported as οὐινδικτᾶ{κ}τοϲ ἀπελεύθ(εροϲ), which is suspicious, though the papyrus certainly has οὐινδικτακτοϲ, as I know from a photograph kindly supplied by the Österreichische Nationalbibliothek. In the *Suda* and in another lexicon

---

[1] On manumission by *vindicta* in Egypt see Taubenschlag, *Law*², p. 99. This passage casts doubt on his statement that it disappeared after the *constitutio Antoniniana*.

(Lex. Rom. Barocc.) there is an entry οὐΐνδικτος. ὁ κατὰ οὐΐνδικτον ἐλευθερούμενος. In the last it seems inevitable that we should emend at least to κατὰ οὐΐνδίκταν (cf. οὐι⟨ν⟩δίκταν P. Gnom. 21), and the *lemma* is also suspect.

This isolated reference to a slave freed in the formal manner indicates that the freedmen not so specifically described were freed by the *manumissio minus iusta* and were consequently *Latini* rather than full Roman citizens. It is doubtful what other conclusions can be reliably drawn, but against my theory that the liturgy was a means of acquiring citizen rights (Introd. pp. 4, 12) it might be argued that the place given to this man among the ἀπελεύθεροι λελειτουργηκότες shows that he had no more rights than they. I would maintain the possibility that he did not have to perform a liturgy but was listed here because he could not be properly listed in any other category.

## 2938. RECEIPT

35 4B.71/H(1–3)c                    8·2 × 10·5 cm.                    A.D. 256–261?

The name of Calpurnius Eusebius, see 2925 2, is the only reason for publishing this scrap in connection with the corn dole archive. He is acting as an agent (3), and it is clearly attractive to restore the text on the theory that here too he is the πραγμα-τευτής of Calpurnius Horion. The lower rank of his principal may be explained by the hypothesis that this text falls earlier in Horion's career than the documents of the archive. This would fit the possibility that in line 7 there is a reference to Mussius Aemilianus, *praefectus Aegypti* A.D. 256/7–261.

The verso has remains of two columns of a daily account of personal expenditure on such items as water, beer, vegetables, and baths.

Καλπούρνιος Ὡρί]ων ἱππεὺς Ῥωμαίων νεωκόρος
τοῦ μεγάλου Cαράπι]δος ἐξηγη(τεύσας) βουλ(ευτὴς) τῆς λαμ(προτάτης) πόλεως
τῶν Ἀλεξανδρέων καὶ] ὡς χρημ(ατίζει) δι' ἐμοῦ Καλ(πουρνίου) Εὐσεβίου
. . . . . . . . . . . . .]. Cαραπίωνι τραπεζείτῃ κολ-
5     λυβιστικῆς τραπ]έζης χαίρειν· ἔσχον παρὰ σοῦ
. . . . . . . . . . . . . . . . .].ον τῷ κυριακῷ λόγῳ ἀκο-
. . . . . . . . . . . . . . . . . . .].ου Αἰμιλι ..[
. . . . . . . . . . . . . . . . . . . . .]. ασεξ[
. . . . . . . . . . . . . . . . . . . . . .].. [

          ·          ·          ·          ·          ·          ·

1 ἱππευς          2 εξηγη⁷?, βουλ, λαμ∫          3 χρη^μ, καλ^λ

'(Calpurnius Horion?), Roman knight, temple attendant of the great Sarapis, former *exegetes*, senator of the most glorious city (of the Alexandrians) and however he is officially styled, through me Calpurnius Eusebius, (agent?), to Sarapion, banker of an exchange bank, greeting. I have received from you . . . (to?) the imperial account in accordance with (orders given by Mussius Aemilianus?) . . .'

2 ἐξηγῆ(τεύσας). If it is right to restore Horion's name in 1, this document was apparently drawn up before he became *hypomnematographus*.

4 Probably πραγματευτο]ῦ, cf. 2925 2, will be enough. The handwriting is too irregular to allow any but a rough estimate of the numbers of missing letters. But this word is not indispensable and there

are other possibilities; for instance, the banker's name may have been longer. It is possible that he should be identified with the man mentioned in **2925** 4, in which case the line would read Αὐρηλίῳ Ἡρᾷ τῷ κα]ὶ̣ Cαραπίωνι. However, the traces, though minute, are against *iota* because they are at the top level and there is blank papyrus directly beneath them, where one would expect to see a descender.

6–7 It is very tempting to restore something like ἀκο⁷[λούθως τοῖς κελευσθεῖσιν ὑπὸ Μουςς]ίο̣υ Αἰμιλιά̣ν[οῦ. This would supply an approximate date in or not long after the prefecture of Aemilianus, but Αἰμιλίο̣υ is not absolutely excluded, though less likely, and another Aemilianus is also possible.

8 ]..ac. ]α̣τας looks best; not δρα]χμάς, or -χι]λ̣ίας or -κο]ς̣ίας.

### 2939–2940. EXTRACTS FROM ARCHIVES[1]

Texts of this type are not uncommon: see **1649** 1 n. They illustrate how various was the information available in the βιβλιοθήκη δημοσίων λόγων. The extracts were made by or for individuals, who needed them as documentary evidence in negotiations with the administration: see Hombert–Préaux, *Recensement*, pp. 144 seqq. **2939** documents the *epicrisis* of a boy, **2940** service as a liturgist. **2940** refers to Dec./Jan. A.D. 270/1; there is no reason to think the copy much later than this, though the regnal year number for Vaballathus suggests that it is somewhat later. The earliest non-retrospective dating with a double regnal year number is of Phamenoth 18, 1 Aur. 4 Vab., in P. Strasb. inv. gr. 1238 in *Recherches* iii 62–3, no. 8. It is tempting to link it with the corn dole which is now documented for Oxyrhynchus for the years A.D. 269–72. Liturgical service was one of the qualifications for the dole; the ὀνηλαςία is several times cited by applicants (**2904** 10, **2906** ii 9, **2909** 10, **2915** 13, **2917** 9); one includes in his application an extract from his nomination to office (**2915** 11 seqq.); it is at least possible that others added separate certificates (ἐν ἐκτάκτῳ, **2913** iii 9, **2915** ii 2?). It may be that **2939** had a similar purpose; proof of *epicrisis* had often to be offered, e.g. **2898** ii 15–16. Both these documents were found during the third season at Oxyrhynchus, like much of the corn dole archive. The closeness of the inventory numbers may indicate that they were all found not far apart.

#### 2939

23 3B.11/D(10–11)b                    7 × 29·2 cm                    Third cent.

ἔκλημψις ἐκ
δημοςίας βιβλ(ιοθήκης)
ἐκ κατ᾽ ἄνδρα ἐπὶ
ἀμφόδου Βορρᾶ
5    Κρηπεῖδος
κολ(λήματος) μθ⁻ μετ᾽ ἄλλα.

2 βιβλ        6 κδ

[1] Mr. Parsons was preparing these papyri for publication when he read a draft of this volume. Recognizing the probability that they were connected with the corn dole he kindly offered to allow me to append them here. I have drawn very largely on his typescripts, while making some alterations to take account of the rest of the archive.

Διονύсιος Πινδάρου
μη(τρὸς) Φαυστείνης
καὶ προσγείνεται τῷ
10    γ (ἔτει) ἀπὸ ἀφηλίκων
προσβ(ὰς) εἰς (τεσσαρεσκαιδεκαετεῖς) τῷ
αὐτῷ γ (ἔτει)

8 μη'     10 γ𐆓″     11 προσβ', ιδ𐆓⁻     12 γ𐆓″

'Extract from the public record-office. From the list of individuals registered in the North Quay quarter, sheet 49, after other matter: Dionysius son of Pindarus, mother Faustina; and he joins the list in the 3rd year, from the (list of) minors, having advanced into the category of fourteen-year-olds in the same 3rd year.'

12 After the last line of writing there are *c.* 18 cm. of papyrus blank, which might imply that the writer intended to copy more.

## 2940

23 3B.11/D(22-4)b          8 × 13 cm.          A.D. 270/1 or later

This extract is written in red ink. The first entry ends with line 9; there is then a space; a second entry must have followed, of which there remains only one trace at the bottom right of the main fragment, and three detached illegible scraps.

ἔγλημψις ἐκ δημοσίας
βιβ[λ]ι[ο]θήκης
ἐκ προ[σα]γγελμάτων
α (ἔτους) [κ]αὶ δ (ἔτους) Τῦβι
5    εἰς ὀνηλασίαν μητρο-
πόλεως
Εὔπορος Ἑρμείνου
καὶ ὡς χρηματί-
ζει    ὄνου    (τέταρτον)
.    .    .    .

4 α𐆓, δ𐆓     9 d⁻

'Extract from the public record-office. From nominations made in the 1st and 4th year, Tybi, for metropolite donkey-transport: Euporus son of Herminus (and the rest of his official nomenclature) ¼ donkey.'

3-6 Cf. **2915** 11 seqq.

4 Of [κ]αί nothing is really visible except the final long descender; but δ is almost certain. Year 1 of Aurelian and 4 of Vaballathus, A.D. 270/1: see Introd. p. 24.

5 This liturgy is mentioned in **2131** 11 ff., and in the Corn Dole texts cited in the introduction to **2939-40**; in **2131** the nomination is made by the *amphodogrammateus*. The evidence is more extensive for the villages, where the nomination was made by the comarchs (Börner, *Staatliche Korntransport*, pp. 18 seq.). Except for **2915** 17 I find nothing similar to line 9, which presumably implies that four liturgists together were responsible for providing one donkey (or its monetary equivalent?).

### 2941–2942. Communications to a Nomarch

These two documents came to light while the volume was in the press, during the continuous process of cataloguing the collection. Both are addressed to a hitherto unknown nomarch of Antinoopolis and both are so mutilated at the foot that the purpose of them is entirely unknown. One (**2941**) preserves just enough text to let us know that the sender had been appointed by the council of Antinoopolis to supervise distribution of loaves for one of the city's tribes—distribution, moreover, which took place both inside and outside the framework of a ϲιτηρέϲιον.

For the date of the documents we have a fixed *terminus post quem* in the foundation of Antinoopolis, A.D. 130 (Kühn, *Antinoopolis*, p. 8). Neither of the senders has adopted the *nomen* Aurelius, from which we can probably conclude that these official documents date from before the *constitutio Antoniniana*, A.D. 214 (*JEA* xlviii (1962), pp. 124–31). The cursive hands in which they are written would naturally be assigned to the end of the second century or the beginning of the third and so do not contradict the other indications. The persons remain unidentified and I have detected no other element of evidence of the date.[1]

I had hazarded the guess that the sort of ϲιτηρέϲιον that we find in Oxyrhynchus would be likely to be confined to the city of Rome until Roman citizenship had been vastly extended by the *constitutio Antoniniana* (Introd. p. 9). If this Antinoite ϲιτηρέϲιον is of the same sort, that guess was probably wrong. We may, however, find it easier to envisage a different sort of procedure here if we remember that Antinoopolis was not founded on the model of the Egyptian nome capitals, but as a city of the Greek type. So the dole may have been modelled on the private largesses that were usual in Greek cities, for which see A. R. Hands, *Charities*, pp. 88 seqq. It may, for instance, have been an endowment by Hadrian, like the foundation he set up for the maintenance of the children of Antinoite citizens (SB v 7602).

[1] A more precise date for the existence of a ϲιτηρέϲιον in Antinoopolis can now be supplied from P. Mich. 629, the text of which was generously made available to me in advance of publication by Dr. G. M. Browne. Though the document has lost its foot, where a date clause may well have stood, it is a petition addressed to the epistrategus Lucceius Ofellianus, known to have been in office from A.D. 166 to 169 (M. Vandoni, *Gli epistrategi*, p. 31). The petitioner describes himself in the prescript as τῶν ἐκτὸϲ ϲιτηρεϲίου ἀναγορευομένων. No light is shed on this rather mysterious turn of phrase by the body of the text, which is an application for an extension of leave of absence from Antinoopolis.

ADDENDUM. Nos. **2941** and **2942** can now be approximately dated by the belated discovery that the nomarch Nicippus has appeared in a papyrus of A.D. 154, see *Recherches de Papyrologie*, III, pp. 26–7 n.1. The text has been reprinted as SB viii 9904, but the name does not appear in the index in SB ix because the reading was doubtful. It is now made certain by the new documents.

## 2941

45 5B.59/G(5–7)b       5.8 × 8.2 cm.       Second/third century

On the left of the sheet there are remains of a join. Probably there was a τόμος cυγκολλήcιμος of related documents, from which **2942** also came.

.[
Νικίππωι νομάρχ(η)
τῆc Ἀντινόου
παρὰ Ἀπολλωνίου
5   Ἀ]πολλωνίου τοῦ Ἀμμω-
νίου Νερουιανείου τοῦ κ(αὶ)
Εἰρηνιέωc προχειριc-
θέντοc ὑπὸ τῆc κρ(ατίcτηc) βουλ(ῆc)
ἐπ’ ἀ]ναδόcεωc ἄρτων
10   ... .ς φυλ(ῆc) Νερουιανῆc
τῶν τε ἐν τῷ cιτηρε-
cί]ῳ καὶ ἐκτὸc cιτηρε-
cί]ου ..δ.......

·    ·    ·    ·    ·

2 νομαρχ    6 τουκ    8 κρς βου    10 φυλ

'To Nicippus, nomarch of Antinoopolis, from Apollonius, son of Apollonius, grandson of Ammonius, of the Nervian tribe and the Eirenian deme, appointed by the most excellent council (to be) in charge of distribution of loaves ... for the Nervian tribe, both those within the corn dole and those outside the corn dole ...'

1 .[. In this place a file number is expected, see **2942** 1 n.

2 Νικίππωι. It may be that this hitherto unknown official was an Oxyrhynchite who brought these documents home among his papers.

9 ἐπ’ ἀ]ναδόcεωc. For the terminology compare the known appointment ἐπ’ ἀναδόcεωc cπερμάτων; see N. Lewis, *Inventory of Compulsory Services*, s.v. ἀνάδοcιc; cf. *BASP* v (1968), p. 86.

10 ... .ς. Before the curved stroke, which has very various uses as a symbol, there appears to be a figure, ς = 6 or ε = 5. The stroke above probably means that this number is an ordinal, (πέμπτου) or (ἕκτου). One possibility might be τοῦ ς (ἔτουc), another χρς = γρ(άμματοc) ες. There were divisions of the city called γράμματα, subdivided further into πλινθεῖα, also numbered. So far, however, only four γράμματα are attested (Kühn, *Antinoopolis*, p. 28; Pistorius, *Indices Ant.*, p. 48). There were five γράμματα at Alexandria (Kühn, pp. 26–7). If this is the service of a sixth or fifth year, the most likely would be 5 or 6 Severus (A.D. 196/7, 197/8), and 5 or 6 Marcus and Verus (A.D. 164/5, 165/6).[1]

[1] A new possibility is suggested by P. Mich. 629, see p. 117 n. 1, namely τῶν ξς (sc. ἀνδρῶν). Then the sense would be 'to be in charge of the distribution of loaves for the 200 men of the Nervian tribe, both those in the corn dole and those outside the corn dole'. This cannot be confirmed as a reading, but as a hypothesis it has the advantage of making τῶν ... ἐκτὸc cιτηρεcίου refer to persons, as in P. Mich. 629. It is certain, however, that ἀναγορευομένων cannot be read in 13.

## 2942

45 5B.54/D(2–4)a                    7·5 × 6 cm.                    Second/third century

(m. 2) χ

(m. 1) Νικίππωι νομάρχηι
Ἀντινόου πόλεωc
π]α[ρὰ] Βηcαρίωνοc τοῦ καὶ
5      ...]. ἀνδροc Ἀπίωνοc
Cα]βινίου τοῦ κ(αὶ) Τροφω-
νιέω]c προχειριcθέντ[ο]c
ὑπὸ τῆc κρατί]cτηc βουλ(ῆc)
............].·[
·      ·      ·      ·      ·

6 τουᵏ          8 βουλ

'(2nd hand) 600 (?). (1st hand). To Nicippus, nomarch of Antinoopolis, from Besarion alias . . . , son of Apion, of the Sabinian tribe and the Trophonian deme, appointed by the most excellent council . . .'

1 In this position one would expect a file number, but χ represents 600. Six hundred documents of the same width as this one would make a roll of nearly 45 metres in length, which is impossibly long. Perhaps the numeration of items was continued over several rolls.

5 Presumably -ἀνδροc is a mistake for -ἀνδρου. If so, there are many possible names, see Dornseiff–Hansen, *Rückläufiges Wörterbuch d. gr. Eigennamen.*

# INDEXES

(Figures in small raised type refer to fragments, small roman numerals to columns. Square brackets indicate that a word is wholly or partly supplied from other sources or by conjecture. The article and καί are not indexed.)

## I. EMPERORS AND REGNAL YEARS

SEVERUS ALEXANDER

   ... Ἀλέξανδρος Year 4 **2899** 13.

PHILIPPI

   Μάρκοι Ἰούλιοι Year unknown [**2913** iii 4].

DECIUS AND HERENNIUS

   Δέκιοι Year 1 **2913** ii 9.

GALLIENUS

   Γαλλιηνός Year 13 **2903** 7.

CLAUDIUS II

   Κλαύδιος Year 2 **2929** 2.

   Αὐτοκράτωρ Καῖσαρ Μάρκος Αὐρήλιος Κλαύδιος, Εὐσεβής, Εὐτυχής, Σεβαστός Year 1 **2901** 10–13 **2913** ii 18–20, iii 14–18 **2914** i 22–5, ii 8–11 Year 2 **2892** i 16–18, 32, ii 15–18, 31 **2893** i 18–21 **2894** ii 24–8, iii 22–5 **2895** i 14–17, ii 23–5 Year uncertain **2896** 10–12 **2897** 12.

AURELIAN AND VABALLATHUS

   Αὐτοκράτωρ Καῖσαρ Λούκιος Δομίττιος Αὐρηλιανός, Εὐσεβής, Εὐτυχής, Σεβαστός καὶ Ἰούλιος Αὐρήλιος Σεπτίμιος Οὐαβάλλαθος Ἀθηνόδωρος ὁ λαμπρότατος βασιλεύς, ὕπατος, αὐτοκράτωρ, στρατηγὸς Ῥωμαίων Year 1 **2898** 23–8 **2906** i 21–6 **2908** ii 20–5, iii 29–33 **2921** 6–11 Year 2 and 5 **2904** 15–23 **2936** 25–8 Year uncertain **2916** 12–13 **2922** 1–5.

AURELIAN

   Αὐτοκράτωρ Καῖσαρ Λούκιος Δομίττιος Αὐρηλιανός, Γουνθικὸς μέγιστος, Εὐσεβής, Εὐτυχής, Σεβαστός Year 3 **2902** 17–19 Year uncertain **2903** 16–18.

## II. CONSULS

ἐπὶ ὑπάτων τοῦ ἐνεστῶτος ἔτους (A.D. 270) **2906** ii 19–20 **2907** i 5–7, ii 12–13.

## III. MONTHS

(Month names appear *passim* in **2934–2937**.)

Ἀθύρ **2906** ii 20 **2907** i 7, ii 13 **2930** 10 **2933** 8.
Ἐπείφ **2930** 10, 11.
Θώθ **2892** i 19, ii 18 **2893** i 21 [**2930** 11].
Μεχείρ **2894** iii 25 **2913** ii 21, iii 18 **2914** [i 25], ii 11 [**2932** 7].
Παῦνι **2902** 19 **2929** 2 **2932** 7 **2933** 16.

Τῦβι **2894** ii 28 **2895** ii 26 **2901** 13 **2908** ii 26 **2922** 6 **2930** 10, 10 **2940** 4.
Φαμενώθ **2930** 10.
Φαρμοῦθι **2904** 24 **2933** 12.
Φαῶφι **2892** i 32, ii 31 **2896** 12 **2930** 10.
Χοιάκ **2921** 11 **2930** 10 **2933** 14.

# IV. PERSONAL NAMES

(d. = daughter; f. = father; gd.f. = grandfather; m. = mother; s. = son.)

Ἀσκληπιάδης, s. of Germanus, gd.s. of Dioscorus, m. Tayris **2934** 36.
Ἀτρῆς, alias Didymus, s. of Sontoous **2936** ii 1.
Αὐνῆς (s. of?) Plution **2935** ii 10.
Αὐρηλιανός see Index I (Aurelian and Vaballathus, Aurelian).
Αὐρήλιος... **2893** ii 2 **2898** 30–1 **2901** 14 **2909** 4 **2912** 3 **2913** iii 20 **2914** ii 12 **2921** 13, 14 **2931** 1.
Αὐρήλιός τις **2927** 11, 13, [16], [18], 21.
Αὐρήλιος see Ἀβινοῦνις, Ἀγαθὸς Δαίμων, Ἀμυντιανός, Ἀνίκητος, Ἀντίνοος, Ἀντώνιος, Ἀπίων, Ἀπολλοδίδυμος, Ἀπολλώνιος, Ἄρειος, Ἀσκλ..., Ἀφύγχις, Ἀχιλλεύς, Βησάμμων, Δίδυμος, Διονύcιος, Διοσκουρίδης, Εὐδαίμων, Εὐφροσύνης, Ζωιλ..., Ζωίλος, Ἡρακλείδης, Ἡρακλέων, Ἡρακλῆς, Ἡρακλιανός, Ἡρᾶς, Θε[, Θέων, Θῶνις, Ἰcίδωρος, Κερδάμμων, Κοπρεύς, Λογγῖνος, Μέλας, Νεμεσιανός, Πανάρης, Παυc[, Πεκύcιος, Πλουτίων, Cαραπάμμων, Cαραπιάδης, Cαραπίων, Cαρᾶς, Cερῆνος, Cιλβανός, Cτέφανος, Τούρβων, ...αμμων, ...ρίων.
Αὐρήλιος see Index I (Claudius II, Aurelian and Vaballathus).
Ἀφύγχις, Aur., s. of Dioscorus, m. Philete **2908** iii 8–9.
Ἀφύγχις, s. of Thonis, gd.s. of Antiochus, m. Isidora **2934** 18.
Ἀφύγχις see Ἁμόις, s. of Aphynchis.
Ἀφύγχις see Cιλβανός.
Ἀχιλλᾶς see Θῶνις.
Ἀχιλλεύς, M. Aur., alias A(mmonius?) [**2899** ii 2?] **2915** 1 **2918** 1 **2920** 1.
Ἀχιλλεύς see Ἡρακλέων.
Α..., s. of Sarapion, gd.s. of Horion, m. Sarallium, d. of ...nius alias Sara(pion?), ex-cosmetes, councillor **2935** ii 5.
Α...εινος, s. of Hermeeis(?), m. Tan... **2936** ii 4.
Α...ιανός alias Horion, s. of Artemidorus alias Chaeremon, m. Thatres **2935** ii 14.

Βερενίκη see Ἀσκληπιάδης, s. of Didymus.
Βησάμμων, Aur., nominator **2894** ii 36, iii 33.
Βησάμμων see Χαιρήμων.
Βησαρίων, alias ...ander(?), s. of Apion **2942** 4.
Βηcᾶς see Ὀννῶφρις.

Γάιος see Πτολεμαῖος.
Γεμελλᾶς(?), witness of identity **2922** 14.
Γεννάδιος see Ἁμόις, alias G.
Γερμανός see Ἀσκληπιάδης.

Δημήτριος **2937** 1 i 12.
Δημήτριος, alias Alexander see Ἀκύλας.

Δημήτριος see Ἀγαθὸς Δαίμων, alias Thonis, Ἁρποκρατίων, Ἐπαφρόδιτος, Ἡρακλῆς, Πράκτικος.
Διδ[ see Διονύcιος, freedman of Theon alias Did...
Διδύμη see Ἀγαθὸς Δαίμων, alias Thonis, Ἰcίδωρος, Κοπρεύς, Cαραπιάδης.
Δίδυμος, Aur., former phylarch **2892** i 25, ii 22 **2930** 2.
Δίδυμος, Aur., s. of Hermias, m. Thaesis **2905** 5–6.
Δίδυμος see Ἀβινοῦνις, Ἀσκληπιάδης, s. of Didymus, Ἀτρῆς alias Didymus.
Διεῦς, d. of Theon see Ἀνταιόδωρος.
Διεῦς see Ἐπιμαχοῦς.
Διο..., Septimius see Ὡρίων, Septimius alias Diogenes.
Διογένης, Ammonius (alias?) see Μέλας.
Διογένης, (?) s. of Thonis see Ἀρητίων.
Διογένης see Ἀντίοχος, Ἀπίων, Aur., Ἀπολλώνιος, s. of Theon, Εὐφροσύνης, Ὡρίων, Septimius.
Διογενίς see Ἀλῦπις alias Plutarch, Λογγῖνος.
Διονυcία **2937** 1 i 15.
Διονυcία, m. of Thonis **2920** 6.
Διονύcιος, Aur., s. of Sarapion, etc., Althaean deme **2911** 4–6.
Διονύcιος, freedman of Theon alias Did... **2936** ii 20.
Διονύcιος, s. of Pindar, m. Faustina **2939** 7–8.
Διονύcιος see Ἁμόις alias Dionysius.
Διόσκορος **2937** 1 i 1, 8, 3 10.
Διόσκορος, freedman of Tanenteris, priestess **2937** ii 11.
Διόσκορος see Ἀσκληπιάδης, s. of Germanus, Ἀφύγχις, Aur.
Διοσκουρίδης, Aur. **2904** 25–6.
Διοσκουρίδης see Θέων, s. of Dioscurides.
Δομίττιος see Index I (Aurelian and Vaballathus, Aurelian).

Ἑλένη **2937** 1 i 18.
Ἑλένη see Ἄμμων, m. Helen.
Ἑλλάδιος see Εὐδαίμων.
Ἐπαφρόδιτος, freedman of Demetrius **2936** ii 17.
Ἐπιμαχοῦς, alias Dieus **2925** 13.
Ἑρμίας see Δίδυμος, Aur., s. of Hermias.
Ἑρμῖνος see Εὔπορος, s. of Herminus.
Ἑρμιόνη see Ἀπολλώνιος.
Ἔρως see Cαραπίων, Aur., s. of Eros.
Εὐδαίμων, Aur., alias Helladius **2904** 2.
Εὐδαίμων, s. of Sarapion **2915** 14–15.
Εὔπορος, s. of Herminus **2940** 7.
Εὐσέβιος see Καλπούρνιος Ε.
Εὐτύχιος(?), freedman of Nilus **2937** ii 14.
Εὐφροσύνης, Aur., freedman(?) of Diogenes, (ex-?) exegetes **2906** ii 4, 21.

Οὐαβάλλαθος see Index I (Aurelian and Vaballathus).
Ὀφέλλιος, Lucius Ofellius Sarapion see Ἀπίων.
Ὀφέλλιος Μάξιμος, f. of Thonis 2920 5.
Ὀφέλλιος see Cαραπιάδης.

Παᾶπις see Ἀμόις alias Dionysius.
Παμβῆκις, (s. of?) Apion 2935 ii 8.
Πανάρης, Aur. 2936 ii 28.
Παυ[ see Παῦλος.
Παῦλος, s. of Socrates, gr.s. of . . ., m. Παυ... 2896 4.
Παυς[..., Aur., 2913 iii 19.
Παυσανίας see Ἀμμώνιος, s. of Horion.
Παυςᾶς 2935 ii 12.
Παυςειρίων see Ἀρείων.
Πείνη see Ἀντώνιος.
Πέκυλλος(?), witness of identity 2922 14.
Πεκύςιος, Aur., s. of Sarapion, gd.s. of . . ., m. Θεωνίς 2895 ii 1–3, 27.
Πίνδαρος see Διονύςιος, s. of Pindar, Κτίςτης.
Πλούταρχος see Ἀλῦπις alias Plutarch.
Πλουτίων, alias Horion see Ἀπίων, Aur.
Πλουτίων, Aur. 2908 ii 28.
Πλουτίων, Aur., alias . . . 2908 ii 37.
Πλουτίων, Aur., secretary of the corn dole 2892 i 3, ii 2 2893 i 1, ii 1 2894 ii 1, iii 1 2905 3 2906 ii 2 2911 ii 2 2916 2 2926 1.
Πλουτίων see Αὐνῆς.
Ποταμ[ 2893 ii 5.
Πράκτικος alias Serapiacus, freedman of Demetrius 2936 ii 14.
Πτολεμαῖος, C. Julius [2928 ii 1–2].
Πτολεμαῖος see Cαραπίων.

Ῥωμανός see Ἀμόις, s. of Romanus.

Cαρα[ 2937 ¹ i 21.
Cαράλλιον see Α..., s. of Sarapion.
Cαραπάμμων, Aur., gd.s.? of Alexander 2918 5–6.
Cαραπάμμων see Ἀμόις, s. of Romanos, Ἀμόις, s. of Sarapammon, Ἀνίκητος.
Cαραπιάδης, Aur., s. of Ophellius, m. Didyme 2908 iii 4–5, 34.
Cαραπίας 2937 ¹ i 8.
Cαραπίας see Ἀμόις, s. of Sarapammon.
Cαραπίων, Aur., s. of Eros 2894 ii [3], 29.
Cαραπίων, Aur., s. of . . ., gd.s of Ptolemy, m. Thaesis 2903 3–4.
Cαραπίων, banker 2938 4.
Cαραπίων, L. Ofellius Sarapion see Ἀπίων, s. of Serenus.
Cαραπίων see Ἀγαθὸς Δαίμων, Aur., Ἀνταιόδωρος, Ἀπολλώνιος, Aur., alias Nemesi..., Α..., s. of

Sarapion, Διονύςιος, Aur., Εὐδαίμων, s. of Sarapion, Ἡρακλῆς, Aur., Ἡρᾶς, Aur., Θῶνις, Aur., alias Achillas, Πεκύςιος.
Cαρα(πίων?) see Α..., s. of Sarapion.
Cαρᾶς, Aur., alias Isidorus, witness of identity 2892 i 30, ii 29.
Cενψόις see Ἀγαθὸς Δαίμων.
Cεουῆρος see Ἀμόις alias Dionysius, Ἀππιανός.
Cεπτίμιος see Ἀλέξανδρος, Septimius, Ὠρίων, Septimius, Index I (Aurelian and Vaballathus).
Cεραπιακός see Πράκτικος alias Serapiacus.
Cερῆνος, Aur., epicrites 2892 i 23, ii 25 2894 ii 34, iii 31 2895 i 22 2902 20.
Cερῆνος, Aur., witness of identity 2908 ii 44, iii 42.
Cερῆνος, nominator 2936 ii 9, 12, 15, 18, 21, 30.
Cερῆνος see Ἀλῦπις, Ἀπίων, s. of Serenus.
Cιλβανός, Aur., witness of identity 2902 22.
Cιλβανός, s. (or gd.s.?) of Aphynchis 2897 7–8.
Cιλβανός see Ἀμμωνᾶς.
Cινθῶνις see Cτέφανος.
Cοῆρις 2937 ¹ i 4.
Cοντώους, s. of Horus, m. Thatres 2936 ii 11.
Cοντώους see Ἀτρῆς alias Didymus.
Cτατίλιος Ἀμμιανός, praefectus Aegypti 2923 8.
Cτέφανος, Aur., s. of Harachthes alias Agathinus, m. Sinthonis 2923 2–3, 10–11.
Cτέφανος see Ἀβάςκαντος.
Cτρατονίκη see Ἀπολλώνιος, s. of Theon.
Cῦρος see Ἀμόις, s. of Syrus.
Cωκράτης see Παῦλος.

Τααποῦς 2935 ii 12.
Ταμόις see Ἀπολλώνιος.
Τανεντῆρις, priestess 2937 ii 11.
Ταῦρις see Ἀβινοῦνις, Ἀμόις alias Dionysius, Ἁρποκρατίων, s. of Demetrius, Ἀςκληπιάδης, s. of Germanus.
Ταυςεῖρις see Ἀμόις, s. of Syrus.
Ταφίλων 2937 ¹ i 12.
Τερεῦς see Ἀμόις alias Gennadius.
Τεχῶςις 2912 5.
Τιθοῆς 2937 ¹ i 4.
Τούρβων, Aur., strategus 2923 1.
Τρύφων, s. of Apollonius, gd.s. of Apollonius, m. Xenarchis 2894 iii 15–17.

Φαυςτῖνα see Διονύςιος, s. of Pindar.
Φιλέας 2925 10.
Φιλήτη see Ἀφύγχις, Aur.

Χαιρημονίς see Ἀπίων, Aur.
Χαιρήμων, alias Besammon 2895 i 9–10.

Χαιρήμων, Artemidorus alias C. *see A . . . ιανός* alias Horion.

Ὠρίων, alias Plution *see Ἀπίων*, Aur.
Ὠρίων, Septimius, alias Diogenes, ex-gymnasiarch 2924 1 [2925 10?].
Ὠρίων, steersman 2926 2, 10.
Ὠρίων *see Ἀμμώνιος* s. of Horion, Ἀπίων, Aur., *A . . .*, s. of Sarapion, *A . . . ιανός* alias Horion, Καλπούρνιος Ὠ.

Ὦρος *see Ϲοντῶους*, s. of Horus.
. . . αμμων 2896 13, 14.
. . . αμμων, Aur. 2913 ii 23.
. . . αντίνοος *see Ἀντίνοος*.
. . . νιος alias Sara(pion?) ex-cosmetes, councillor 2935 ii 6.
. . . ριων, Aur., witness of identity 2895 i 29.
. . . ρος, s. of Aur. Zoilus 2908 iii 40.
. . . , s. of Justus, m. Cyrilla 2930 9.
. . . , s. of . . . clas, gd.s. of Theon 2892 ii 9–10.

# V. GEOGRAPHICAL

## (a) Countries, Nomes, Toparchies, Cities, etc.

Αἴγυπτος 2923 9.
Ἀλεξάνδρεια 2904 3 2937 ii 14.
Ἀλεξανδρεύς 2901 6 2915 18 2916 4, 7 2927 3 [2932 5].
Ἀλεξανδρέων, ἡ λαμπροτάτη πόλις τῶν 2898 3–4 2925 12 2938 2–3.
Ἀντινοεύς 2917 6, 10.
Ἀντινόου (πόλεως) 2941 3 2942 3.
Γουνθικός *see* Index I (Aurelian).
Ὀξυρυγχειτῶν πόλις 2892 i 6, ii 4 2893 i 6 2894 ii 6, iii 6 [2895 ii 4] 2898 7 2903 5 2906 i 5, ii 6

2908 ii 7 [2909 5] [2912 5] 2913 ii 5 2923 4, [11] 2925 11.
Ὀξυρυγχίτης (citizen) 2892 i 7, ii 5 2923 12.
Ὀξυρυγχίτης (nome) 2923 1.
Ὀξυρύγχων πόλις 2899 9 2908 iii 6 2916 6 2920 7.
Ὀξυρυγχ( ) πόλις 2905 7.
Πηλούσιον 2926 4.
Ῥωμαῖος 2915 18 2927 3 [2932 5] 2938 1.
Ῥωμαῖος *see* Index I (Aurelian and Vaballathus).

## (b) ἄμφοδα of Oxyrhynchus

Βορρᾶ Δρόμου 2916 8 2917 8 2928 i 5, ii 7 2929 11 [2933 6, 17].
Βορρᾶ Κρηπῖδος 2928 i 7, ii 9 2929 5 2939 4.
Δρόμου Γυμνασίου 2893 i 8, [ii 5] 2894 ii 8, iii 8.
Δρόμος Θοήριδος 2892 i 8, 34, ii 7, 32 2910 ii 6 2928 i 6, ii 8 2929 14 2930 1, 3, 8, 15.
Ἑρμαίου 2903 6 2906 i 10, ii 7 2922 17 2928 i 9, ii 11 2929 13.
Ἡρακλέους τόπων 2912 7.
Ἡρῴου 2905 9 2928 i 2, ii 4 [2929 9].
Ἱππέων (Παρεμβολῆς) 2923 13 2928 i 4, ii 6 [2929 6].
Κρητικοῦ [2899 11] 2928 i 11, ii 13 2929 10.

Λυκίων Παρεμβολῆς [2930 3].
Μητρῴου [2900 3].
Μυροβαλάνου 2898 9 2915 6, 20 2928 i 13, ii 15 2929 3.
Νότου Δρόμου 2913 ii 7.
Νότου Κρηπῖδος 2908 ii 8–9, iii 11 2928 i 8, ii 10 2929 8.
Παμμένους (Παραδείσου) 2928 i 12, ii 14 2929 4 2931 2.
Παρεμβολῆς (Ἱππέων? Λυκίων?) 2913 iii 3.
Πλατείας 2928 i 10, ii 12 2929 12.
Ποιμενικῆς 2904 10 2928 i 3, ii 5 2929 7 2932 1.
Τεμιούθεως 2895 ii 8 2918 7.

## (c) Tribes and Demes

Ἀλθαιεύς 2911 6 2915 [4], 17, 22.
Εἰρηνιεύς 2941 7.
Ἡραιεύς 2917 6.
Νεοκόσμιος 2915 3, 16, [22].

Νερουιάνειος 2941 6.
Νερουιανή 2941 10.
Ϲαβείνιος 2917 5 2942 6.
Τροφωνιεύς 2942 6.

# VI. RELIGION

ἱέρισσα 2937 ii 11.
νεωκόρος τοῦ μεγάλου Ϲαράπιδος 2899 3–4 2909

1–2 2917 1–2 [2938 2].
Ϲάραπις 2899 3–4 2909 2 2917 2 2938 2.

# VII. OFFICIAL AND MILITARY TERMS AND TITLES

ἀναγορεύειν 2892 i 24, 26, ii 24, 26  2894 ii 35, 39,
iii 32  [2895 i 23]  2896 17  [2899 27]  2900 17
2901 5  2902 21  2913 ii 15, iii 11  2914 [i 10], ii 4.
ἀναγορία 2902 24  2903 10  2908 ii 13, 40, iii 39
[2909 13]  2910 ii 10  2922 12  2927 2, 6, 10, 12,
14, 17, [20], 22  2930 7  [2931 5]  [2932 4]  2936
ii 29, 31.
ἀναγράφειν 2893 i 7, ii 5  2894 ii 7, iii 7  2895 ii 6
2897 2  2905 8  2906 ii 7  2908 ii 8, iii 10  2912 6
2913 ii 6, [iii 1]  [2918 6]  2923 12.
ἀνεπίκριτος 2908 iii 12.
ἀπογράφειν [2912 7]  2913 ii 7  2927 4.
ἀπογραφή 2912 8 (l. ἀπὸ {απο}γρ[αφῆς?).
ἄρχειν (ἄρξας) 2904 2.
ἀρχεῖον 2925 15.
ἄρχων 2913 ii 2  2924 3.

βιβλίδιον 2921 3  2923 4.
βιβλιοθήκη 2907 ii 21  2919 4  2927 1, 5, 9, 19, 22
2930 5  2931 4  [2932 3]  2939 2  2940 2.
βιβλίον 2895 ii 13  2898 12, 18  2900 4  2902 12, 13
2903 9  2905 14  2906 i 14, 16, ii 15, 23  2907
ii 3  2908 ii 16, iii 24  [2909 12]  2910 ii 9  2912 12
2913 ii 10, 11, iii 7  2914 i 4, [9]  2918 10
2920 8  2925 5.
βουλευτής 2898 3  2904 3  2935 ii 6  2937 ii 14
2938 2.
βουλή 2894 ii 13, iii 13  [2896 1]  2898 21  [2899
6, 17]  2900 6  2903 15  2904 6  2906 i 7, [19]
2907 ii 11  [2909 6, 18]  2910 i 6, ii 14  2911
7  2912 17  [2914 i 7]  [2916 7], [2918 3]  [2921 5]
2924 5  2941 8  2942 8.

γνωρίζειν 2892 i 29, 31, ii 29, [30]  2894 ii 42, 44
[2895 i 28, 31]  2902 22  2914 i [21], ii 19
2922 14  2927 13.
γνωστεύειν 2908 ii 44, iii 42.
γνωστήρ 2892 i 28, 30, ii 28, [29]  2894 ii 41, 43
2895 i 26, 29  2902 22  2908 ii 32, 44, iii 42
2914 [i 19], ii 17  2922 14  2927 13.
γραμματεὺς σιτηρεσίου 2892 i 3, ii 2  2893 i 1,
[ii 1]  [2894 ii 1, iii 2]  2905 4  2906 ii 2  2911 3
2916 2  2926 1, 9.
γραφή 2912 8?  2913 ii 8  2915 9, 18  2927 4, 18.
γυμνασιαρχεῖν 2924 1.

διάδοσις 2892 i 16, [ii 14]  2895 i 13  2900 4  [2910
i 4, ii 13]  2913 ii 15, [iii 11]  2914 i 11, ii 5
2918 4  2924 3, 6.
διακρίνειν 2892 i 28, 31, ii 28, 30  2894 ii 39, 42,
44  [2895 i 28, 31]  [2899 20]  2900 9  2902
24  2914 [i 20], ii 18  2927 2, 5, 9, 11, 16, 19, 22
[2930 6]  2931 4  2932 3  2936 ii 29.

διάκρισις 2898 12.
διακριτής 2899 6  2913 ii 2.
διάσημος 2923 8.

ἐξηγ[ 2906 ii 5.
ἐξηγητεύειν 2938 2.
ἔπαρχος Αἰγύπτου 2923 9.
ἐπικ( ) 2908 ii 40.
ἐπικρίνειν 2892 i 7, 23, ii [6], 26  2893 i 8, [ii 6]
2894 ii 8, 35, iii 9, 31  2895 i 1, 23, ii 6  [2896 17]
2897 3  2898 1, 8, 20  2899 10  2902 4, 7, 14, 20
2903 6  2908 ii 1, 9, 36  [2913 iii 3]  2918 8  2927
1, 1, 11, 16  2931 3  2932 2.
ἐπίκρισις 2895 ii 9  2898 15  2902 11.
ἐπικριτής 2892 i 23, ii 25  2894 ii 34, iii 31  2895
i 22  2896 16  2902 20  2927 11.

ἡγεμονία 2923 5.

ἱππεὺς Ῥωμαίων 2938 1.
ἱππικός 2925 2.

κανονικάριος (?; κανανικλαριωι pap.) 2925 1.
κατ' ἄνδρα 2898 11  [2906 i 14]  2908 iii 14  2912 11
2927 1, 4, 7  2928 i 1  2929 1  2930 4  2931 3
2932 2  2933 3  2939 3.
καταχωρισμός 2913 ii 9  [2914 i 4].
κλῆρος 2892 i 9, [ii 8]  2893 i 11, [ii 8]  2894 ii 11,
iii 11  2895 i 8.
κοσμητεύειν 2935 ii 6.
κυριακὸς λόγος 2938 6.

λαγχάνειν 2893 i 11, [ii 8]  2894 ii 14, iii 13
2896 2  2897 6.
λογιστήριον [2925 22?].

μητρόπολις 2904 11  2906 i 11  2940 5.
μητροπολίτης 2895 ii 5.

νεωκόρος 2899 3–4  2909 1–2  2917 1–2  [2938 2].
νομάρχης 2941 2  2942 2.

ὁμόλογος 2912 11  2927 4, 18  2928 ii 3.
ὀνηλασία 2904 10  2906 ii 9  [2909 10]  2915 13
2917 9  2940 5.

πολιτεία 2908 ii 33.
πολίτης 2892 i 14, ii 13  2902 12.
πραγματευτής 2925 2.
προσβαίνειν 2898 8  2903 5  2912 8  2913 ii 7
2927 4, 18  2939 11.

# VIII. PROFESSIONS, TRADES, AND OCCUPATIONS

# IX. MEASURES

# X. GENERAL INDEX OF WORDS

PLATE I

PLATE II

2904

2915

PLATE III

2921

2941

2924

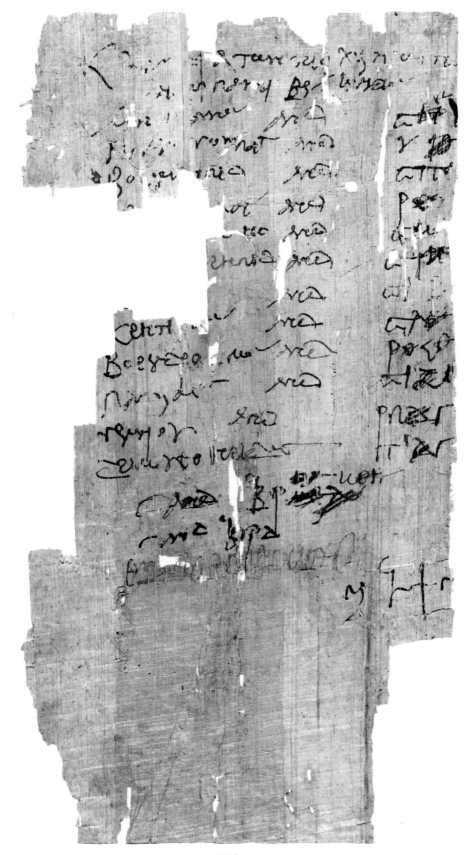

PLATE IV

PLATE V

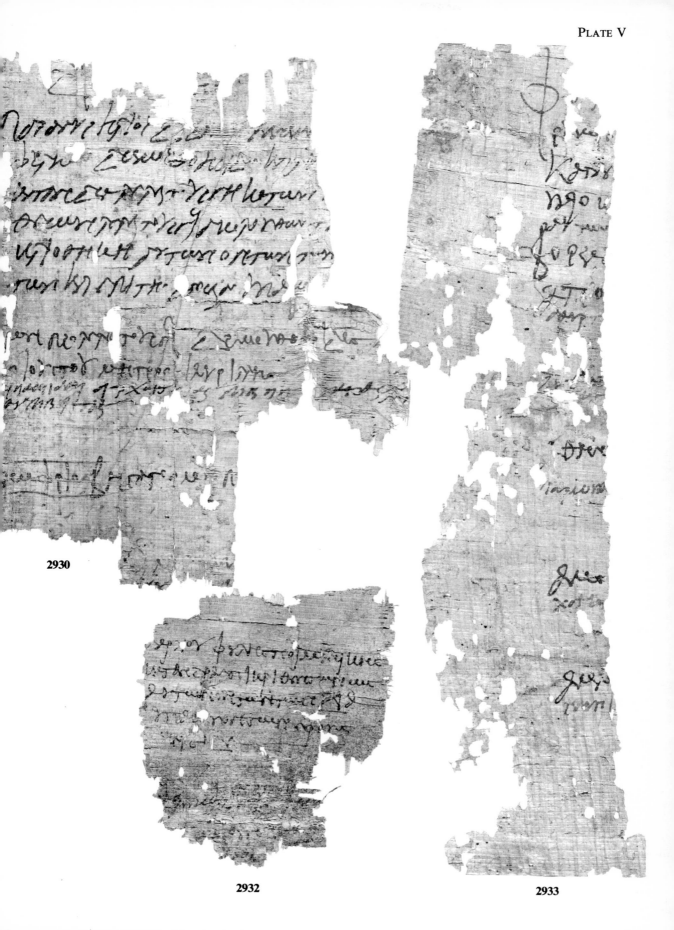

2930

2932

2933

PLATE VI

PLATE VII

PLATE VIII

2938

2931

2942

2940

2007.04.23                    (9.95)